Woodrow Wilson, Josephus Daniels

Woodrow Wilson: Speeches, Inaugural Addresses, State of the Union Addresses, Executive Decisions & Messages to Congress

Madison & Adams Press 2019

Woodrow Wilson
Essays of Woodrow Wilson

Woodrow Wilson
George Washington

Woodrow Wilson, Josephus Daniels
The Collected Works of Woodrow Wilson

Charles Eastman
The Life of Charles Eastman OhiyeS'a: Indian Boyhood & From the Deep
Woods to Civilization (Volume 1&2)

James Madison Page
The True Story of Andersonville Prison

John Alexander Logan
The Great Conspiracy: Its Origin and History (Illustrated Edition)

Samuel R. Watkins
Co. Aytch: Maury Grays First Tennessee Regiment

John Singleton Mosby
Mosby's War Reminiscences - Stuart's Cavalry Campaigns

Thomas Wentworth Higginson
Army Life in a Black Regiment

Thomas Coleman Younger
The Story of Cole Younger: An Autobiography of the Missouri Guerrilla
Captain and Outlaw

Woodrow Wilson, Josephus Daniels

Woodrow Wilson: Speeches, Inaugural Addresses, State of the Union Addresses, Executive Decisions & Messages to Congress

Madison & Adams Press, 2019.
Contact: info@madisonadamspress.com

ISBN 978-80-273-3436-0

This is a publication of Madison & Adams Press. Our production consists of thoroughly prepared educational & informative editions: Advice & How-To Books, Encyclopedias, Law Anthologies, Declassified Documents, Legal & Criminal Files, Historical Books, Scientific & Medical Publications, Technical Handbooks and Manuals. All our publications are meticulously edited and formatted to the highest digital standard. The main goal of Madison & Adams Press is to make all informative books and records accessible to everyone in a high quality digital and print form.

Contents

Biography of Woodrow Wilson

Woodrow Wilson

By Josephus Daniels

Woodrow Wilson is descended from a Scotch-Irish ancestry noted for its culture and its intensity of religious conviction. Some of his Scot forbears died for their faith. Immediately, he comes from a line of ministers and editors. William Duane, democrat and friend of Jefferson, had a hand in the training of James Wilson, grandfather of Woodrow Wilson, who came from County Down, Ireland, lured as a youth of twenty-two to the land of opportunity in the New World. Landing at Philadelphia in the year 1808, he quickly found a congenial task in the work rooms of Duane's militant "Daily Aurora." The joy of his new toil was enhanced by the fact that a fine Irish lass, who had sailed on the same ship with him, was watching him make his fortune; and within four years he was able to claim Ann Adams as his wife. The happy pair could not be disobedient to the enticing vision of the developing West, and in 1812 James Wilson founded the Western Herald at Steubenville, Ohio, and soon afterward the Pennsylvania Advocate at Pittsburg, Pennsylvania, and divided his time between the two newspapers.

As Providence would have it, Joseph Ruggles Wilson, youngest of seven sons and three daughters, was marked to be the scholar of the family. Trained by his parents, and especially by his mother, who was a Presbyterian of the "straitest sect," it was not surprising that he turned to the Gospel ministry as his calling. The stair steps in his education were the Steubenville Academy; Jefferson College, afterwards Washington and Jefferson College, where he took first honors; and a year each at Western Theological Seminary at Allegheny, Pennsylvania, and Princeton Seminary.

The Reverend Doctor Thomas Woodrow, English-descended but Scotch-born, some years before had left his church at Carlisle, England, to become a missionary in the New World, and had finally come to Chillicothe, Ohio. It came about that he sent his pretty and sprightly daughter, Janet, sometimes called Jessie, to the girls school at Steubenville at the same time that Joseph R. Wilson had returned to that place to teach for a couple of years in the male academy. Finding their tastes congenial and their ideals alike, these two were happily married on June 7, 1849, and after teaching rhetoric for a year at Jefferson College, and chemistry and the natural sciences for four years at Hampden Sidney College, Virginia, the young husband accepted a call to the pastorate of the Presbyterian church at Staunton, Virginia, in the year 1855, and moved there with his wife and two small daughters, Marian and Annie Josephine.

Staunton was the birthplace of Woodrow Wilson. As his father left there when he was two years old to accept a call to the important First Presbyterian church of Augusta, Georgia, he had no recollection of the home of his nativity in the beautiful valley of Virginia, but he will never forget the reception tendered him by citizens of that city upon the fifty-seventh anniversary of his birth, on December 28, 1912, when he was President-elect of the United States, and when he was quartered in the little room in the manse where he first saw the light.

Both at Augusta and at Columbia, South Carolina, where Doctor Wilson in 1870 accepted the chair of pastoral and evangelistic theology at the Southern Presbyterian Theological Seminary, Woodrow attended excellent private schools, but his real instructor was his father. Doctor Wilson was one of the brilliant leaders of the Presbyterian Church in the south. For forty years he was Stated Clerk of the Southern General Assembly. He was Moderator of the Assembly of 1879. Well-informed upon the news of the day and well-balanced and fair-minded, the father was keen to judge a new book, to analyze a political situation, to shatter a sham with irony, or to scorn a pretender. From him all the while the boy was unconsciously absorbing the ability to do the same things.

Wilson's decision as to his life purpose was formed suddenly. He had spent a year at Davidson College, North Carolina, an excellent institution with a strong faculty, and then a year at his new home in Wilmington, North Carolina, whither his father had been called from Columbia to the Presbyterian pastorate. In the early fall of 1875 he entered Princeton, then under the presidency of Doctor James McCosh. About three months had passed when young Wilson, while browsing in the library, took down a file of the Gentlemen's Magazine and turned to the series of articles entitled "Men and Manners in Parliament," written by "The Member for Chiltern Hundreds," the anonymous successor of Doctor Johnson. Wilson was captivated by these vivid reports of the parliamentary debates participated in by Gladstone, Disraeli, John Bright, Earl Granville, Sir William Vernon Harcourt and other figures in the public eye of England at that time. He eagerly devoured the entire series, and went on to the earnest study of English political history. He does not hesitate to confess that this was a turning point in his life and that no other circumstance did so much to make public life the purpose of his existence. In his senior year, Wilson embodied his conclusions in an article entitled "Cabinet Government in the United States," which was instantly accepted by the International Review and published in August, 1879. His criticism was that in Congress the important legislation was shaped in committee; and secrecy, he contended, is the atmosphere in which all corruption and evil flourish. To remedy the evil of committee government, which he attributed to lack of leaders, he devised a plan whereby Cabinet members should be entitled to a seat in Congress, and the right to participate in the debates, even if it were deemed advisable not to give them the right to vote. All through his later voluminous writings, Wilson clung to this theory and put the idea into practice, so far as he could, with marked effect, when he came to be the head of the nation, by personally appearing before joint meetings of both houses of Congress and reading his messages.

One effect of Wilson's selection of a career so early in his college course was to induce him to select all his studies with a view to it, and to reject as unsuited both to his tastes and his needs the rigid and inflexible curriculum then prescribed at Princeton. As illustrating how he reached for anything which would help him in his career, he went outside the campus to learn stenography so that he might the more easily make notes during his library work. This acquirement has proved an invaluable aid to him throughout his life, and all his public papers were originally prepared in the characters of the stenographic art. He was a famous and dreaded debater, belonging to Whig Hall, at Princeton, and it was conceded that he stood the best chance to win the Lynde Debate, an extemporaneous discussion participated in by three representatives from each of the two literary societies. But when in the preliminary trial in his society he drew out of the hat a slip labeled "Protection," requiring him to defend that side, he refused to participate in the debate at all, because he could not advocate what he did not believe.

Conceiving that the law guaranteed the surest promise of a useful career, Wilson took his law course at the University of Virginia. Meanwhile, however, he continued his studies of English government and contributed articles to the University Magazine on John Bright and Gladstone.

A year of rest with his parents at Wilmington followed his leaving college, and then young Wilson engaged in the practice of law at Atlanta, Georgia, but, after a waiting experience of eighteen months in which clients were slow in putting in an appearance, he decided that he would continue his studies in the science of government at Johns Hopkins University. They were mainly directed by Herbert B. Adams in history, and Richard T. Ely in political economy. A second year at Hopkins was spent as the holder of the Historical Fellowship. A brilliant composition at this time was a study of Adam Smith, while early in 1885 appeared his first important volume, "Congressional Government, a Study of Government by Committee." It was the first time a thorough consideration not only of the theory but of the actual working of the Constitution of the United States had ever been prepared in book form. It was the result of ten years of absorbing study. It met with immediate success, and Ambassador Bryce in the preface to his "American Commonwealth" acknowledges his indebtedness to the work. It brought him invitations to several college chairs, and, while still continuing his Hopkins studies, he accepted the place of associate in history and political economy at the new college for the higher education of women — Bryn Mawr. Mr. Wilson's course of lectures was one of the most popular in the college. In 1886 he took his Ph.D. from Johns Hopkins, his work on "Congressional Government" being accepted as his thesis, and one year later the University offered him a lectureship which took him to Baltimore once a week for twenty-five weeks.

Leaving Bryn Mawr, he was two years at Wesleyan University as professor of history and political economy, during which time he wrote "The State," and in 1890 he accepted an offer of the chair of jurisprudence and politics in Princeton University. After fifteen years the young professor who had received the inspiration for his life work in the Princeton Library was back on the campus of his Alma Mater as a member of the faculty. His lectures sprang into popularity here as well as with his earlier professorships. Princeton had never in all its brilliant history had a teacher who so captivated his classes. Upwards of four hundred students in all were in attendance, absorbing his carefully ascertained and impressively presented facts of history, or fascinated by his original views of current events. His teaching was enlightened by sprightly humor. He spoke with the greatest freedom, often with utter abandon, concerning modern events and those concerned in them, putting the students on their honor not to report him and none of them ever violated his confidences.

Twelve years went by. It was a period of development with Woodrow Wilson. His mind mellowed. There was a ripening into maturity. As he continued his studies along the line of his bent a number of new books came from his pen. They were: "The State," "Division and Reunion," "An Old Master," "Mere Literature" and "George Washington." Later still appeared his masterly "History of the American People." As he compared the conditions of government in this day with the ideals of government set up by the fathers of the Republic, and as he noted points of failure in the realization of these ideals, he was fired with a holy zeal to champion the cause of social justice.

In June, 1902, Woodrow Wilson was elected president of Princeton University. His thorough equipment, his proven capacity for leadership, his splendid scholarship, his eloquence and popularity as a speaker, his already widespread fame, his judgment and executive ability marked him as the man of the hour. His mettle had been tested in the faculty meetings when he had quickly made himself felt in his readiness in debate over the problems affecting the welfare of the campus and the college. His discernment, his preparedness for emergency, his loyalty, had been amply proven. He was the logical man for the place — this first layman in a list of presidents reaching back for one hundred and sixty years.

By his election a man who had no peer for genuine democracy was placed in supreme power in probably the most aristocratic educational institution in the United States. And this leaven of democracy mixed in with the fine flour of college aristocracy began soon to "work." After a year of quiet but earnest study of conditions from the new point of view of the presidency, Doctor Wilson initiated and carried through to rapid success certain reforms. After seeing to it that the actual scholarship and discipline corresponded properly to what they were scheduled in the catalogue to be, demanding genuine work to win a diploma and banishing the social pull that had theretofore existed, Doctor Wilson laid his hand to the revision of the course of study. Princeton must not only be a place of work, but of work which should be intelligent and calculated to put the worker in a position best to serve society in the twentieth century.

The new president next secured the preceptorial system. Out of one hundred and sixty-eight hours a week, fifteen hours a week in the classroom were not considered sufficient by President Wilson for the proper education of the students entrusted to Princeton's care. They were no longer to be allowed to drift aimlessly through the weeks and the years. The institution was to give better attention toward direction of their spare time. To this end preceptors were employed at a great expense — for the new system involved an annual cost of about one hundred thousand dollars — and they were to supply friendly companionship and have oversight of studies. The informal, personal contact of the students with these preceptors has been of infinite value. The new system proved its worth from the outset, and the eyes of the educational world were turned upon Princeton which was thus forging to the front with a forcefully constructive programme.

President Wilson next attempted a reorganization of the social life of the campus. For ten years he had been turning over in his mind a plan by which the exclusive clubs patronized by the wealthier of the upper classmen might be superseded by a number of "quadrangles," dormitories in which a certain number of men from each class together with several instructors should have their domicile. This would assure a commingling of all the students, the upper classmen demonstrating the value of the college training they were receiving and the lower classmen, through personal contact, receiving an impetus and inspiration for their further college career. As it was, Princeton had a dozen "swell" club-houses, to which only students possessed of large means could afford to belong. The aggregate value of these buildings and their elegant furnishings was upwards of a million dollars. The membership averaged about fifteen seniors and fifteen juniors each, the members of these two classes alone being eligible. Some three hundred or more other members of the senior and junior classes were excluded. Freshmen and especially sophomores engaged in fierce rivalry in their efforts to "make" a club. Their spirit was the dominant character-forming influence on the Princeton campus. It can readily be imagined how eagerly the democratic heart of President Wilson was throbbing in his desire to overthrow this pernicious system so alien to the American ideal.

A committee of seven trustees presented a report at the commencement of 1907, endorsing the President's plan for "the social co-ordination of the University" and the report was accepted. There were twenty-seven trustees. Twenty-five voted for the plan and one against. One member was absent. A circular outlining the plan was sent to the clubs and was read there by hundreds of returned alumni on the Friday night before commencement of the same year 1907. A cry of protest went up and continued through the year. The Alumni Weekly carried communications attacking the President for his high-handed attempts to "make a gentleman chum with a mucker," or to force men "to submit to dictation as to their table companions." The trustees, frightened by the noise the alumni had raised, on October 17 requested President Wilson to withdraw the proposition.

16

The Home of president Woodrow Wilson, Princeton, N. J., during his professorship.
Built by Mr. & Mrs. Wilson

Yet another matter of serious controversy arose with the question of the establishment of a Graduate College. Bequests made for this purpose contained conditions which seemed to require of President Wilson that he should abrogate powers which he believed it his duty to exercise, and this he refused to do. It ended in Princeton getting her magnificent Graduate College — and losing her president. Mr. Wilson felt that he could be of no more service to Old Nassau. When therefore an opportunity to serve his fellow men came with the Democratic nomination to the governorship of New Jersey, he accepted it, and doubtless gladly, for it opened the avenues of statesmanship and public service for which his whole life had been an unconscious preparation.

New Jersey had begun to feel the effects of the great political reform movement sweeping the country and Democratic leaders knew that the state could not be won for their party unless a strong, clean man led the ticket. Woodrow Wilson's splendid campaign to make Princeton a truly American institution had caught the eye of the whole country. He had been a life long Democrat. New Jersey had within her borders the very man the party needed. The state was at the mercy of the big interests. Mr. Wilson hesitated to give his consent to consider the nomination, and was outspoken in the statement that he would make no promises and if elected he must be the accepted leader of his party. This latter condition he rightly regarded as essential to the carrying out of the reforms needed. When asked whether, if he were elected, he would refuse to listen to organization leaders and acknowledge the party organization, Mr. Wilson replied in this wise: "I have always been a believer in party organizations. If I were elected Governor I should be very glad to consult with the leaders of the Democratic organization. I should refuse to listen to no man but I should be especially glad to hear and duly consider the suggestions of the leaders of my party. If on my own independent investigation, I found that recommendations for appointment made to me by the organization leaders named the best possible men, I should naturally prefer, other things being equal, to appoint them, as the men pointed out by the combined counsels of the party." On July 15 he published a statement to the effect that he would accept the nomination if it were the desire "of a decided majority of the thoughtful Democrats of the State." He was enthusiastically nominated and made a brilliant campaign, convincing the people everywhere of his sincerity of purpose and of his freedom from leading strings. He was elected by 49,150 plurality, which marked a notable political revolution, for Taft had carried New Jersey before by a plurality of 82,000.

A primary for United States senator had been held the same day of the election of governor. Not dreaming that Democratic success would extend to the Legislature, the Democratic primary for senator had been allowed to go by default, or at least to take care of itself. The total Democratic vote was 73,000 and James E. Martine had received 54,000 of these. After a bitter fight, in which Governor Wilson showed he was the real leader of his party and able to cope successfully with the old politicians who did not know that a new day and a new leader had arrived, the Legislature elected Mr. Martine, who had led in the primary, giving him forty votes, while James Smith, Jr., who insisted upon becoming a candidate, when he had declared before election he would not run, received only four. It was a preliminary victory which greatly encouraged the new general and his soldiery for coming battles. For battles there must needs be, because not only was there Republican opposition to contend with but some of the old Democratic organization leaders could not soon forget the Governor's triumph in the defeat of their old leader. Governor Wilson found the Legislature to be constituted as follows: Senate: Republicans 12, Democrats 9; Assembly: Republicans 18, Democrats 42. The platform on which the party had won promised four vital reforms, a direct primary bill, a corrupt practices act, a public service commission with power to fix rates, and an employer's liability and workingmen's compensation law. Bitter opposition to these reforms developed, secretly even among some Democratic members who were supposed to be pledged to them. Few believed the Governor could force them through. When informed that it would be the end of the session before they could be reached, he replied that if that were the case an extra session would be called to pass them. He invited Republican as well as Democratic members to call upon him at his offices. If they did not come he sent for them. He won over some by his logical reasoning, others by his magnetic personality. To some who were extremely stubborn he proposed canvassing their own districts with them. Once in a message he intimated that he might be compelled to name publicly the balking members but as a matter of fact he never had to do so. He never made ugly threats but he often smilingly suggested that Jersey public opinion was back of his arguments.

In a legislative session of three months, in spite of the fact that the upper house of the legislature was of the opposite party to him, Governor Wilson fulfilled every demand of the people in securing this important legislation:

(1) The reform of the election laws was achieved by a Corrupt Practices Act, which makes it impossible for any corporation to contribute in any way towards the election of any candidate, and likewise makes the use of money on election-day unlawful and difficult; direct primaries for all elective state, county and municipal offices; direct primaries for United States senator and delegates to national conventions, with popular expression for choice for president; civil service tests for election officers and personal registration for all voters; non-partisan ballots in both primaries and elections.

(2) The better regulation of corporations was accomplished by a comprehensive Public Utilities Law, fixing the responsibility on officers of corporations for all violations, and vesting power in a commission to make rates and physical valuation of public service companies.

(3) Accidents to workingmen were provided for by a workmen's compensation law, providing for automatic payments for injuries or loss of life, in all industries, and doing away with the old fellow-servant responsibility of the common law.

(4) An act was passed enabling cities to adopt the commission form of government.

(5) A law was passed providing for the complete reorganization of the complicated state school system, whereby politics was eliminated.

(6) A law was passed regulating cold storage and other laws to purify the milk supply and to keep oysters from contamination.

Governor Wilson's extraordinary success in putting reforms through the New Jersey legislature gave him a strong lead for the Democratic nomination for the Presidency, and when the Democratic convention met at Baltimore on June 25, 1912, the New Jersey Executive was in a forward position as one of the people's favorites. Feeling that he was not the representative of progressive politics, the selection of Judge Parker as temporary chairman was earnestly opposed by Honorable William J. Bryan, who sent telegrams to every presidential candidate asking whether Parker was satisfactory for this position. To this telegram Wilson did not hesitate to reply without equivocation that he felt that the choice of Parker would be a mistake. That telegram, sent contrary to the dictates of the old political method of trimming, was a master stroke. It showed that Wilson was no opportunist, but was ready to declare his position when silence or straddling was recommended. Parker won, and it seemed at first as if those who opposed him were doomed to defeat. The deadlock, which lasted from June 25 until July 2, gave Bryan his opportunity, for it allowed the story of the fight that was being made for Wilson as the most militant leader of Progressive measures to find its way back to the uttermost corners of the country. The national Democracy was thrilled. The people began to telegraph their wishes to the delegates, and they strongly favored the nomination of Wilson. It is said that one hundred and ten thousand telegrams were received by delegates. Mr. Bryan himself receiving 1,112 signed by more than thirty thousand persons. Mr. Bryan became the leading spirit of the Convention and he threw his support to Governor Wilson, who made slow but steady gains until his final triumph. On the first ballot he received three hundred and twenty-four votes, and on the forty-sixth, which nominated, nine hundred and ninety.

Upon accepting the nomination for the presidency, Mr. Wilson thus succinctly summarized in his speech at Sea Girt the two great things he would undertake to do:

"There are two great things to do. One is to set up the rule of justice and of right in such matters as the tariff, the regulation of the trusts and the prevention of monopoly, the adaptation of our banking and currency laws to the varied uses to which our people must put them, the treatment of those who do the daily labor in our factories and mines and throughout all our great industrial and commercial undertakings, and the political life of the people of the Philippines, for whom we hold governmental power in trust for their service, not our own. The other, the additional duty, is the great task of protecting our people and our resources and of keeping open to the whole people the doors of opportunity through which they must, generation by generation, pass if they are to make conquest of their fortunes in health, in freedom, in peace and in contentment. In the performance of this second great duty we are face to face with questions of conservation and of development, questions of forests and water powers and mines and waterways, of the building of an adequate merchant marine, and the opening of every highway and facility and the setting up of every safeguard needed by a great, industrious, expanding nation."

In this speech Governor Wilson contended that representative government is nothing more nor less than an effort to give voice to the great, struggling body of the masses — the learned and the fortunate, as well as the uneducated — through spokesmen chosen out of every grade and class. He declared it to be a fact which it would be dangerous to ignore that, "We stand in the presence of an awakened nation — awake to the knowledge that she has lost certain cherished liberties and has wasted priceless resources which she had solemnly under taken to hold in trust for posterity and for all mankind; and she stands confronted with an occasion for constructive statesmanship such as has not arisen since the days in which the Government was set up." . . . "We are servants of the people, the whole people. The Nation has been unnecessarily, unreasonably at war within itself. Interest has clashed with interest when there were common principles of right and of fair dealing which might and should have bound them all together, not as rivals, but as partners. As the servants of all, we are bound to undertake the great duty of accommodation and adjustment."

The Nominee was outspoken in his conviction that the tariff should be revised. Said he:

"Tariff duties, as they have employed them, have not been a means of setting up an equitable system of protection. They have been, on the contrary, a method of fostering special privilege. They have made it easy to establish monopoly in our domestic markets. Trusts have owed their origin and their secure power to them. The economic freedom of our people, our prosperity in trade, our untrammeled energy in manufacture depend upon their reconsideration from top to bottom in an entirely different spirit. . . . It is obvious that the changes we make should be made only at such a rate and in such a way as will least interfere with the normal and healthful course of commerce and manufacture. But we shall not on that account act with timidity, as if we did not know our own minds, for we are certain of our ground and of our object. There should be an immediate revision, and it should be downward, unhesitatingly and steadily downward." . . .

President Wilson made an inspiring campaign, delivering a number of speeches at strategic centers in the various states. The triangular character of the race made it the most interesting in American history since Lincoln's time. Wilson got 6,293,454 of the popular vote; Roosevelt 4,119,538, and Taft 3,484,980, but the New Jersey Executive got an overwhelming majority in the Electoral College, the vote standing thus: Wilson 435, Roosevelt 88, and Taft 8.

The marrow of the man is his sincerity. His carrying out of every pledge made in New Jersey presaged his course as President. He kept the rudder true in his State in a storm that beat its fury upon the Commonwealth and threatened to divide and defeat his party, victorious for the first time in a dozen years. In his inaugural address, in which his sincere and genuine appeal to "all forward-looking men" fell upon ears that were glad to hear the pledge of the New Freedom he had come to inaugurate in our Republic, the new President showed that his campaign pledges were the sacred covenants between the new executive and the people.

His inaugural illustrated the truth that he was sailing by the chart which he himself had prepared in the campaign: After insisting that the change of government meant that the nation now sought to use the Democratic party to interpret a change in its own plans and point of view; after asserting that some old, familiar things have dropped their disguises and shown themselves alien and sinister, and that some new things have come to assume the aspect of things long believed in and familiar, he declared we had come to a work of restoration, and continued:

"We have itemized with some degree of particularity the things that ought to be altered and here are some of the chief items: A tariff which cuts us off from our proper part in the commerce of the world, violates the just principles of taxation, and makes the Government a facile instrument in the hands of private interests; a banking and currency system based upon the necessity of the Government to sell its bonds fifty years ago and perfectly adapted to concentrating cash and restricting credits; an industrial system which, take it on all sides, financial as well as administrative, holds capital in leading strings, restricts the liberties and limits the opportunities of labor, and exploits without renewing or conserving the natural resources of the country; a body of agricultural activities never yet given the efficiency of great business undertakings or served as it should be through the instrumentality of science taken directly to the farm, or afforded the facilities of credit best suited to its practical needs; water-courses undeveloped, waste places unreclaimed, forests untended, fast disappearing without plan or prospect of renewal, unregarded waste heaps at every mine. We have studied as perhaps no other nation has the most effective means of production, but we have not studied cost or economy as we should either as organizers of industry, as statesmen, or as individuals."

The inaugural address concluded with this appeal for co-operation in the great task upon which he was entering:

"This is not a day of triumph; it is a day of dedication. Here muster, not the forces of party, but the forces of humanity. Men's hearts wait upon us; men's lives hang in the balance; men's hopes call upon us to say what we will do. Who shall live up to the great trust? Who dares fail to try? I summon all honest men, all patriotic, all forward-looking men, to my side. God helping me, I will not fail them, if they will but counsel and sustain me!"

When the 63rd Congress was called in extraordinary session the President's proclamation did not limit the purpose to tariff reduction, as many party leaders desired, but it was primarily convened to revise and reduce the tariff. The previous Republican administration had revised but not reduced, and suffered a crushing defeat in the elections of 1910 and 1912. Wilson, moreover, had before his vision the mistakes of the late President Cleveland to aid him in determining to permit no new question or no reasonings to divert him from the paramount duty of responding to the double mandate of the voters to reduce the tariff and unfetter trade. His every utterance emphasized tariff as the first great reform to be carried out. He was in frequent conference with the leaders of the House, both before Congress assembled and when it convened. He led in the Nation in making and invoking public sentiment as he had successfully led when he was Governor of New Jersey. To emphasize his tariff program and impress the argument for genuine reduction, he astonished the country by going in person and reading his message to Congress, reviving an early custom which went into innocuous desuetude because Jefferson, who had no taste and little gift for public speaking, sent his message to be read by a clerk, instead of delivering it in person. There were those who declared this return to an old order suggested a king giving orders to Congress. They predicted that the innovation smacked of a return to Federalism. But on the day that Wilson entered the House to read his message every seat was occupied. Hundreds could not gain admission. Those who witnessed the contrast between the clear enunciation and impressive presentation of his convictions and recommendations, and the old humdrum reading, when clerks droned through a message, and the tense interest when the new leader enunciated his own views and the pledges of the majority party, rejoiced at the new freedom that ushered in the delivery in the flesh of a fresh message to the American people.

Wilson was in direct touch with Mr. Underwood and other members of the Ways and Means Committee and other leaders of the House in the preparation of the Underwood Bill. He did not shirk labor or responsibility, nor assume the duty resting upon others. But, in consonance with the duty which the leadership of the dominant party, to which he had been called, demanded, he helped to shape the character of the legislation on the schedules upon which there was the most difference of opinion. He freely discussed these schedules with those who had a claim upon his consideration of their views. The sugar people were the most active and earnest in trying to secure a reversal of the program of free sugar. They sought to impress the President with the view that a protective duty, which would bring in large revenue, should remain on sugar. He heard, he conferred, he debated, and declared that free sugar must be a part of the bill, and free sugar is in the Underwood-Simmons bill. The famous Schedule K, long called the key to the protection arch, had given so much trouble to the Democrats in the prior Congress that they had to be content to levy some tax on wool, much to the regret of the many who for more than a quarter of a century had been fighting for free wool. The advocates of a tariff on wool wished to enact the same wool schedule that passed the Sixty-second Congress, but the President stood firmly for free wool, as did nearly all the newly elected Congressmen, and free wool is in the bill. The old plan of permitting the beneficiaries of the tariff to write the tariff schedules, which put money in their purses, had come to an end. The President, with the overwhelming majority of his party in Congress, subordinated every local consideration to the passage of a tariff act drafted along the lines indicated in the pre-election promises of the President. In the tariff, as in important matters in which he was interested in New Jersey, he accepted no compromise. The Tariff act of 1913 owes much of its value to the wise and courageous President in the White House. To him is largely due the credit of a united party, with a narrow margin in the Senate, refusing to change in one jot or tittle the bill agreed upon in party council and approved by the Chief Executive. In 1894, with a like slender majority in the Senate, Mr. Cleveland was unable to lead his party in the famous tariff struggle. They divided and compromised so that, when the Senate finally passed a tariff bill which the House felt forced to accept, the President refused to sign it. He declared it to represent "party perfidy and party dishonor." But the Democratic party went into long exile as the result of party dissensions over tariff and currency legislation. There were those who predicted that history would repeat itself and that the Democratic Congress would so divide in 1913 as to invite another long exile such as the one that began in 1894 and lasted until 1912. To the President, in cordial co-operation with the leaders of his party in Congress, the historian will give the credit for the united action that insured tariff and currency legislation[1] without party dissension or serious financial disturbance.

It is well known that every revision of the tariff in the past half a century has been accompanied by a strong lobby of the interests which had commercial or industrial issues at stake. After the Underwood bill had gone to the Senate, President Wilson had occasion to inform the Senate that he had information that "a numerous, industrious and insidious lobby" was at work. The President's statement, which aroused the country, was, in full, as follows:

"I think that the public ought to know the extraordinary exertions being made by the lobby in Washington to gain recognition for certain alterations of the tariff bill. Washington has seldom seen so numerous, so industrious, or so insidious a lobby. The newspapers are being filled with paid advertisements calculated to mislead the judgment of public men not only, but also the public opinion of the country itself. There is every evidence that money without limit is being spent to sustain this lobby and to create an appearance of a pressure of public opinion antagonistic to some of the chief items of the tariff bill. It is of serious interest to the country that the people at large should have no lobby and be voiceless in these matters while great bodies of astute men seek to create an artificial opinion and to overcome the interests of the public for their private profit. It is thoroughly worth the while of the people of this country to take knowledge of this matter. Only public opinion can check and destroy it.

"The Government in all its branches ought to be relieved from this intolerable burden and this constant interruption to the calm progress of debate. I know that in this I am speaking for the members of the two Houses, who would rejoice as much as I would to be released from this unbearable situation."

The statement, at first, was received by a portion of the press and people with incredulity but, as the lobby investigating committee, headed by Senator Overman, proceeded with its work, it became plainly evident that the President was entirely correct in his charge and in his description of the nature of the lobby. Evidence adduced showed that the sugar-growing interests spent as much as $100,000 in agitation against free sugar, though there was no proof that this particular item was illegally expended. It was in evidence that more than 1,000,000 documents had been mailed under the franks of Congressmen in opposition to free sugar. In one quarter, charges were made that a long list of members of both branches of Congress had accepted money considerations in exchange for their influence in committees of Congress which had labor legislation in charge. Undue influence was exerted upon other members, it was alleged, by means of "business, political and sympathetic" reasons. It was proven that one shameless lobbyist had impersonated, over the long-distance telephone, several of the leading members of Congress and had offered in their name to influence pending legislation. Evidence was multiplied that strong bodies of men united to defeat members of Congress who opposed the legislation they desired, or sought to put laws on the statute books not favored by them. The trail of the lobbyist was found in a score of ways. The charge of the President of the existence of "a numerous, industrious and insidious lobby" was more than established by the evidence. The President was vindicated. The President's warning and the work of the lobby committee served to put Congress and the people on their guard, and history will doubtless record that the Underwood-Simmons tariff bill was freer from attack by this old enemy of tariff reduction than any other tariff measure passed for many years.

As soon as it became certain that a tariff bill, in accordance with the promises of the Baltimore platform, would pass the extra session, the President bent his energies toward co-operating with Congress to secure the passage of a currency reform measure. The bill, which was christened with the names of Representative Glass and Senator Owen, had the sanction of the Administration.

The President undertook to overcome the feeling of those members of the Senate that remaining in session through the hot summer in order to pass the tariff bill was sufficient achievement for one session and that the currency bill could go over to the regular session. With all the earnestness of his nature, the President urged that there would never be a more favorable opportunity to pass a currency reform measure than the present. He appeared personally before Congress in joint session for the second time and read his message on the currency. "When the work to be done is so pressing and so fraught with big consequence," he said, "we know that we are not at liberty to weigh against it any point of personal sacrifice." In making men free to employ individual initiative by removing the trammels of the protection tariff, the President held, there will be necessary some readjustments of purpose and point of view. Then will follow a period of expansion and new enterprise, and "it is for us to determine whether it shall be rapid and facile and of easy accomplishment. This it cannot be unless the resourceful business men who are to deal with the new circumstances are to have at hand and ready for use the instrumentalities and conveniences of free enterprise which independent men need when acting on their own initiative." One of the chief things business needs now is "the proper means by which readily to vitalize its credit, corporate and individual, and its originative brains. The tyrannies of business, big and little, lie within the field of credit. We know that. Shall we not act upon the knowledge? Do we not know how to act upon it? If a man cannot make his assets available at pleasure, his assets of capacity and character and resource, what satisfaction is it to him to see opportunity beckoning to him on every hand, when others have the keys of credit in their pockets and treat them as all but their own private possession?"

It is imperative, therefore, to act immediately and upon clear principles. "The country has sought and seen its path in this matter within the last few years — sees it more clearly now than it ever saw it before — much more clearly than when the last legislative proposals on the subject were made. We must have a currency, not rigid as now, but readily, elastically responsive to sound credit, the expanding and contracting credits of everyday transactions, the normal ebb and flow of personal and corporate dealings. Our banking laws must mobilize reserves; must not permit the concentration anywhere in a few hands of the monetary resources of the country or their use for speculative purposes in such volume as to hinder or impede or stand in the way of other more legitimate, more fruitful uses. And the control of the system of banking and of issue which our new laws are to set up must be public, not private, must be vested in the Government itself, so that the banks may be the instruments, not the masters, of business and of individual enterprise and initiative."

The Wilson administration, in its earliest stages, was called upon to consider diplomatic questions that at once gave the people a clear understanding of its foreign policy. With firmness and dignity, unmoved by jingoism or hesitation, the President made clear his determination to make friendliness and justice to other nations the duty and mission of the Republic. In his brief inaugural, Mr. Wilson did not touch upon foreign questions but confined himself to the few economic home problems that pressed for solution. He may have thought, as did most of the people, that no international complications would come up until the needed tariff and currency legislation had been enacted, and he doubtless hoped that not even a small cloud would appear upon the horizon to threaten our cordial and friendly relations with other nations. But there soon came rumors of threatened trouble in one or more Republics to the south of us. There seemed to be a feeling that, after a long period of Republican rule at Washington, the new Administration's induction into office would encourage self-imposed officials to seek to obtain the reins of government. What should the attitude of the Administration be toward our neighbor countries in Central and South America? The President deemed the answer to that question important enough to make a declaration that attracted world-wide attention. He said:

"One of the chief objects of my administration will be to cultivate the friendship and deserve the confidence of our sister republics of Central and South America, and to promote in every proper and honorable way the interests which are common to the peoples of the two continents. I earnestly desire the most cordial understanding and co-operation between the peoples and leaders of America and, therefore, deem it my duty to make this brief statement.

"Co-operation is possible only when supported at every turn by the orderly processes of just government based upon law, not upon arbitrary or irregular force. We hold, as I am sure all thoughtful leaders of republican government everywhere hold, that just government rests always upon the consent of the governed, and that there can be no freedom without order based upon law and upon the public conscience and approval. We shall look to make these principles the basis of mutual intercourse, respect and helpfulness between our sister republics and ourselves. We shall lend our influence of every kind to the realization of these principles in fact and practice, knowing that disorder, personal intrigues, and defiance of constitutional rights weaken and discredit government and injure none so much as the people who are unfortunate enough to have their common life and their common affairs so tainted and disturbed. We can have no sympathy with those who seek to seize the power of government to advance their own personal interests or ambition. We are the friends of peace, but we know that there can be no lasting or stable peace in such circumstances. As friends, therefore, we shall prefer those who act in the interest of peace and honor, who protect private rights, and respect the restraints of constitutional provision. Mutual respect seems to us the indispensable foundation of friendships between states, as between individuals.

"The United States has nothing to seek in Central and South America except the lasting interests of the peoples of the two continents, the security of governments intended for the people and for no special group or interest, and the development of personal and trade relationships between the two continents which shall redound to the profit and advantage of both and interfere with the rights and liberties of neither."

At the same time, the world was given to under stand that what is known as "dollar diplomacy" would not be countenanced by the Administration. During the Presidential campaign there had been much criticism of this policy and many had attributed to it a growing irritation in some of our sister republics.

The people of China had but latterly changed the form of their government into a republic, patterned after the United States. No great nation had recognized the Republic, and there was doubt whether it would maintain itself. The President determined not to join hands with other nations in a loan coupled with conditions that denied the government of China a free hand. He resolved also that as soon as the Chinese legislative branch was organized he would recognize the new Republic. The people of the United States rejoiced in the recognition, and shortly other nations followed. In extending the recognition of the greatest western Republic to the oldest nation that had put on the robes of self-government, the addresses by the new President of China and the American representative in China gave a thrill to all who believe that all governments derive their just powers from the consent of the governed. The words of President Wilson constitute the best expression of American thought. He wrote:

"The Government and people of the United States of America having abundantly testified their sympathy with the people of China upon their assumption of the attributes and powers of self-government deem it opportune at this time, when the representative National Assembly has met to discharge the high duty of setting the seal of full accomplishment upon the aspirations of the Chinese people, that I extend, in the name of my Government and of my countrymen, a greeting of welcome to the New China thus entering into the family of nations. In taking this step, I entertain the confident hope and expectation that in perfecting a republican form of government the Chinese nation will attain to the highest degree of development and well-being, and that under the new rule all the established obligations of China which passed to the Provisional Government will, in turn, pass to and be observed by the Government established by the Assembly."

Early in the history of the Administration, the Japanese Minister lodged a protest with the Department of State against the proposed passage of an anti-alien land law bill by the California Legislature. The claim of the Japanese Government was that such a measure would violate treaty rights. "To lease land for commercial purposes" is granted to Japanese subjects in our treaty with Japan. It was claimed by the California Legislature that the Japanese were increasing their leases and their ownership of lands, particularly agricultural lands, in California. President Wilson set himself to see that the treaty rights of Japan should be respected. In a telegram to Governor Johnson, of California, the President "very respectfully but most earnestly advised against" the use of the words "ineligible to citizenship," which were used in one or more of the bills pending. In a second telegram to Governor Johnson, he appealed to the Executive, the Legislature, and the people of California, "to act in the matter under consideration in a manner that cannot from any point of view be fairly challenged or called in question. If they deem it necessary to exclude all aliens who have not declared their intention to become citizens from the privilege of land ownership, they can do so along the lines already followed in the laws of many foreign countries including Japan itself. Invidious discrimination will inevitably draw in question the treaty obligations of the Government of the United States." The President added that he was "confident the people and the legislative authorities of California would generously respond the moment the matter was presented to them as a question of national policy and national honor."

Upon the receipt of a reply from Governor Johnson, President Wilson telegraphed to the Governor asking whether, on account of the difficulty from a distance of understanding fully the situation with regard to the sentiments and circumstances lying back of the pending proposition concerning the ownership of land in California, it would be agreeable to him and the Legislature to have the Secretary of State visit Sacramento for the purpose of counseling with the Governor and the members of the Legislature and co-operating in the framing of a law which would meet the views of the people of the State and yet leave untouched the international obligations of the United States.

Mr. Bryan went to California and conferred with the Governor and Legislature, but it soon be came clearly apparent that the Legislature was bent upon passing a law forbidding ownership of agricultural land by the Japanese.

Mr. Bryan's suggestions to the Legislature were the following:

1. Delay immediate action and permit the State Department to try to frame a new treaty with Japan.

2. Delay immediate action and appoint a legislative commission to investigate alien land ownership and act with President Wilson in gaining relief.

3. Enact a law similar to the Illinois statute, which allows all aliens to hold land six years.

4. Enact a law similar to the Federal statute in the District of Columbia, which applies to all aliens.

Mr. Bryan presented these suggestions with this happy statement: "Each State in the Union acts in a dual capacity. It is the guardian of local affairs of its people and in a sense the only guardian, and yet each State is a member of the Union and one of the sisterhood of States. Therefore, in acting upon questions of local conditions, the State always recognizes that it is its duty to share the responsibility with other States in actions affecting the nation's relations with foreign nations."

The Legislature passed an act that was regarded by Japan as a discrimination against that country. For a time there was a feeling that the friendly relations long existing between the two countries would be sundered. But the policy of the Federal Administration, couched in friendly and courteous terms, convinced the Japanese people of its genuine friendship and of its sincere desire to treat that country with justice and consideration. The tense feeling in both countries was relieved by the spirit of amity and justice shown in every act and note of the Wilson administration.

A second delicate diplomatic situation with which the President had to deal concerned Mexico. The Ambassador at Mexico City, Mr. Henry Lane Wilson, was an appointee of the previous Administration, and in his desire to have this country recognize the de facto Huerta government, which followed the Madero régime, he did not represent the views of President Wilson. Ambassador Wilson was summoned to Washington to confer with the President, but a variance of views developing between him and the Administration, his resignation was eventually accepted. The situation was one of grave difficulty. The President was constrained to send a personal representative to deal with it at first hand and for this delicate mission selected ex-Governor John Lind of Minnesota, who was sent to Mexico. He was sent as adviser of the United States Embassy at Mexico City, and he began his negotiations with the Huerta administration through the United States chargé d'affaires. General Huerta showed little inclination, however, to accept the good offices tendered by this country through Mr. Lind. At this juncture, President Wilson for the third time took the Congress and people of the United States into his counsels by appearing personally before the joint session of both houses and making public his purpose and plans in dealing with the Mexican situation and with the results that followed his efforts.

His address revealed how the Huerta provisional government had rejected the friendly offices of the United States, told of its effort to aid in the establishment of peace, and of a government which could be recognized by this nation, and which would be obeyed and respected by Mexico's own people. For the first time since Washington's administration, a President appeared before Congress to discuss foreign affairs. His cordial reception by members from all sides, and the endorsement of his course by a large majority of the members of Congress, the press, and of the people of the Union, showed how strongly public opinion was behind him in his efforts. He sounded a high note when he stated at the outset:

"The peace, prosperity and contentment of Mexico mean more, much more, to us than merely an enlarged field for our commerce and enterprise. They mean an enlargement of the field of self-government and the realization of the hopes and rights of a nation with whose best aspirations, so long suppressed and disappointed, we deeply sympathize. We shall yet prove to the Mexican people that we know how to serve them without first thinking how we shall serve ourselves."

May 19, 1913.

THE WHITE HOUSE
WASHINGTON

My dear General Wilson,

I wish most sincerely that it were possible for me to be present at the dedication of the Maine Monument. My thoughts will be very much with you that day, as will, I am sure, the thoughts of the whole country.

All Americans must look back to the tragedy of the Maine with the profoundest sentiments of sorrow for the fine men who then so tragically and unexpectedly lost their lives, and must always feel that to have been one of the turning points of our consciousness of what was involved in the struggle for human liberty.

Cordially and Sincerely Yours,

Woodrow Wilson

General James Grant Wilson

[Fac-simile letter from President Woodrow Wilson to Gen. James Grant Wilson]

26

Mr. Lind was sent with the following instructions:

"Press very earnestly upon the attention of those who are now exercising authority or wielding influence in Mexico the following considerations and advice:

"The Government of the United States does not stand in the same case with the other great governments of the world in respect of what is happening or what is likely to happen in Mexico. We offer our good offices, not only because of our genuine desire to play the part of a friend, but also because we are expected by the powers of the world to act as Mexico's nearest friend.

"We wish to act in these circumstances in the spirit of the most earnest and disinterested friendship. It is our purpose in whatever we do or propose in this perplexing and distressing situation not only to pay the most scrupulous regard to the sovereignty and independence of Mexico — that we take as a matter of course to which we are bound by every obligation of right and honor — but also to give every possible evidence that we act in the interest of Mexico alone, and not in the interest of any person or body of persons who may have personal or property claims in Mexico which they may feel that they have a right to press. We are seeking to counsel Mexico for her own good and in the interest of her own peace, and not for any other purpose whatever. The Government of the United States would deem itself discredited if it had any selfish or ulterior purpose in transactions where the peace, happiness, and prosperity of a whole people are involved. It is acting as its friendship for Mexico, not as any selfish interest, dictates.

"The present situation in Mexico is incompatible with the fulfillment of international obligations on the part of Mexico, with the civilized development of Mexico herself, and with the maintenance of tolerable political and economic conditions in Central America. It is upon no common occasion therefore that the United States offers her counsel and assistance. All America cries out for a settlement.

"A satisfactory settlement seems to us to be conditioned on —

"(a) An immediate cessation of fighting throughout Mexico, a definite armistice solemnly entered into and scrupulously observed;

"(b) Security given for an early and free election in which all will agree to take part;

"(c) The consent of General Huerta to bind himself not to be a candidate for election as president of the republic at this election; and

"(d) The agreement of all parties to abide by the results of the election and co-operate in the most loyal way in organizing and supporting the new administration."

The Mexican Government was to be assured that the United States wished to play any part in this settlement which it could play honorably and consistently. It pledged itself to recognize and assist an administration so set up. Could Mexico give the civilized world a good reason for rejecting these good offices?

Mr. Lind executed his delicate mission with singular tact, firmness and good judgment, but the proposals he submitted were rejected in a note of Foreign Minister Gamboa which was laid before the Congress in printed form. This rejection the President was constrained to believe was due to misinformation, first, as to the friendly spirit of the American people in this matter, and, second, because they did not believe that the present Administration spoke for the people of the United States. "The effect of this unfortunate misunderstanding on their part," he continued in his message, "is to leave them singularly isolated and without friends who can effectually aid them. So long as the misunderstanding continues, we can only await the time of their awakening to a realization of the actual facts. We cannot thrust our good offices upon them. The situation must be given a little more time to work itself out in the new circumstances; and I believe that only a little time will be necessary. For the circumstances are new. The rejection of our friendship makes them new and will inevitably bring its own alterations in the whole aspect of affairs. The actual situation of the authorities at Mexico City will presently be revealed." Meantime, "we can afford to exercise the self-restraint of a really great nation which realizes its own strength and scorns to misuse it." With increased activity on the part of contending factions in Mexico would come increased danger to non-combatants, and therefore the President earnestly urged all Americans to leave Mexico at once. We should assist them in getting away, but, at the same time, let every one who assumed authority know, in the most unequivocal way, "that we shall vigilantly watch the fortunes of those Americans who cannot get away and shall hold those responsible for their sufferings and losses to a definite reckoning." For the rest, the President would forbid the exportation of arms or munitions of war from the United States into any part of the Republic of Mexico. His policy of justice, patience and friendship in all dealings with Mexico won the approval of the whole world. This policy, dictated by neighborly regard and freedom from any spirit of aggression, has, it is believed, gone far to make for the enduring friendship of the neighboring republics when the present unhappy struggles in Mexico have given way to honorable peace.

Inaugural Addresses

First Inaugural Address

There has been a change of government. It began two years ago, when the House of Representatives became Democratic by a decisive majority. It has now been completed. The Senate about to assemble will also be Democratic. The offices of President and Vice-President have been put into the hands of Democrats. What does the change mean? That is the question that is uppermost in our minds to-day. That is the question I am going to try to answer, in order, if I may, to interpret the occasion.

It means much more than the mere success of a party. The success of a party means little except when the Nation is using that party for a large and definite purpose. No one can mistake the purpose for which the Nation now seeks to use the Democratic Party. It seeks to use it to interpret a change in its own plans and point of view. Some old things with which we had grown familiar, and which had begun to creep into the very habit of our thought and of our lives, have altered their aspect as we have latterly looked critically upon them, with fresh, awakened eyes; have dropped their disguises and shown themselves alien and sinister. Some new things, as we look frankly upon them, willing to comprehend their real character, have come to assume the aspect of things long believed in and familiar, stuff of our own convictions. We have been refreshed by a new insight into our own life.

We see that in many things that life is very great. It is incomparably great in its material aspects, in its body of wealth, in the diversity and sweep of its energy, in the industries which have been conceived and built up by the genius of individual men and the limitless enterprise of groups of men. It is great, also, very great, in its moral force. Nowhere else in the world have noble men and women exhibited in more striking forms the beauty and the energy of sympathy and helpfulness and counsel in their efforts to rectify wrong, alleviate suffering, and set the weak in the way of strength and hope. We have built up, moreover, a great system of government, which has stood through a long age as in many respects a model for those who seek to set liberty upon foundations that will endure against fortuitous change, against storm and accident. Our life contains every great thing, and contains it in rich abundance.

But the evil has come with the good, and much fine gold has been corroded. With riches has come inexcusable waste. We have squandered a great part of what we might have used, and have not stopped to conserve the exceeding bounty of nature, without which our genius for enterprise would have been worthless and impotent, scorning to be careful, shamefully prodigal as well as admirably efficient. We have been proud of our industrial achievements, but we have not hitherto stopped thoughtfully enough to count the human cost, the cost of lives snuffed out, of energies overtaxed and broken, the fearful physical and spiritual cost to the men and women and children upon whom the dead weight and burden of it all has fallen pitilessly the years through. The groans and agony of it all had not yet reached our ears, the solemn, moving undertone of our life, coming up out of the mines and factories, and out of every home where the struggle had its intimate and familiar seat. With the great Government went many deep secret things which we too long delayed to look into and scrutinize with candid, fearless eyes. The great Government we loved has too often been made use of for private and selfish purposes, and those who used it had forgotten the people.

At last a vision has been vouchsafed us of our life as a whole. We see the bad with the good, the debased and decadent with the sound and vital. With this vision we approach new affairs. Our duty is to cleanse, to reconsider, to restore, to correct the evil without impairing the good, to purify and humanize every process of our common life without weakening or sentimentalizing it. There has been something crude and heartless and unfeeling in our haste to succeed and be great. Our thought has been "Let every man look out for himself, let every generation look out for itself," while we reared giant machinery which made it impossible that any but those who stood at the levers of control should have a chance to look out for themselves. We had not forgotten our morals. We remembered well enough that we had set up a policy which was meant to serve the humblest as well as the most powerful, with an eye single to the standards of justice and fair play, and remembered it with pride. But we were very heedless and in a hurry to be great.

We have come now to the sober second thought. The scales of heedlessness have fallen from our eyes. We have made up our minds to square every process of our national life again with the standards we so proudly set up at the beginning and have always carried at our hearts. Our work is a work of restoration.

We have itemized with some degree of particularity the things that ought to be altered and here are some of the chief items: A tariff which cuts us off from our proper part in the commerce of the world, violates the just principles of taxation, and makes the Government a facile instrument in the hand of private interests; a banking and currency system based upon the necessity of the Government to sell its bonds fifty years ago and perfectly adapted to concentrating cash and restricting credits; an industrial system which, take it on all its sides, financial as well as administrative, holds capital in leading strings, restricts the liberties and limits the opportunities of labor, and exploits without renewing or conserving the natural resources of the country; a body of agricultural activities never yet given the efficiency of great business undertakings or served as it should be through the instrumentality of science taken directly to the farm, or afforded the facilities of credit best suited to its practical needs; watercourses undeveloped, waste places unreclaimed, forests untended, fast disappearing without plan or prospect of renewal, unregarded waste heaps at every mine. We have studied as perhaps no other nation has the most effective means of production, but we have not studied cost or economy as we should either as organizers of industry, as statesmen, or as individuals.

Nor have we studied and perfected the means by which government may be put at the service of humanity, in safeguarding the health of the Nation, the health of its men and its women and its children, as well as their rights in the struggle for existence. This is no sentimental duty. The firm basis of government is justice, not pity. These are matters of justice. There can be no equality or opportunity, the first essential of justice in the body politic, if men and women and children be not shielded in their lives, their very vitality, from the consequences of great industrial and social processes which they can not alter, control, or singly cope with. Society must see to it that it does not itself crush or weaken or damage its own constituent parts. The first duty of law is to keep sound the society it serves. Sanitary laws, pure food laws, and laws determining conditions of labor which individuals are powerless to determine for themselves are intimate parts of the very business of justice and legal efficiency.

These are some of the things we ought to do, and not leave the others undone, the old-fashioned, never-to-be-neglected, fundamental safeguarding of property and of individual right. This is the high enterprise of the new day: To lift everything that concerns our life as a Nation to the light that shines from the hearthfire of every man's conscience and vision of the right. It is inconceivable that we should do this as partisans; it is inconceivable we should do it in ignorance of the facts as they are or in blind haste. We shall restore, not destroy. We shall deal with our economic system as it is and as it may be modified, not as it might be if we had a clean sheet of paper to write upon; and step by step we shall make it what it should be, in the spirit of those who question their own wisdom and seek counsel and knowledge, not shallow self-satisfaction or the excitement of excursions whither they can not tell. Justice, and only justice, shall always be our motto.

And yet it will be no cool process of mere science. The Nation has been deeply stirred, stirred by a solemn passion, stirred by the knowledge of wrong, of ideals lost, of government too often debauched and made an instrument of evil. The feelings with which we face this new age of right and opportunity sweep across our heartstrings like some air out of God's own presence, where justice and mercy are reconciled and the judge and the brother are one. We know our task to be no mere task of politics but a task which shall search us through and through, whether we be able to understand our time and the need of our people, whether we be indeed their spokesmen and interpreters, whether we have the pure heart to comprehend and the rectified will to choose our high course of action.

This is not a day of triumph; it is a day of dedication. Here muster, not the forces of party, but the forces of humanity. Men's hearts wait upon us; men's lives hang in the balance; men's hopes call upon us to say what we will do. Who shall live up to the great trust? Who dares fail to try? I summon all honest men, all patriotic, all forward-looking men, to my side. God helping me, I will not fail them, if they will but counsel and sustain me!

Second Inaugural Address

My Fellow Citizens:

The four years which have elapsed since last I stood in this place have been crowded with counsel and action of the most vital interest and consequence. Perhaps no equal period in our history has been so fruitful of important reforms in our economic and industrial life or so full of significant changes in the spirit and purpose of our political action. We have sought very thoughtfully to set our house in order, correct the grosser errors and abuses of our industrial life, liberate and quicken the processes of our national genius and energy, and lift our politics to a broader view of the people's essential interests.

It is a record of singular variety and singular distinction. But I shall not attempt to review it. It speaks for itself and will be of increasing influence as the years go by. This is not the time for retrospect. It is time rather to speak our thoughts and purposes concerning the present and the immediate future.

Although we have centered counsel and action with such unusual concentration and success upon the great problems of domestic legislation to which we addressed ourselves four years ago, other matters have more and more forced themselves upon our attention — matters lying outside our own life as a nation and over which we had no control, but which, despite our wish to keep free of them, have drawn us more and more irresistibly into their own current and influence.

It has been impossible to avoid them. They have affected the life of the whole world. They have shaken men everywhere with a passion and an apprehension they never knew before. It has been hard to preserve calm counsel while the thought of our own people swayed this way and that under their influence. We are a composite and cosmopolitan people. We are of the blood of all the nations that are at war. The currents of our thoughts as well as the currents of our trade run quick at all seasons back and forth between us and them. The war inevitably set its mark from the first alike upon our minds, our industries, our commerce, our politics and our social action. To be indifferent to it, or independent of it, was out of the question.

And yet all the while we have been conscious that we were not part of it. In that consciousness, despite many divisions, we have drawn closer together. We have been deeply wronged upon the seas, but we have not wished to wrong or injure in return; have retained throughout the consciousness of standing in some sort apart, intent upon an interest that transcended the immediate issues of the war itself.

As some of the injuries done us have become intolerable we have still been clear that we wished nothing for ourselves that we were not ready to demand for all mankind-fair dealing, justice, the freedom to live and to be at ease against organized wrong.

It is in this spirit and with this thought that we have grown more and more aware, more and more certain that the part we wished to play was the part of those who mean to vindicate and fortify peace. We have been obliged to arm ourselves to make good our claim to a certain minimum of right and of freedom of action. We stand firm in armed neutrality since it seems that in no other way we can demonstrate what it is we insist upon and cannot forget. We may even be drawn on, by circumstances, not by our own purpose or desire, to a more active assertion of our rights as we see them and a more immediate association with the great struggle itself. But nothing will alter our thought or our purpose. They are too clear to be obscured. They are too deeply rooted in the principles of our national life to be altered. We desire neither conquest nor advantage. We wish nothing that can be had only at the cost of another people. We always professed unselfish purpose and we covet the opportunity to prove our professions are sincere.

There are many things still to be done at home, to clarify our own politics and add new vitality to the industrial processes of our own life, and we shall do them as time and opportunity serve, but we realize that the greatest things that remain to be done must be done with the whole world for stage and in cooperation with the wide and universal forces of mankind, and we are making our spirits ready for those things.

We are provincials no longer. The tragic events of the thirty months of vital turmoil through which we have just passed have made us citizens of the world. There can be no turning back. Our own fortunes as a nation are involved whether we would have it so or not.

And yet we are not the less Americans on that account. We shall be the more American if we but remain true to the principles in which we have been bred. They are not the principles of a province or of a single continent. We have known and boasted all along that they were the principles of a liberated mankind. These, therefore, are the things we shall stand for, whether in war or in peace:

That all nations are equally interested in the peace of the world and in the political stability of free peoples, and equally responsible for their maintenance; that the essential principle of peace is the actual equality of nations in all matters of right or privilege; that peace cannot securely or justly rest upon an armed balance of power; that governments derive all their just powers from the consent of the governed and that no other powers should be supported by the common thought, purpose or power of the family of nations; that the seas should be equally free and safe for the use of all peoples, under rules set up by common agreement and consent, and that, so far as practicable, they should be accessible to all upon equal terms; that national armaments shall be limited to the necessities of national order and domestic safety; that the community of interest and of power upon which peace must henceforth depend imposes upon each nation the duty of seeing to it that all influences proceeding from its own citizens meant to encourage or assist revolution in other states should be sternly and effectually suppressed and prevented.

I need not argue these principles to you, my fellow countrymen; they are your own part and parcel of your own thinking and your own motives in affairs. They spring up native amongst us. Upon this as a platform of purpose and of action we can stand together. And it is imperative that we should stand together. We are being forged into a new unity amidst the fires that now blaze throughout the world. In their ardent heat we shall, in God's Providence, let us hope, be purged of faction and division, purified of the errant humors of party and of private interest, and shall stand forth in the days to come with a new dignity of national pride and spirit. Let each man see to it that the dedication is in his own heart, the high purpose of the nation in his own mind, ruler of his own will and desire.

I stand here and have taken the high and solemn oath to which you have been audience because the people of the United States have chosen me for this august delegation of power and have by their gracious judgment named me their leader in affairs.

I know now what the task means. I realize to the full the responsibility which it involves. I pray God I may be given the wisdom and the prudence to do my duty in the true spirit of this great people. I am their servant and can succeed only as they sustain and guide me by their confidence and their counsel. The thing I shall count upon, the thing without which neither counsel nor action will avail, is the unity of America-an America united in feeling, in purpose and in its vision of duty, of opportunity and of service.

We are to beware of all men who would turn the tasks and the necessities of the nation to their own private profit or use them for the building up of private power.

United alike in the conception of our duty and in the high resolve to perform it in the face of all men, let us dedicate ourselves to the great task to which we must now set our hand. For myself I beg your tolerance, your countenance and your united aid.

The shadows that now lie dark upon our path will soon be dispelled, and we shall walk with the light all about us if we be but true to ourselves-to ourselves as we have wished to be known in the counsels of the world and in the thought of all those who love liberty and justice and the right exalted.

State of the Union Addresses

First State of the Union address

December 2, 1913

Gentlemen of the Congress:

In pursuance of my constitutional duty to "give to the Congress information of the state of the Union," I take the liberty of addressing you on several matters which ought, as it seems to me, particularly to engage the attention of your honorable bodies, as of all who study the welfare and progress of the Nation.

I shall ask your indulgence if I venture to depart in some degree from the usual custom of setting before you in formal review the many matters which have engaged the attention and called for the action of the several departments of the Government or which look to them for early treatment in the future, because the list is long, very long, and would suffer in the abbreviation to which I should have to subject it. I shall submit to you the reports of the heads of the several departments, in which these subjects are set forth in careful detail, and beg that they may receive the thoughtful attention of your committees and of all Members of the Congress who may have the leisure to study them. Their obvious importance, as constituting the very substance of the business of the Government, makes comment and emphasis on my part unnecessary.

The country, I am thankful to say, is at peace with all the world, and many happy manifestations multiply about us of a growing cordiality and sense of community of interest among the nations, foreshadowing an age of settled peace and good will. More and more readily each decade do the nations manifest their willingness to bind themselves by solemn treaty to the processes of peace, the processes of frankness and fair concession. So far the United States has stood at the front of such negotiations. She will, I earnestly hope and confidently believe, give fresh proof of her sincere adherence to the cause of international friendship by ratifying the several treaties of arbitration awaiting renewal by the Senate. In addition to these, it has been the privilege of the Department of State to gain the assent, in principle, of no less than 31 nations, representing four-fifths of the population of the world, to the negotiation of treaties by which it shall be agreed that whenever differences of interest or of policy arise which can not be resolved by the ordinary processes of diplomacy they shall be publicly analyzed, discussed, and reported upon by a tribunal chosen by the parties before either nation determines its course of action.

There is only one possible standard by which to determine controversies between the United States and other nations, and that is compounded of these two elements: Our own honor and our obligations to the peace of the world. A test so compounded ought easily to be made to govern both the establishment of new treaty obligations and the interpretation of those already assumed.

There is but one cloud upon our horizon. That has shown itself to the south of us, and hangs over Mexico. There can be no certain prospect of peace in America until Gen. Huerta has surrendered his usurped authority in Mexico; until it is understood on all hands, indeed, that such pretended governments will not be countenanced or dealt with by-the Government of the United States. We are the friends of constitutional government in America; we are more than its friends, we are its champions; because in no other way can our neighbors, to whom we would wish in every way to make proof of our friendship, work out their own development in peace and liberty. Mexico has no Government. The attempt to maintain one at the City of Mexico has broken down, and a mere military despotism has been set up which has hardly more than the semblance of national authority. It originated in the usurpation of Victoriano Huerta, who, after a brief attempt to play the part of constitutional President, has at last cast aside even the pretense of legal right and declared himself dictator. As a consequence, a condition of affairs now exists in Mexico which has made it doubtful whether even the most elementary and fundamental rights either of her own people or of the citizens of other countries resident within her territory can long be successfully safeguarded, and which threatens, if long continued, to imperil the interests of peace, order, and tolerable life in the lands immediately to the south of us. Even if the usurper had succeeded in his purposes, in despite of the constitution of the Republic and the rights of its people, he would have set up nothing but a precarious and hateful power, which could have lasted but a little while, and whose eventual downfall would have left the country in a more deplorable condition than ever. But he has not succeeded. He has forfeited the respect and the moral support even of those who were at one time willing to see him succeed. Little by little he has been completely isolated. By a little every day his power and prestige are crumbling and the collapse is not far away. We shall not, I believe, be obliged to alter our policy of watchful waiting. And then, when the end comes, we shall hope to see constitutional order restored in distressed Mexico by the concert and energy of such of her leaders as prefer the liberty of their people to their own ambitions.

I turn to matters of domestic concern. You already have under consideration a bill for the reform of our system of banking and currency, for which the country waits with impatience, as for something fundamental to its whole business life and necessary to set credit free from arbitrary and artificial restraints. I need not say how earnestly I hope for its early enactment into law. I take leave to beg that the whole energy and attention of the Senate be concentrated upon it till the matter is successfully disposed of. And yet I feel that the request is not needed-that the Members of that great House need no urging in this service to the country.

I present to you, in addition, the urgent necessity that special provision be made also for facilitating the credits needed by the farmers of the country. The pending currency bill does the farmers a great service. It puts them upon an equal footing with other business men and masters of enterprise, as it should; and upon its passage they will find themselves quit of many of the difficulties which now hamper them in the field of credit. The farmers, of course, ask and should be given no special privilege, such as extending to them the credit of the Government itself. What they need and should obtain is legislation which will make their own abundant and substantial credit resources available as a foundation for joint, concerted local action in their own behalf in getting the capital they must use. It is to this we should now address ourselves.

It has, singularly enough, come to pass that we have allowed the industry of our farms to lag behind the other activities of the country in its development. I need not stop to tell you how fundamental to the life of the Nation is the production of its food. Our thoughts may ordinarily be concentrated upon the cities and the hives of industry, upon the cries of the crowded market place and the clangor of the factory, but it is from the quiet interspaces of the open valleys and the free hillsides that we draw the sources of life and of prosperity, from the farm and the ranch, from the forest and the mine. Without these every street would be silent, every office deserted, every factory fallen into disrepair. And yet the farmer does not stand upon the same footing with the forester and the miner in the market of credit. He is the servant of the seasons. Nature determines how long he must wait for his crops, and will not be hurried in her processes. He may give his note, but the season of its maturity depends upon the season when his crop matures, lies at the gates of the market where his products are sold. And the security he gives is of a character not known in the broker's office or as familiarly as it might be on the counter of the banker.

The Agricultural Department of the Government is seeking to assist as never before to make farming an efficient business, of wide co-operative effort, in quick touch with the markets for foodstuffs. The farmers and the Government will henceforth work together as real partners in this field, where we now begin to see our way very clearly and where many intelligent plans are already being put into execution. The Treasury of the United States has, by a timely and well-considered distribution of its deposits, facilitated the moving of the crops in the present season and prevented the scarcity of available funds too often experienced at such times. But we must not allow ourselves to depend upon extraordinary expedients. We must add the means by which the, farmer may make his credit constantly and easily available and command when he will the capital by which to support and expand his business. We lag behind many other great countries of the modern world in attempting to do this. Systems of rural credit have been studied and developed on the other side of the water while we left our farmers to shift for themselves in the ordinary money market. You have but to look about you in any rural district to see the result, the handicap and embarrassment which have been put upon those who produce our food.

Conscious of this backwardness and neglect on our part, the Congress recently authorized the creation of a special commission to study the various systems of rural credit which have been put into operation in Europe, and this commission is already prepared to report. Its report ought to make it easier for us to determine what methods will be best suited to our own farmers. I hope and believe that the committees of the Senate and House will address themselves to this matter with the most fruitful results, and I believe that the studies and recently formed plans of the Department of Agriculture may be made to serve them very greatly in their work of framing appropriate and adequate legislation. It would be indiscreet and presumptuous in anyone to dogmatize upon so great and many-sided a question, but I feel confident that common counsel will produce the results we must all desire.

Turn from the farm to the world of business which centers in the city and in the factory, and I think that all thoughtful observers will agree that the immediate service we owe the business communities of the country is to prevent private monopoly more effectually than it has yet been prevented. I think it will be easily agreed that we should let the Sherman anti-trust law stand, unaltered, as it is, with its debatable ground about it, but that we should as much as possible reduce the area of that debatable ground by further and more explicit legislation; and should also supplement that great act by legislation which will not only clarify it but also facilitate its administration and make it fairer to all concerned. No doubt we shall all wish, and the country will expect, this to be the central subject of our deliberations during the present session; but it is a subject so many-sided and so deserving of careful and discriminating discussion that I shall take the liberty of addressing you upon it in a special message at a later date than this. It is of capital importance that the business men of this country should be relieved of all uncertainties of law with regard to their enterprises and investments and a clear path indicated which they can travel without anxiety. It is as important that they should be relieved of embarrassment and set free to prosper as that private monopoly should be destroyed. The ways of action should be thrown wide open.

I turn to a subject which I hope can be handled promptly and without serious controversy of any kind. I mean the method of selecting nominees for the Presidency of the United States. I feel confident that I do not misinterpret the wishes or the expectations of the country when I urge the prompt enactment of legislation which will provide for primary elections throughout the country at which the voters of the several parties may choose their nominees for the Presidency without the intervention of nominating conventions. I venture the suggestion that this legislation should provide for the retention of party conventions, but only for the purpose of declaring and accepting the verdict of the primaries and formulating the platforms of the parties; and I suggest that these conventions should consist not of delegates chosen for this single purpose, but of the nominees for Congress, the nominees for vacant seats in the Senate of the United States, the Senators whose terms have not yet closed, the national committees, and the candidates for the Presidency themselves, in order that platforms may be framed by those responsible to the people for carrying them into effect.

These are all matters of vital domestic concern, and besides them, outside the charmed circle of our own national life in which our affections command us, as well as our consciences, there stand out our obligations toward our territories over sea. Here we are trustees. Porto Rico, Hawaii, the Philippines, are ours, indeed, but not ours to do what we please with. Such territories, once regarded as mere possessions, are no longer to be selfishly exploited; they are part of the domain of public conscience and of serviceable and enlightened statesmanship. We must administer them for the people who live in them and with the same sense of responsibility to them as toward our own people in our domestic affairs. No doubt we shall successfully enough bind Porto Rico and the Hawaiian Islands to ourselves by ties of justice and interest and affection, but the performance of our duty toward the Philippines is a more difficult and debatable matter. We can satisfy the obligations of generous justice toward the people of Porto Rico by giving them the ample and familiar rights and privileges accorded our own citizens in our own territories and our obligations toward the people of Hawaii by perfecting the provisions for self-government already granted them, but in the Philippines we must go further. We must hold steadily in view their ultimate independence, and we must move toward the time of that independence as steadily as the way can be cleared and the foundations thoughtfully and permanently laid.

Acting under the authority conferred upon the President by Congress, I have already accorded the people of the islands a majority in both houses of their legislative body by appointing five instead of four native citizens to the membership of the commission. I believe that in this way we shall make proof of their capacity in counsel and their sense of responsibility in the exercise of political power, and that the success of this step will be sure to clear our view for the steps which are to follow. Step by step we should extend and perfect the system of self-government in the islands, making test of them and modifying them as experience discloses their successes and their failures; that we should more and more put under the control of the native citizens of the archipelago the essential instruments of their life, their local instrumentalities of government, their schools, all the common interests of their communities, and so by counsel and experience set up a government which all the world will see to be suitable to a people whose affairs are under their own control. At last, I hope and believe, we are beginning to gain the confidence of the Filipino peoples. By their counsel and experience, rather than by our own, we shall learn how best to serve them and how soon it will be possible and wise to withdraw our supervision. Let us once find the path and set out with firm and confident tread upon it and we shall not wander from it or linger upon it.

A duty faces us with regard to Alaska which seems to me very pressing and very imperative; perhaps I should say a double duty, for it concerns both the political and the material development of the Territory. The people of Alaska should be given the full Territorial form of government, and Alaska, as a storehouse, should be unlocked. One key to it is a system of railways. These the Government should itself build and administer, and the ports and terminals it should itself control in the interest of all who wish to use them for the service and development of the country and its people.

But the construction of railways is only the first step; is only thrusting in the key to the storehouse and throwing back the lock and opening the door. How the tempting resources of the country are to be exploited is another matter, to which I shall take the liberty of from time to time calling your attention, for it is a policy which must be worked out by well-considered stages, not upon theory, but upon lines of practical expediency. It is part of our general problem of conservation. We have a freer hand in working out the problem in Alaska than in the States of the Union; and yet the principle and object are the same, wherever we touch it. We must use the resources of the country, not lock them up. There need be no conflict or jealousy as between State and Federal authorities, for there can be no essential difference of purpose between them. The resources in question must be used, but not destroyed or wasted; used, but not monopolized upon any narrow idea of individual rights as against the abiding interests of communities. That a policy can be worked out by conference and concession which will release these resources and yet not jeopard or dissipate them, I for one have no doubt; and it can be done on lines of regulation which need be no less acceptable to the people and governments of the States concerned than to the people and Government of the Nation at large, whose heritage these resources are. We must bend our counsels to this end. A common purpose ought to make agreement easy.

Three or four matters of special importance and significance I beg, that you will permit me to mention in closing.

Our Bureau of Mines ought to be equipped and empowered to render even more effectual service than it renders now in improving the conditions of mine labor and making the mines more economically productive as well as more safe. This is an all-important part of the work of conservation; and the conservation of human life and energy lies even nearer to our interests than the preservation from waste of our material resources.

We owe it, in mere justice to the railway employees of the country, to provide for them a fair and effective employers' liability act; and a law that we can stand by in this matter will be no less to the advantage of those who administer the railroads of the country than to the advantage of those whom they employ. The experience of a large number of the States abundantly proves that.

We ought to devote ourselves to meeting pressing demands of plain justice like this as earnestly as to the accomplishment of political and economic reforms. Social justice comes first. Law is the machinery for its realization and is vital only as it expresses and embodies it.

An international congress for the discussion of all questions that affect safety at sea is now sitting in London at the suggestion of our own Government. So soon as the conclusions of that congress can be learned and considered we ought to address ourselves, among other things, to the prompt alleviation of the very unsafe, unjust, and burdensome conditions which now surround the employment of sailors and render it extremely difficult to obtain the services of spirited and competent men such as every ship needs if it is to be safely handled and brought to port.

May I not express the very real pleas-are I have experienced in co-operating with this Congress and sharing with it the labors of common service to which it has devoted itself so unreservedly during the past seven months of uncomplaining concentration upon the business of legislation? Surely it is a proper and pertinent part of my report on "the state of the Union" to express my admiration for the diligence, the good temper, and the full comprehension of public duty which has already been manifested by both the Houses; and I hope that it may not be deemed an impertinent intrusion of myself into the picture if I say with how much and how constant satisfaction I have availed myself of the privilege of putting my time and energy at their disposal alike in counsel and in action.

Second State of the Union address

Woodrow Wilson

December 8, 1914

GENTLEMEN OF THE CONGRESS:

The session upon which you are now entering will be the closing session of the Sixty-third Congress, a Congress, I venture to say, which will long be remembered for the great body of thoughtful and constructive work which it has done, in loyal response to the thought and needs of the country. I should like in this address to review the notable record and try to make adequate assessment of it; but no doubt we stand too near the work that has been done and are ourselves too much part of it to play the part of historians toward it.

Our program of legislation with regard to the regulation of business is now virtually complete. It has been put forth, as we intended, as a whole, and leaves no conjecture as to what is to follow. The road at last lies clear and firm before business. It is a road which it can travel without fear or embarrassment. It is the road to ungrudged, unclouded success. In it every honest man, every man who believes that the public interest is part of his own interest, may walk with perfect confidence.

Moreover, our thoughts are now more of the future than of the past. While we have worked at our tasks of peace the circumstances of the whole age have been altered by war. What we have done for our own land and our own people we did with the best that was in us, whether of character or of intelligence, with sober enthusiasm and a confidence in the principles upon which we were acting which sustained us at every step of the difficult undertaking; but it is done. It has passed from our hands. It is now an established part of the legislation of the country. Its usefulness, its effects will disclose themselves in experience. What chiefly strikes us now, as we look about us during these closing days of a year which will be forever memorable in the history of the world, is that we face new tasks, have been facing them these six months, must face them in the months to come,-face them without partisan feeling, like men who have forgotten everything but a common duty and the fact that we are representatives of a great people whose thought is not of us but of what America owes to herself and to all mankind in such circumstances as these upon which we look amazed and anxious.

War has interrupted the means of trade not only but also the processes of production. In Europe it is destroying men and resources wholesale and upon a scale unprecedented and ap-palling, There is reason to fear that the time is near, if it be not already at hand, when several of the countries of Europe will find it difficult to do for their people what they have hitherto been always easily able to do,-many essential and fundamental things. At any rate, they will need our help and our manifold services as they have never needed them before; and we should be ready, more fit and ready than we have ever been.

It is of equal consequence that the nations whom Europe has usually supplied with innu-merable articles of manufacture and commerce of which they are in constant need and without which their economic development halts and stands still can now get only a small part of what they formerly imported and eagerly look to us to supply their all but empty markets. This is particularly true of our own neighbors, the States, great and small, of Central and South America. Their lines of trade have hitherto run chiefly athwart the seas, not to our ports but to the ports of Great Britain and of the older continent of Europe. I do not stop to inquire why, or to make any comment on probable causes. What interests us just now is not the explanation but the fact, and our duty and opportunity in the presence of it. Here are markets which we must supply, and we must find the means of action. The United States, this great people for whom we speak and act, should be ready, as never before, to serve itself and to serve mankind; ready with its resources, its energies, its forces of production, and its means of distribution.

It is a very practical matter, a matter of ways and means. We have the resources, but are we fully ready to use them? And, if we can make ready what we have, have we the means at hand to distribute it? We are not fully ready; neither have we the means of distribution. We are willing, but we are not fully able. We have the wish to serve and to serve greatly, generously; but we are not prepared as we should be. We are not ready to mobilize our resources at once. We are not prepared to use them immediately and at their best, without delay and without waste.

To speak plainly, we have grossly erred in the way in which we have stunted and hindered the development of our merchant marine. And now, when we need ships, we have not got them. We have year after year debated, without end or conclusion, the best policy to pursue with regard to the use of the ores and forests and water powers of our national domain in the rich States of the West, when we should have acted; and they are still locked up. The key is still turned upon them, the door shut fast at which thousands of vigorous men, full of initiative, knock clamorously for admittance. The water power of our navigable streams outside the national domain also, even in the eastern States, where we have worked and planned for generations, is still not used as it might be, because we will and we won't; because the laws we have made do not intelligently balance encouragement against restraint. We withhold by regulation.

I have come to ask you to remedy and correct these mistakes and omissions, even at this short session of a Congress which would certainly seem to have done all the work that could reasonably be expected of it. The time and the circumstances are extraordinary, and so must our efforts be also.

Fortunately, two great measures, finely conceived, the one to unlock, with proper safeguards, the resources of the national domain, the other to encourage the use of the navigable waters outside that domain for the generation of power, have already passed the House of Representatives and are ready for immediate consideration and action by the Senate. With the deepest earnestness I urge their prompt passage. In them both we turn our backs upon hesitation and makeshift and formulate a genuine policy of use and conservation, in the best sense of those words. We owe the one measure not only to the people of that great western country for whose free and systematic development, as it seems to me, our legislation has done so little, but also to the people of the Nation as a whole; and we as clearly owe the other fulfillment of our repeated promises that the water power of the country should in fact as well as in name be put at the disposal of great industries which can make economical and profitable use of it, the rights of the public being adequately guarded the while, and monopoly in the use prevented. To have begun such measures and not completed them would indeed mar the record of this great Congress very seriously. I hope and confidently believe that they will be completed.

And there is another great piece of legislation which awaits and should receive the sanction of the Senate: I mean the bill which gives a larger measure of self-government to the people of the Philippines. How better, in this time of anxious questioning and perplexed policy, could we show our confidence in the principles of liberty, as the source as well as the expression of life, how better could we demonstrate our own self-possession and steadfastness in the courses of justice and disinterestedness than by thus going calmly forward to fulfill our promises to a dependent people, who will now look more anxiously than ever to see whether we have indeed the liberality, the unselfishness, the courage, the faith we have boasted and professed. I can not believe that the Senate will let this great measure of constructive justice await the action of another Congress. Its passage would nobly crown the record of these two years of memorable labor.

But I think that you will agree with me that this does not complete the toll of our duty. How are we to carry our goods to the empty markets of which I have spoken if we have not the ships? How are we to build up a great trade if we have not the certain and constant means of transportation upon which all profitable and useful commerce depends? And how are we to get the ships if we wait for the trade to develop without them? To correct the many mistakes by which we have discouraged and all but destroyed the merchant marine of the country, to retrace the steps by which we have.. it seems almost deliberately, withdrawn our flag from the seas.. except where, here and there, a ship of war is bidden carry it or some wandering yacht displays it, would take a long time and involve many detailed items of legislation, and the trade which we ought immediately to handle would disappear or find other channels while we debated the items.

The case is not unlike that which confronted us when our own continent was to be opened up to settlement and industry, and we needed long lines of railway, extended means of transportation prepared beforehand, if development was not to lag intolerably and wait interminably. We lavishly subsidized the building of transcontinental railroads. We look back upon that with regret now, because the subsidies led to many scandals of which we are ashamed; but we know that the railroads had to be built, and if we had it to do over again we should of course build them, but in another way. Therefore I propose another way of providing the means of transportation, which must precede, not tardily follow, the development of our trade with our neighbor states of America. It may seem a reversal of the natural order of things, but it is true, that the routes of trade must be actually opened-by many ships and regular sailings and moderate charges-before streams of merchandise will flow freely and profitably through them.

Hence the pending shipping bill, discussed at the last session but as yet passed by neither House. In my judgment such legislation is imperatively needed and can not wisely be postponed. The Government must open these gates of trade, and open them wide; open them before it is altogether profitable to open them, or altogether reasonable to ask private capital to open them at a venture. It is not a question of the Government monopolizing the field. It should take action to make it certain that transportation at reasonable rates will be promptly provided, even where the carriage is not at first profitable; and then, when the carriage has become sufficiently profitable to attract and engage private capital, and engage it in abundance, the Government ought to withdraw. I very earnestly hope that the Congress will be of this opinion, and that both Houses will adopt this exceedingly important bill.

The great subject of rural credits still remains to be dealt with, and it is a matter of deep regret that the difficulties of the subject have seemed to render it impossible to complete a bill for passage at this session. But it can not be perfected yet, and therefore there are no other constructive measures the necessity for which I will at this time call your attention to; but I would be negligent of a very manifest duty were I not to call the attention of the Senate to the fact that the proposed convention for safety at sea awaits its confirmation and that the limit fixed in the convention itself for its acceptance is the last day of the present month. The conference in which this convention originated was called by the United States; the representatives of the United States played a very influential part indeed in framing the provisions of the proposed convention; and those provisions are in themselves for the most part admirable. It would hardly be consistent with the part we have played in the whole matter to let it drop and go by the board as if forgotten and neglected. It was ratified in May by the German Government and in August by the Parliament of Great Britain. It marks a most hopeful and decided advance in international civilization. We should show our earnest good faith in a great matter by adding our own acceptance of it.

There is another matter of which I must make special mention, if I am to discharge my conscience, lest it should escape your attention. It may seem a very small thing. It affects only a single item of appropriation. But many human lives and many great enterprises hang upon it. It is the matter of making adequate provision for the survey and charting of our coasts. It is immediately pressing and exigent in connection with the immense coast line of Alaska, a coast line greater than that of the United States themselves, though it is also very important indeed with regard to the older coasts of the continent. We can not use our great Alaskan domain, ships will not ply thither, if those coasts and their many hidden dangers are not thoroughly surveyed and charted. The work is incomplete at almost every point. Ships and lives have been lost in threading what were supposed to be well-known main channels. We have not provided adequate vessels or adequate machinery for the survey and charting. We have used old vessels that were not big enough or strong enough and which were so nearly unseaworthy that our inspectors would not have allowed private owners to send them to sea. This is a matter which, as I have said, seems small, but is in reality very great. Its importance has only to be looked into to be appreciated.

Before I close may I say a few words upon two topics, much discussed out of doors, upon which it is highly important that our judgment should be clear, definite, and steadfast?

One of these is economy in government expenditures. The duty of economy is not debatable. It is manifest and imperative. In the appropriations we pass we are spending the money of the great people whose servants we are,–not our own. We are trustees and responsible stewards in the spending. The only thing debatable and upon which we should be careful to make our thought and purpose clear is the kind of economy demanded of us. I assert with the greatest confidence that the people of the United States are not jealous of the amount their Government costs if they are sure that they get what they need and desire for the outlay, that the money is being spent for objects of which they approve, and that it is being applied with good business sense and management.

Governments grow, piecemeal, both in their tasks and in the means by which those tasks are to be performed, and very few Governments are organized, I venture to say, as wise and experienced business men would organize them if they had a clean sheet of paper to write upon. Certainly the Government of the United States is not. I think that it is generally agreed that there should be a systematic reorganization and reassembling of its parts so as to secure greater efficiency and effect considerable savings in expense. But the amount of money saved in that way would, I believe, though no doubt considerable in itself, running, it may be, into the millions, be relatively small,–small, I mean, in proportion to the total necessary outlays of the Government. It would be thoroughly worth effecting, as every saving would, great or small. Our duty is not altered by the scale of the saving. But my point is that the people of the United States do not wish to curtail the activities of this Government; they wish, rather, to enlarge them; and with every enlargement, with the mere growth, indeed, of the country itself, there must come, of course, the inevitable increase of expense. The sort of economy we ought to practice may be effected, and ought to be effected, by a careful study and assessment of the tasks to be performed; and the money spent ought to be made to yield the best possible returns in efficiency and achievement. And, like good stewards, we should so account for every dollar of our appropriations as to make it perfectly evident what it was spent for and in what way it was spent.

It is not expenditure but extravagance that we should fear being criticized for; not paying for the legitimate enterprise and undertakings of a great Government whose people command what it should do, but adding what will benefit only a few or pouring money out for what need not have been undertaken at all or might have been postponed or better and more economically conceived and carried out. The Nation is not niggardly; it is very generous. It will chide us only if we forget for whom we pay money out and whose money it is we pay. These are large and general standards, but they are not very difficult of application to particular cases.

The other topic I shall take leave to mention goes deeper into the principles of our national life and policy. It is the subject of national defense.

It can not be discussed without first answering some very searching questions. It is said in some quarters that we are not prepared for war. What is meant by being prepared? Is it meant that we are not ready upon brief notice to put a nation in the field, a nation of men trained to arms? Of course we are not ready to do that; and we shall never be in time of peace so long as we retain our present political principles and institutions. And what is it that it is suggested we should be prepared to do? To defend ourselves against attack? We have always found means to do that, and shall find them whenever it is necessary without calling our people away from their necessary tasks to render compulsory military service in times of peace.

Allow me to speak with great plainness and directness upon this great matter and to avow my convictions with deep earnestness. I have tried to know what America is, what her people think, what they are, what they most cherish and hold dear. I hope that some of their finer passions are in my own heart,–some of the great conceptions and desires which gave birth to this Government and which have made the voice of this people a voice of peace and hope and liberty among the peoples of the world, and that, speaking my own thoughts, I shall, at least in part, speak theirs also, however faintly and inadequately, upon this vital matter.

We are at peace with all the world. No one who speaks counsel based on fact or drawn from a just and candid interpretation of realities can say that there is reason to fear that from any quarter our independence or the integrity of our territory is threatened. Dread of the power of any other nation we are incapable of. We are not jealous of rivalry in the fields of commerce or of any other peaceful achievement. We mean to live our own lives as we will; but we mean also to let live. We are, indeed, a true friend to all the nations of the world, because we threaten none, covet the possessions of none, desire the overthrow of none. Our friendship can be accepted and is accepted without reservation, because it is offered in a spirit and for a purpose which no one need ever question or suspect. Therein lies our greatness. We are the champions of peace and of concord. And we should be very jealous of this distinction which we have sought to earn. Just now we should be particularly jealous of it because it is our dearest present hope that this character and reputation may presently, in God's providence, bring us an opportunity such as has seldom been vouchsafed any nation, the opportunity to counsel and obtain peace in the world and reconciliation and a healing settlement of many a matter that has cooled and interrupted the friendship of nations. This is the time above all others when we should wish and resolve to keep our strength by self-possession, our influence by preserving our ancient principles of action.

From the first we have had a clear and settled policy with regard to military establishments. We never have had, and while we retain our present principles and ideals we never shall have, a large standing army. If asked, Are you ready to defend yourselves? we reply, Most assuredly, to the utmost; and yet we shall not turn America into a military camp. We will not ask our young men to spend the best years of their lives making soldiers of themselves. There is another sort of energy in us. It will know how to declare itself and make itself effective should occasion arise. And especially when half the world is on fire we shall be careful to make our moral insurance against the spread of the conflagration very definite and certain and adequate indeed.

Let us remind ourselves, therefore, of the only thing we can do or will do. We must depend in every time of national peril, in the future as in the past, not upon a standing army, nor yet upon a reserve army, but upon a citizenry trained and accustomed to arms. It will be right enough, right American policy, based upon our accustomed principles and practices, to provide a system by which every citizen who will volunteer for the training may be made familiar with the use of modern arms, the rudiments of drill and maneuver, and the maintenance and sanitation of camps. We should encourage such training and make it a means of discipline which our young men will learn to value. It is right that we should provide it not only, but that we should make it as attractive as possible, and so induce our young men to undergo it at such times as they can command a little freedom and can seek the physical development they need, for mere health's sake, if for nothing more. Every means by which such things can be stimulated is legitimate, and such a method smacks of true American ideas. It is right, too, that the National Guard of the States should be developed and strengthened by every means which is not inconsistent with our obligations to our own people or with the established policy of our Government. And this, also, not because the time or occasion specially calls for such measures, but because it should be our constant policy to make these provisions for our national peace and safety.

More than this carries with it a reversal of the whole history and character of our polity. More than this, proposed at this time, permit me to say, would mean merely that we had lost our self-possession, that we had been thrown off our balance by a war with which we have nothing to do, whose causes can not touch us, whose very existence affords us opportunities of friendship and disinterested service which should make us ashamed of any thought of hostility or fearful preparation for trouble. This is assuredly the opportunity for which a people and a government like ours were raised up, the opportunity not only to speak but actually to embody and exemplify the counsels of peace and amity and the lasting concord which is based on justice and fair and generous dealing.

A powerful navy we have always regarded as our proper and natural means of defense, and it has always been of defense that we have thought, never of aggression or of conquest. But who shall tell us now what sort of navy to build? We shall take leave to be strong upon the seas, in the future as in the past; and there will be no thought of offense or of provocation in that. Our ships are our natural bulwarks. When will the experts tell us just what kind we should construct-and when will they be right for ten years together, if the relative efficiency of craft of different kinds and uses continues to change as we have seen it change under our very eyes in these last few months?

But I turn away from the subject. It is not new. There is no new need to discuss it. We shall not alter our attitude toward it because some amongst us are nervous and excited. We shall easily and sensibly agree upon a policy of defense. The question has not changed its aspects because the times are not normal. Our policy will not be for an occasion. It will be conceived as a permanent and settled thing, which we will pursue at all seasons, without haste and after a fashion perfectly consistent with the peace of the world, the abiding friendship of states, and the unhampered freedom of all with whom we deal. Let there be no misconception. The country has been misinformed. We have not been negligent of national defense. We are not unmindful of the great responsibility resting upon us. We shall learn and profit by the lesson of every experience and every new circumstance; and what is needed will be adequately done.

I close, as I began, by reminding you of the great tasks and duties of peace which challenge our best powers and invite us to build what will last, the tasks to which we can address ourselves now and at all times with free-hearted zest and with all the finest gifts of constructive wisdom we possess. To develop our life and our resources; to supply our own people, and the people of the world as their need arises, from the abundant plenty of our fields and our marts of trade to enrich the commerce of our own States and of the world with the products of our mines, our farms, and our factories, with the creations of our thought and the fruits of our character,-this is what will hold our attention and our enthusiasm steadily, now and in the years to come, as we strive to show in our life as a nation what liberty and the inspirations of an emancipated spirit may do for men and for societies, for individuals, for states, and for mankind.

Third State of the Union address

Woodrow Wilson

December 7, 1915

GENTLEMEN OF THE CONGRESS:

Since I last had the privilege of addressing you on the state of the Union the war of nations on the other side of the sea, which had then only begun to disclose its portentous proportions, has extended its threatening and sinister scope until it has swept within its flame some portion of every quarter of the globe, not excepting our own hemisphere, has altered the whole face of international affairs, and now presents a prospect of reorganization and reconstruction such as statesmen and peoples have never been called upon to attempt before.

We have stood apart, studiously neutral. It was our manifest duty to do so. Not only did we have no part or interest in the policies which seem to have brought the conflict on; it was necessary, if a universal catastrophe was to be avoided, that a limit should be set to the sweep of destructive war and that some part of the great family of nations should keep the processes of peace alive, if only to prevent collective economic ruin and the breakdown throughout the world of the industries by which its populations are fed and sustained. It was manifestly the duty of the self-governed nations of this hemisphere to redress, if possible, the balance of economic loss and confusion in the other, if they could do nothing more. In the day of readjustment and recuperation we earnestly hope and believe that they can be of infinite service.

In this neutrality, to which they were bidden not only by their separate life and their habitual detachment from the politics of Europe but also by a clear perception of international duty, the states of America have become conscious of a new and more vital community of interest and moral partnership in affairs, more clearly conscious of the many common sympathies and interests and duties which bid them stand together.

There was a time in the early days of our own great nation and of the republics fighting their way to independence in Central and South America when the government of the United States looked upon itself as in some sort the guardian of the republics to the South of her as against any encroachments or efforts at political control from the other side of the water; felt it its duty to play the part even without invitation from them; and I think that we can claim that the task was undertaken with a true and disinterested enthusiasm for the freedom of the Americas and the unmolested Self-government of her independent peoples. But it was always difficult to maintain such a role without offense to the pride of the peoples whose freedom of action we sought to protect, and without provoking serious misconceptions of our motives, and every thoughtful man of affairs must welcome the altered circumstances of the new day in whose light we now stand, when there is no claim of guardianship or thought of wards but, instead, a full and honorable association as of partners between ourselves and our neighbors, in the interest of all America, north and south. Our concern for the independence and prosperity of the states of Central and South America is not altered. We retain unabated the spirit that has inspired us throughout the whole life of our government and which was so frankly put into words by President Monroe. We still mean always to make a common cause of national independence and of political liberty in America. But that purpose is now better understood so far as it concerns ourselves. It is known not to be a selfish purpose. It is known to have in it no thought of taking advantage of any government in this hemisphere or playing its political fortunes for our own benefit. All the governments of America stand, so far as we are concerned, upon a footing of genuine equality and unquestioned independence.

We have been put to the test in the case of Mexico, and we have stood the test. Whether we have benefited Mexico by the course we have pursued remains to be seen. Her fortunes are in her own hands. But we have at least proved that we will not take advantage of her in her distress and undertake to impose upon her an order and government of our own choosing. Liberty is often a fierce and intractable thing, to which no bounds can be set, and to which no bounds of a few men's choosing ought ever to be set. Every American who has drunk at the true fountains of principle and tradition must subscribe without reservation to the high doctrine of the Virginia Bill of Rights, which in the great days in which our government was set up was everywhere amongst us accepted as the creed of free men. That doctrine is, "That government is, or ought to be, instituted for the common benefit, protection, and security of the people, nation, or community"; that "of all the various modes and forms of government, that is the best which is capable of producing the greatest degree of happiness and safety, and is most effectually secured against the danger of maladministration; and that, when any government shall be found inadequate or contrary to these purposes, a majority of the community hath an indubitable, inalienable, and indefeasible right to reform, alter, or abolish it, in such manner as shall be judged most conducive to the public weal." We have unhesitatingly applied that heroic principle to the case of Mexico, and now hopefully await the rebirth of the troubled Republic, which had so much of which to purge itself and so little sympathy from any outside quarter in the radical but necessary process. We will aid and befriend Mexico, but we will not coerce her; and our course with regard to her ought to be sufficient proof to all America that we seek no political suzerainty or selfish control.

The moral is, that the states of America are not hostile rivals but cooperating friends, and that their growing sense of community or interest, alike in matters political and in matters economic, is likely to give them a new significance as factors in international affairs and in the political history of the world. It presents them as in a very deep and true sense a unit in world affairs, spiritual partners, standing together because thinking together, quick with common sympathies and common ideals. Separated they are subject to all the cross currents of the confused politics of a world of hostile rivalries; united in spirit and purpose they cannot be disappointed of their peaceful destiny.

This is Pan-Americanism. It has none of the spirit of empire in it. It is the embodiment, the effectual embodiment, of the spirit of law and independence and liberty and mutual service.

A very notable body of men recently met in the City of Washington, at the invitation and as the guests of this Government, whose deliberations are likely to be looked back to as marking a memorable turning point in the history of America. They were representative spokesmen of the several independent states of this hemisphere and were assembled to discuss the financial and commercial relations of the republics of the two continents which nature and political fortune have so intimately linked together. I earnestly recommend to your perusal the reports of their proceedings and of the actions of their committees. You will get from them, I think, a fresh conception of the ease and intelligence and advantage with which Americans of both continents may draw together in practical cooperation and of what the material foundations of this hopeful partnership of interest must consist,-of how we should build them and of how necessary it is that we should hasten their building.

There is, I venture to point out, an especial significance just now attaching to this whole matter of drawing the Americans together in bonds of honorable partnership and mutual advantage because of the economic readjustments which the world must inevitably witness within the next generation, when peace shall have at last resumed its healthful tasks. In the performance of these tasks I believe the Americas to be destined to play their parts together. I am interested to fix your attention on this prospect now because unless you take it within your view and permit the full significance of it to command your thought I cannot find the right light in which to set forth the particular matter that lies at the very font of my whole thought as I address you to-day. I mean national defense.

No one who really comprehends the spirit of the great people for whom we are appointed to speak can fail to perceive that their passion is for peace, their genius best displayed in the practice of the arts of peace. Great democracies are not belligerent. They do not seek or desire war. Their thought is of individual liberty and of the free labor that supports life and the uncensored thought that quickens it. Conquest and dominion are not in our reckoning, or agreeable to our principles. But just because we demand unmolested development and the undisturbed government of our own lives upon our own principles of right and liberty, we resent, from whatever quarter it may come, the aggression we ourselves will not practice. We insist upon security in prosecuting our self-chosen lines of national development. We do more than that. We demand it also for others. We do not confine our enthusiasm for individual liberty and free national development to the incidents and movements of affairs which affect only ourselves. We feel it wherever there is a people that tries to walk in these difficult paths of independence and right. From the first we have made common cause with all partisans of liberty on this side the sea, and have deemed it as important that our neighbors should be free from all outside domination as that we ourselves should be. We have set America aside as a whole for the uses of independent nations and political freemen.

Out of such thoughts grow all our policies. We regard war merely as a means of asserting the rights of a people against aggression. And we are as fiercely jealous of coercive or dictatorial power within our own nation as of aggression from without. We will not maintain a standing army except for uses which are as necessary in times of peace as in times of war; and we shall always see to it that our military peace establishment is no larger than is actually and continuously needed for the uses of days in which no enemies move against us. But we do believe in a body of free citizens ready and sufficient to take care of themselves and of the governments which they have set up to serve them. In our constitutions themselves we have commanded that "the right of the people to keep and bear arms shall not be infringed," and our confidence has been that our safety in times of danger would lie in the rising of the nation to take care of itself, as the farmers rose at Lexington.

But war has never been a mere matter of men and guns. It is a thing of disciplined might. If our citizens are ever to fight effectively upon a sudden summons, they must know how modern fighting is done, and what to do when the summons comes to render themselves immediately available and immediately effective. And the government must be their servant in this matter, must supply them with the training they need to take care of themselves and of it. The military arm of their government, which they will not allow to direct them, they may properly use to serve them and make their independence secure,-and not their own independence merely but the rights also of those with whom they have made common cause, should they also be put in jeopardy. They must be fitted to play the great role in the world, and particularly in this hemisphere, for which they are qualified by principle and by chastened ambition to play.

It is with these ideals in mind that the plans of the Department of War for more adequate national defense were conceived which will be laid before you, and which I urge you to sanction and put into effect as soon as they can be properly scrutinized and discussed. They seem to me the essential first steps, and they seem to me for the present sufficient.

They contemplate an increase of the standing force of the regular army from its present strength of five thousand and twenty-three officers and one hundred and two thousand nine hundred and eighty-five enlisted men of all services to a strength of seven thousand one hundred and thirty-six officers and one hundred and thirty-four thousand seven hundred and seven enlisted men, or 141,843, all told, all services, rank and file, by the addition of fifty-two companies of coast artillery, fifteen companies of engineers, ten regiments of infantry, four regiments of field artillery, and four aero squadrons, besides seven hundred and fifty officers required for a great variety of extra service, especially the all important duty of training the citizen force of which I shall presently speak, seven hundred and ninety-two noncommissioned officers for service in drill, recruiting and the like, and the necessary quota of enlisted men for the Quartermaster Corps, the Hospital Corps, the Ordnance Department, and other similar auxiliary services. These are the additions necessary to render the army adequate for its present duties, duties which it has to perform not only upon our own continental coasts and borders and at our interior army posts, but also in the Philippines, in the Hawaiian Islands, at the Isthmus, and in Porto Rico.

By way of making the country ready to assert some part of its real power promptly and upon a larger scale, should occasion arise, the plan also contemplates supplementing the army by a force of four hundred thousand disciplined citizens, raised in increments of one hundred and thirty-three thousand a year throughout a period of three years. This it is proposed to do by a process of enlistment under which the serviceable men of the country would be asked to bind themselves to serve with the colors for purposes of training for short periods throughout three years, and to come to the colors at call at any time throughout an additional "furlough" period of three years. This force of four hundred thousand men would be provided with personal accoutrements as fast as enlisted and their equipment for the field made ready to be supplied at any time. They would be assembled for training at stated intervals at convenient places in association with suitable units of the regular army. Their period of annual training would not necessarily exceed two months in the year.

It would depend upon the patriotic feeling of the younger men of the country whether they responded to such a call to service or not. It would depend upon the patriotic spirit of the employers of the country whether they made it possible for the younger men in their employ to respond under favorable conditions or not. I, for one, do not doubt the patriotic devotion either of our young men or of those who give them employment,–those for whose benefit and protection they would in fact enlist. I would look forward to the success of such an experiment with entire confidence.

At least so much by way of preparation for defense seems to me to be absolutely imperative now. We cannot do less.

The programme which will be laid before you by the Secretary of the Navy is similarly conceived. It involves only a shortening of the time within which plans long matured shall be carried out; but it does make definite and explicit a programme which has heretofore been only implicit, held in the minds of the Committees on Naval Affairs and disclosed in the debates of the two Houses but nowhere formulated or formally adopted. It seems to me very clear that it will be to the advantage of the country for the Congress to adopt a comprehensive plan for putting the navy upon a final footing of strength and efficiency and to press that plan to completion within the next five years. We have always looked to the navy of the country as our first and chief line of defense; we have always seen it to be our manifest course of prudence to be strong on the seas. Year by year we have been creating a navy which now ranks very high indeed among the navies of the maritime nations. We should now definitely determine how we shall complete what we have begun, and how soon.

The programme to be laid before you contemplates the construction within five years of ten battleships, six battle cruisers, ten scout cruisers, fifty destroyers, fifteen fleet submarines, eighty-five coast submarines, four gunboats, one hospital ship, two ammunition ships, two fuel oil ships, and one repair ship. It is proposed that of this number we shall the first year provide for the construction of two battleships, two battle cruisers, three scout cruisers, fifteen destroyers, five fleet submarines, twenty-five coast submarines, two gunboats, and one hospital ship; the second year, two battleships, one scout cruiser, ten destroyers, four fleet submarines, fifteen coast submarines, one gunboat, and one fuel oil ship; the third year, two battleships, one battle cruiser, two scout cruisers, five destroyers, two fleet sub marines, and fifteen coast submarines; the fourth year, two battleships, two battle cruisers, two scout cruisers, ten destroyers, two fleet submarines, fifteen coast submarines, one ammunition ship, and one fuel oil ship; and the fifth year, two battleships, one battle cruiser, two scout cruisers, ten destroyers, two fleet submarines, fifteen coast submarines, one gunboat, one ammunition ship, and one repair ship.

The Secretary of the Navy is asking also for the immediate addition to the personnel of the navy of seven thousand five hundred sailors, twenty-five hundred apprentice seamen, and fifteen hundred marines. This increase would be sufficient to care for the ships which are to be completed within the fiscal year 1917 and also for the number of men which must be put in training to man the ships which will be completed early in 1918. It is also necessary that the number of midshipmen at the Naval academy at Annapolis should be increased by at least three hundred in order that the force of officers should be more rapidly added to; and authority is asked to appoint, for engineering duties only, approved graduates of engineering colleges, and for service in the aviation corps a certain number of men taken from civil life.

If this full programme should be carried out we should have built or building in 1921, according to the estimates of survival and standards of classification followed by the General Board of the Department, an effective navy consisting of twenty-seven battleships of the first line, six battle cruisers, twenty-five battleships of the second line, ten armored cruisers, thirteen scout cruisers, five first class cruisers, three second class cruisers, ten third class cruisers, one hundred and eight destroyers, eighteen fleet submarines, one hundred and fifty-seven coast submarines, six monitors, twenty gunboats, four supply ships, fifteen fuel ships, four transports, three tenders to torpedo vessels, eight vessels of special types, and two ammunition ships. This would be a navy fitted to our needs and worthy of our traditions.

But armies and instruments of war are only part of what has to be considered if we are to provide for the supreme matter of national self-sufficiency and security in all its aspects. There are other great matters which will be thrust upon our attention whether we will or not. There is, for example, a very pressing question of trade and shipping involved in this great problem of national adequacy. It is necessary for many weighty reasons of national efficiency and development that we should have a great merchant marine. The great merchant fleet we once used to make us rich, that great body of sturdy sailors who used to carry our flag into every sea, and who were the pride and often the bulwark of the nation, we have almost driven out of existence by inexcusable neglect and indifference and by a hopelessly blind and provincial policy of so-called economic protection. It is high time we repaired our mistake and resumed our commercial independence on the seas.

For it is a question of independence. If other nations go to war or seek to hamper each other's commerce, our merchants, it seems, are at their mercy, to do with as they please. We must use their ships, and use them as they determine. We have not ships enough of our own. We cannot handle our own commerce on the seas. Our independence is provincial, and is only on land and within our own borders. We are not likely to be permitted to use even the ships of other nations in rivalry of their own trade, and are without means to extend our commerce even where the doors are wide open and our goods desired. Such a situation is not to be endured. It is of capital importance not only that the United States should be its own carrier on the seas and enjoy the economic independence which only an adequate merchant marine would give it, but also that the American hemisphere as a whole should enjoy a like independence and self-sufficiency, if it is not to be drawn into the tangle of European affairs. Without such independence the whole question of our political unity and self-determination is very seriously clouded and complicated indeed.

Moreover, we can develop no true or effective American policy without ships of our own,—not ships of war, but ships of peace, carrying goods and carrying much more: creating friendships and rendering indispensable services to all interests on this side the water. They must move constantly back and forth between the Americas. They are the only shuttles that can weave the delicate fabric of sympathy, comprehension, confidence, and mutual dependence in which we wish to clothe our policy of America for Americans.

The task of building up an adequate merchant marine for America private capital must ultimately undertake and achieve, as it has undertaken and achieved every other like task amongst us in the past, with admirable enterprise, intelligence, and vigor; and it seems to me a manifest dictate of wisdom that we should promptly remove every legal obstacle that may stand in the way of this much to be desired revival of our old independence and should facilitate in every possible way the building, purchase, and American registration of ships. But capital cannot accomplish this great task of a sudden. It must embark upon it by degrees, as the opportunities of trade develop. Something must be done at once; done to open routes and develop opportunities where they are as yet undeveloped; done to open the arteries of trade where the currents have not yet learned to run,—especially between the two American continents, where they are, singularly enough, yet to be created and quickened; and it is evident that only the government can undertake such beginnings and assume the initial financial risks. When the risk has passed and private capital begins to find its way in sufficient abundance into these new channels, the government may withdraw. But it cannot omit to begin. It should take the first steps, and should take them at once. Our goods must not lie piled up at our ports and stored upon side tracks in freight cars which are daily needed on the roads; must not be left without means of transport to any foreign quarter. We must not await the permission of foreign ship-owners and foreign governments to send them where we will.

With a view to meeting these pressing necessities of our commerce and availing ourselves at the earliest possible moment of the present unparalleled opportunity of linking the two Americas together in bonds of mutual interest and service, an opportunity which may never return again if we miss it now, proposals will be made to the present Congress for the purchase or construction of ships to be owned and directed by the government similar to those made to the last Congress, but modified in some essential particulars. I recommend these proposals to you for your prompt acceptance with the more confidence because every month that has elapsed since the former proposals were made has made the necessity for such action more and more manifestly imperative. That need was then foreseen; it is now acutely felt and everywhere realized by those for whom trade is waiting but who can find no conveyance for their goods. I am not so much interested in the particulars of the programme as I am in taking immediate advantage of the great opportunity which awaits us if we will but act in this emergency. In this matter, as in all others, a spirit of common counsel should prevail, and out of it should come an early solution of this pressing problem.

There is another matter which seems to me to be very intimately associated with the question of national safety and preparation for defense. That is our policy towards the Philippines and the people of Porto Rico. Our treatment of them and their attitude towards us are manifestly of the first consequence in the development of our duties in the world and in getting a free hand to perform those duties. We must be free from every unnecessary burden or embarrassment; and there is no better way to be clear of embarrassment than to fulfil our promises and promote the interests of those dependent on us to the utmost. Bills for the alteration and reform of the government of the Philippines and for rendering fuller political justice to the people of Porto Rico were submitted to the sixty-third Congress. They will be submitted also to you. I need not particularize their details. You are most of you already familiar with them. But I do recommend them to your early adoption with the sincere conviction that there are few measures you could adopt which would more serviceably clear the way for the great policies by which we wish to make good, now and always, our right to lead in enterprises of peace and good will and economic and political freedom.

The plans for the armed forces of the nation which I have outlined, and for the general policy of adequate preparation for mobilization and defense, involve of course very large additional expenditures of money,-expenditures which will considerably exceed the estimated revenues of the government. It is made my duty by law, whenever the estimates of expenditure exceed the estimates of revenue, to call the attention of the Congress to the fact and suggest any means of meeting the deficiency that it may be wise or possible for me to suggest. I am ready to believe that it would be my duty to do so in any case; and I feel particularly bound to speak of the matter when it appears that the deficiency will arise directly out of the adoption by the Congress of measures which I myself urge it to adopt. Allow me, therefore, to speak briefly of the present state of the Treasury and of the fiscal problems which the next year will probably disclose.

On the thirtieth of June last there was an available balance in the general fund of the Treasury Of $104,170,105.78. The total estimated receipts for the year 1916, on the assumption that the emergency revenue measure passed by the last Congress will not be extended beyond its present limit, the thirty-first of December, 1915, and that the present duty of one cent per pound on sugar will be discontinued after the first of May, 1916, will be $670,365,500. The balance of June last and these estimated revenues come, therefore, to a grand total of $774,535,605-78. The total estimated disbursements for the present fiscal year, including twenty-five millions for the Panama Canal, twelve millions for probable deficiency appropriations, and fifty thousand dollars for miscellaneous debt redemptions, will be $753,891,000; and the balance in the general fund of the Treasury will be reduced to $20,644,605.78. The emergency revenue act, if continued beyond its present time limitation, would produce, during the half year then remaining, about forty-one millions. The duty of one cent per pound on sugar, if continued, would produce during the two months of the fiscal year remaining after the first of May, about fifteen millions. These two sums, amounting together to fifty-six millions, if added to the revenues of the second half of the fiscal year, would yield the Treasury at the end of the year an available balance Of $76,644,605-78.

The additional revenues required to carry out the programme of military and naval preparation of which I have spoken, would, as at present estimated, be for the fiscal year, 1917, $93,800,000. Those figures, taken with the figures for the present fiscal year which I have already given, disclose our financial problem for the year 1917. Assuming that the taxes imposed by the emergency revenue act and the present duty on sugar are to be discontinued, and that the balance at the close of the present fiscal year will be only $20,644,605.78, that the disbursements for the Panama Canal will again be about twenty-five millions, and that the additional expenditures for the army and navy are authorized by the Congress, the deficit in the general fund of the Treasury on the thirtieth of June, 1917, will be nearly two hundred and thirty-five millions. To this sum at least fifty millions should be added to represent a safe working balance for the Treasury, and twelve millions to include the usual deficiency estimates in 1917; and these additions would make a total deficit of some two hundred and ninety-seven millions. If the present taxes should be continued throughout this year and the next, however, there would be a balance in the Treasury of some seventy-six and a half millions at the end of the present fiscal year, and a deficit at the end of the next year of only some fifty millions, or, reckoning in sixty-two millions for deficiency appropriations and a safe Treasury balance at the end of the year, a total deficit of some one hundred and twelve millions. The obvious moral of the figures is that it is a plain counsel of prudence to continue all of the present taxes or their equivalents, and confine ourselves to the problem of providing one hundred and twelve millions of new revenue rather than two hundred and ninety-seven millions.

How shall we obtain the new revenue? We are frequently reminded that there are many millions of bonds which the Treasury is authorized under existing law to sell to reimburse the sums paid out of current revenues for the construction of the Panama Canal; and it is true that bonds to the amount of approximately $222,000,000 are now available for that purpose. Prior to 1913, $134,631,980 of these bonds had actually been sold to recoup the expenditures at the Isthmus; and now constitute a considerable item of the public debt. But I, for one, do not believe that the people of this country approve of postponing the payment of their bills. Borrowing money is short-sighted finance. It can be justified only when permanent things are to be accomplished which many generations will certainly benefit by and which it seems hardly fair that a single generation should pay for. The objects we are now proposing to spend money for cannot be so classified, except in the sense that everything wisely done may be said to be done in the interest of posterity as well as in our own. It seems to me a clear dictate of prudent statesmanship and frank finance that in what we are now, I hope, about to undertake we should pay as we go. The people of the country are entitled to know just what burdens of taxation they are to carry, and to know from the outset, now. The new bills should be paid by internal taxation.

To what sources, then, shall we turn? This is so peculiarly a question which the gentlemen of the House of Representatives are expected under the Constitution to propose an answer to that you will hardly expect me to do more than discuss it in very general terms. We should be following an almost universal example of modern governments if we were to draw the greater part or even the whole of the revenues we need from the income taxes. By somewhat lowering the present limits of exemption and the figure at which the surtax shall begin to be imposed, and by increasing, step by step throughout the present graduation, the surtax itself, the income taxes as at present apportioned would yield sums sufficient to balance the books of the Treasury at the end of the fiscal year 1917 without anywhere making the burden unreasonably or oppressively heavy. The precise reckonings are fully and accurately set out in the report of the Secretary of the Treasury which will be immediately laid before you.

And there are many additional sources of revenue which can justly be resorted to without hampering the industries of the country or putting any too great charge upon individual expenditure. A tax of one cent per gallon on gasoline and naphtha would yield, at the present estimated production, $10,000,000; a tax of fifty cents per horse power on automobiles and internal explosion engines, $15,000,000; a stamp tax on bank cheques, probably $18,000,000; a tax of twenty-five cents per ton on pig iron, $10,000,000; a tax of twenty-five cents per ton on fabricated iron and steel, probably $10,000,000. In a country of great industries like this it ought to be easy to distribute the burdens of taxation without making them anywhere bear too heavily or too exclusively upon any one set of persons or undertakings. What is clear is, that the industry of this generation should pay the bills of this generation.

I have spoken to you to-day, Gentlemen, upon a single theme, the thorough preparation of the nation to care for its own security and to make sure of entire freedom to play the impartial role in this hemisphere and in the world which we all believe to have been providentially assigned to it. I have had in my mind no thought of any immediate or particular danger arising out of our relations with other nations. We are at peace with all the nations of the world, and there is reason to hope that no question in controversy between this and other Governments will lead to any serious breach of amicable relations, grave as some differences of attitude and policy have been land may yet turn out to be. I am sorry to say that the gravest threats against our national peace and safety have been uttered within our own borders. There are citizens of the United States, I blush to admit, born under other flags but welcomed under our generous naturalization laws to the full freedom and opportunity of America, who have poured the poison of disloyalty into the very arteries of our national life; who have sought to bring the authority and good name of our Government into contempt, to destroy our industries wherever they thought it effective for their vindictive purposes to strike at them, and to debase our politics to the uses of foreign intrigue. Their number is not great as compared with the whole number of those sturdy hosts by which our nation has been enriched in recent generations out of virile foreign stock; but it is great enough to have brought deep disgrace upon us and to have made it necessary that we should promptly make use of processes of law by which we may be purged of their corrupt distempers. America never witnessed anything like this before. It never dreamed it possible that men sworn into its own citizenship, men drawn out of great free stocks such as supplied some of the best and strongest elements of that little, but how heroic, nation that in a high day of old staked its very life to free itself from every entanglement that had darkened the fortunes of the older nations and set up a new standard here, that men of such origins and such free choices of allegiance would ever turn in malign reaction against the Government and people who had welcomed and nurtured them and seek to make this proud country once more a hotbed of European passion. A little while ago such a thing would have seemed incredible. Because it was incredible we made no preparation for it. We would have been almost ashamed to prepare for it, as if we were suspicious of ourselves, our own comrades and neighbors! But the ugly and incredible thing has actually come about and we are without adequate federal laws to deal with it. I urge you to enact such laws at the earliest possible moment and feel that in doing so I am urging you to do nothing less than save the honor and self-respect of the nation. Such creatures of passion, disloyalty, and anarchy must be crushed out. They are not many, but they are infinitely malignant, and the hand of our power should close over them at once. They have formed plots to destroy property, they have entered into conspiracies against the neutrality of the Government, they have sought to pry into every confidential transaction of the Government in order to serve interests alien to our own. It is possible to deal with these things very effectually. I need not suggest the terms in which they may be dealt with.

I wish that it could be said that only a few men, misled by mistaken sentiments of allegiance to the governments under which they were born, had been guilty of disturbing the self-possession and misrepresenting the temper and principles of the country during these days of terrible war, when it would seem that every man who was truly an American would instinctively make it his duty and his pride to keep the scales of judgment even and prove himself a partisan of no nation but his own. But it cannot. There are some men among us, and many resident abroad who, though born and bred in the United States and calling themselves Americans, have so forgotten themselves and their honor as citizens as to put their passionate sympathy with one or the other side in the great European conflict above their regard for the peace and dignity of the United States. They also preach and practice disloyalty. No laws, I suppose, can reach corruptions of the mind and heart; but I should not speak of others without also speaking of these and expressing the even deeper humiliation and scorn which every self-possessed and thoughtfully patriotic American must feel when he thinks of them and of the discredit they are daily bringing upon us.

While we speak of the preparation of the nation to make sure of her security and her effective power we must not fall into the patent error of supposing that her real strength comes from armaments and mere safeguards of written law. It comes, of course, from her people, their energy, their success in their undertakings, their free opportunity to use the natural resources of our great home land and of the lands outside our continental borders which look to us for protection, for encouragement, and for assistance in their development; from the organization and freedom and vitality of our economic life. The domestic questions which engaged the attention of the last Congress are more vital to the nation in this its time of test than at any other time. We cannot adequately make ready for any trial of our strength unless we wisely and promptly direct the force of our laws into these all-important fields of domestic action. A matter which it seems to me we should have very much at heart is the creation of the right instrumentalities by which to mobilize our economic resources in any time of national necessity. I take it for granted that I do not need your authority to call into systematic consultation with the directing officers of the army and navy men of recognized leadership and ability from among our citizens who are thoroughly familiar, for example, with the transportation facilities of the country and therefore competent to advise how they may be coordinated when the need arises, those who can suggest the best way in which to bring about prompt cooperation among the manufacturers of the country, should it be necessary, and those who could assist to bring the technical skill of the country to the aid of the Government in the solution of particular problems of defense. I only hope that if I should find it feasible to constitute such an advisory body the Congress would be willing to vote the small sum of money that would be needed to defray the expenses that would probably be necessary to give it the clerical and administrative Machinery with which to do serviceable work.

What is more important is, that the industries and resources of the country should be available and ready for mobilization. It is the more imperatively necessary, therefore, that we should promptly devise means for doing what we have not yet done: that we should give intelligent federal aid and stimulation to industrial and vocational education, as we have long done in the large field of our agricultural industry; that, at the same time that we safeguard and conserve the natural resources of the country we should put them at the disposal of those who will use them promptly and intelligently, as was sought to be done in the admirable bills submitted to the last Congress from its committees on the public lands, bills which I earnestly recommend in principle to your consideration; that we should put into early operation some provision for rural credits which will add to the extensive borrowing facilities already afforded the farmer by the Reserve Bank Act, adequate instrumentalities by which long credits may be obtained on land mortgages; and that we should study more carefully than they have hitherto been studied the right adaptation of our economic arrangements to changing conditions.

Many conditions about which we I-lave repeatedly legislated are being altered from decade to decade, it is evident, under our very eyes, and are likely to change even more rapidly and more radically in the days immediately ahead of us, when peace has returned to the world and the nations of Europe once more take up their tasks of commerce and industry with the energy of those who must bestir themselves to build anew. Just what these changes will be no one can certainly foresee or confidently predict. There are no calculable, because no stable, elements in the problem. The most we can do is to make certain that we have the necessary instrumentalities of information constantly at our service so that we may be sure that we know exactly what we are dealing with when we come to act, if it should be necessary to act at all. We must first certainly know what it is that we are seeking to adapt ourselves to. I may ask the privilege of addressing you more at length on this important matter a little later in your session.

In the meantime may I make this suggestion? The transportation problem is an exceedingly serious and pressing one in this country. There has from time to time of late been reason to fear that our railroads would not much longer be able to cope with it successfully, as at present equipped and coordinated I suggest that it would be wise to provide for a commission of inquiry to ascertain by a thorough canvass of the whole question whether our laws as at present framed and administered are as serviceable as they might be in the solution of the problem. It is obviously a problem that lies at the very foundation of our efficiency as a people. Such an inquiry ought to draw out every circumstance and opinion worth considering and we need to know all sides of the matter if we mean to do anything in the field of federal legislation.

No one, I am sure, would wish to take any backward step. The regulation of the railways of the country by federal commission has had admirable results and has fully justified the hopes and expectations of those by whom the policy of regulation was originally proposed. The question is not what should we undo? It is, whether there is anything else we can do that would supply us with effective means, in the very process of regulation, for bettering the conditions under which the railroads are operated and for making them more useful servants of the country as a whole. It seems to me that it might be the part of wisdom, therefore, before further legislation in this field is attempted, to look at the whole problem of coordination and efficiency in the full light of a fresh assessment of circumstance and opinion, as a guide to dealing with the several parts of it.

For what we are seeking now, what in my mind is the single thought of this message, is national efficiency and security. We serve a great nation. We should serve it in the spirit of its peculiar genius. It is the genius of common men for self-government, industry, justice, liberty and peace. We should see to it that it lacks no instrument, no facility or vigor of law, to make it sufficient to play its part with energy, safety, and assured success. In this we are no partisans but heralds and prophets of a new age.

Fourth State of the Union address

Woodrow Wilson

December 5, 1916

GENTLEMEN OF THE CONGRESS:

In fulfilling at this time the duty laid upon me by the Constitution of communicating to you from time to time information of the state of the Union and recommending to your consideration such legislative measures as may be judged necessary and expedient, I shall continue the practice, which I hope has been acceptable to you, of leaving to the reports of the several heads of the executive departments the elaboration of the detailed needs of the public service and confine myself to those matters of more general public policy with which it seems necessary and feasible to deal at the present session of the Congress.

I realize the limitations of time under which you will necessarily act at this session and shall make my suggestions as few as possible; but there were some things left undone at the last session which there will now be time to complete and which it seems necessary in the interest of the public to do at once.

In the first place, it seems to me imperatively necessary that the earliest possible consideration and action should be accorded the remaining measures of the program of settlement and regulation which I had occasion to recommend to you at the close of your last session in view of the public dangers disclosed by the unaccommodated difficulties which then existed, and which still unhappily continue to exist, between the railroads of the country and their locomotive engineers, conductors and trainmen.

I then recommended:

First, immediate provision for the enlargement and administrative reorganization of the Interstate Commerce Commission along the lines embodied in the bill recently passed by the House of Representatives and now awaiting action by the Senate; in order that the Commission may be enabled to deal with the many great and various duties now devolving upon it with a promptness and thoroughness which are, with its present constitution and means of action, practically impossible.

Second, the establishment of an eight-hour day as the legal basis alike of work and wages in the employment of all railway employes who are actually engaged in the work of operating trains in interstate transportation.

Third, the authorization of the appointment by the President of a small body of men to observe actual results in experience of the adoption of the eight-hour day in railway transportation alike for the men and for the railroads.

Fourth, explicit approval by the Congress of the consideration by the Interstate Commerce Commission of an increase of freight rates to meet such additional expenditures by the railroads as may have been rendered necessary by the adoption of the eight-hour day and which have not been offset by administrative readjustments and economies, should the facts disclosed justify the increase.

Fifth, an amendment of the existing Federal statute which provides for the mediation, conciliation and arbitration of such controversies as the present by adding to it a provision that, in case the methods of accommodation now provided for should fail, a full public investigation of the merits of every such dispute shall be instituted and completed before a strike or lockout may lawfully be attempted.

And, sixth, the lodgment in the hands of the Executive of the power, in case of military necessity, to take control of such portions and such rolling stock of the railways of the country as may be required for military use and to operate them for military purposes, with authority to draft into the military service of the United States such train crews and administrative officials as the circumstances require for their safe and efficient use.

The second and third of these recommendations the Congress immediately acted on: it established the eight-hour day as the legal basis of work and wages in train service and it authorized the appointment of a commission to observe and report upon the practical results, deeming these the measures most immediately needed; but it postponed action upon the other suggestions until an opportunity should be offered for a more deliberate consideration of them.

The fourth recommendation I do not deem it necessary to renew. The power of the Interstate Commerce Commission to grant an increase of rates on the ground referred to is indisputably clear and a recommendation by the Congress with regard to such a matter might seem to draw in question the scope of the commission's authority or its inclination to do justice when there is no reason to doubt either.

The other suggestions-the increase in the Interstate Commerce Commission's membership and in its facilities for performing its manifold duties; the provision for full public investigation and assessment of industrial disputes, and the grant to the Executive of the power to control and operate the railways when necessary in time of war or other like public necessity-I now very earnestly renew.

The necessity for such legislation is manifest and pressing. Those who have entrusted us with the responsibility and duty of serving and safeguarding them in such matters would find it hard, I believe, to excuse a failure to act upon these grave matters or any unnecessary postponement of action upon them.

Not only does the Interstate Commerce Commission now find it practically impossible, with its present membership and organization, to perform its great functions promptly and thoroughly, but it is not unlikely that it may presently be found advisable to add to its duties still others equally heavy and exacting. It must first be perfected as an administrative instrument.

The country cannot and should not consent to remain any longer exposed to profound industrial disturbances for lack of additional means of arbitration and conciliation which the Congress can easily and promptly supply.

And all will agree that there must be no doubt as to the power of the Executive to make immediate and uninterrupted use of the railroads for the concentration of the military forces of the nation wherever they are needed and whenever they are needed.

This is a program of regulation, prevention and administrative efficiency which argues its own case in the mere statement of it. With regard to one of its items, the increase in the efficiency of the Interstate Commerce Commission, the House of Representatives has already acted; its action needs only the concurrence of the Senate.

I would hesitate to recommend, and I dare say the Congress would hesitate to act upon the suggestion should I make it, that any man in any I occupation should be obliged by law to continue in an employment which he desired to leave.

To pass a law which forbade or prevented the individual workman to leave his work before receiving the approval of society in doing so would be to adopt a new principle into our jurisprudence, which I take it for granted we are not prepared to introduce.

But the proposal that the operation of the railways of the country shall not be stopped or interrupted by the concerted action of organized bodies of men until a public investigation shall have been instituted, which shall make the whole question at issue plain for the judgment of the opinion of the nation, is not to propose any such principle.

It is based upon the very different principle that the concerted action of powerful bodies of men shall not be permitted to stop the industrial processes of the nation, at any rate before the nation shall have had an opportunity to acquaint itself with the merits of the case as between employe and employer, time to form its opinion upon an impartial statement of the merits, and opportunity to consider all practicable means of conciliation or arbitration.

I can see nothing in that proposition but the justifiable safeguarding by society of the necessary processes of its very life. There is nothing arbitrary or unjust in it unless it be arbitrarily and unjustly done. It can and should be done with a full and scrupulous regard for the interests and liberties of all concerned as well as for the permanent interests of society itself.

Three matters of capital importance await the action of the Senate which have already been acted upon by the House of Representatives; the bill which seeks to extend greater freedom of combination to those engaged in promoting the foreign commerce of the country than is now thought by some to be legal under the terms of the laws against monopoly; the bill amending the present organic law of Porto Rico; and the bill proposing a more thorough and systematic regulation of the expenditure of money in elections, commonly called the Corrupt Practices Act.

I need not labor my advice that these measures be enacted into law. Their urgency lies in the manifest circumstances which render their adoption at this time not only opportune but necessary. Even delay would seriously jeopard the interests of the country and of the Government.

Immediate passage of the bill to regulate the expenditure of money in elections may seem to be less necessary than the immediate enactment of the other measures to which I refer, because at least two years will elapse before another election in which Federal offices are to be filled; but it would greatly relieve the public mind if this important matter were dealt with while the circumstances and the dangers to the public morals of the present method of obtaining and spending campaign funds stand clear under recent observation, and the methods of expenditure can be frankly studied in the light of present experience; and a delay would have the further very serious disadvantage of postponing action until another election was at hand and some special object connected with it might be thought to be in the mind of those who urged it. Action can be taken now with facts for guidance and without suspicion of partisan purpose.

I shall not argue at length the desirability of giving a freer hand in the matter of combined and concerted effort to those who shall undertake the essential enterprise of building up our export trade. That enterprise will presently, will immediately assume, has indeed already assumed a magnitude unprecedented in our experience. We have not the necessary instrumentalities for its prosecution; it is deemed to be doubtful whether they could be created upon an adequate scale under our present laws.

We should clear away all legal obstacles and create a basis of undoubted law for it which will give freedom without permitting unregulated license. The thing must be done now, because the opportunity is here and may escape us if we hesitate or delay.

The argument for the proposed amendments of the organic law of Porto Rico is brief and conclusive. The present laws governing the island and regulating the rights and privileges of its people are not just. We have created expectations of extended privilege which we have not satisfied. There is uneasiness among the people of the island and even a suspicious doubt with regard to our intentions concerning them which the adoption of the pending measure would happily remove. We do not doubt what we wish to do in any essential particular. We ought to do it at once.

At the last session of the Congress a bill was passed by the Senate which provides for the promotion of vocational and industrial education, which is of vital importance to the whole country because it concerns a matter, too long neglected, upon which the thorough industrial preparation of the country for the critical years of economic development immediately ahead of us in very large measure depends.

May I not urge its early and favorable consideration by the House of Representatives and its early enactment into law? It contains plans which affect all interests and all parts of the country, and I am sure that there is no legislation now pending before the Congress whose passage the country awaits with more thoughtful approval or greater impatience to see a great and admirable thing set in the way of being done.

There are other matters already advanced to the stage of conference between the two houses of which it is not necessary that I should speak. Some practicable basis of agreement concerning them will no doubt be found an action taken upon them.

Inasmuch as this is, gentlemen, probably the last occasion I shall have to address the Sixty-fourth Congress, I hope that you will permit me to say with what genuine pleasure and satisfaction I have co-operated with you in the many measures of constructive policy with which you have enriched the legislative annals of the country. It has been a privilege to labor in such company. I take the liberty of congratulating you upon the completion of a record of rare serviceableness and distinction.

Fifth State of the Union address

Woodrow Wilson

December 4, 1917

GENTLEMEN OF THE CONGRESS:

Eight months have elapsed since I last had the honor of addressing you. They have been months crowded with events of immense and grave significance for us. I shall not undertake to detail or even to summarize those events. The practical particulars of the part we have played in them will be laid before you in the reports of the executive departments. I shall discuss only our present outlook upon these vast affairs, our present duties, and the immediate means of accomplishing the objects we shall hold always in view.

I shall not go back to debate the causes of the war. The intolerable wrongs done and planned against us by the sinister masters of Germany have long since become too grossly obvious and odious to every true American to need to be rehearsed. But I shall ask you to consider again and with a very grave scrutiny our objectives and the measures by which we mean to attain them; for the purpose of discussion here in this place is action, and our action must move straight toward definite ends. Our object is, of course, to win the war; and we shall not slacken or suffer ourselves to be diverted until it is won. But it is worth while asking and answering the question, When shall we consider the war won?

From one point of view it is not necessary to broach this fundamental matter. I do not doubt that the American people know what the war is about and what sort of an outcome they will regard as a realization of their purpose in it.

As a nation we are united in spirit and intention. I pay little heed to those who tell me otherwise. I hear the voices of dissent-who does not? I bear the criticism and the clamor of the noisily thoughtless and troublesome. I also see men here and there fling themselves in impotent disloyalty against the calm, indomitable power of the Nation. I hear men debate peace who understand neither its nature nor the way in which we may attain it with uplifted eyes and unbroken spirits. But I know that none of these speaks for the Nation. They do not touch the heart of anything. They may safely be left to strut their uneasy hour and be forgotten.

But from another point of view I believe that it is necessary to say plainly what we here at the seat of action consider the war to be for and what part we mean to play in the settlement of its searching issues. We are the spokesmen of the American people, and they have a right to know whether their purpose is ours. They desire peace by the overcoming of evil, by the defeat once for all of the sinister forces that interrupt peace and render it impossible, and they wish to know how closely our thought runs with theirs and what action we propose. They are impatient with those who desire peace by any sort of compromise deeply and indignantly impatient--but they will be equally impatient with us if we do not make it plain to them what our objectives are and what we are planning for in seeking to make conquest of peace by arms.

I believe that I speak for them when I say two things: First, that this intolerable thing of which the masters of Germany have shown us the ugly face, this menace of combined intrigue and force which we now see so clearly as the German power, a thing without conscience or honor of capacity for covenanted peace, must be crushed and, if it be not utterly brought to an end, at least shut out from the friendly intercourse of the nations; and second, that when this thing and its power are indeed defeated and the time comes that we can discuss peace when the German people have spokesmen whose word we can believe and when those spokesmen are ready in the name of their people to accept the common judgment of the nations as to what shall henceforth be the bases of law and of covenant for the life of the world-we shall be willing and glad to pay the full price for peace, and pay it ungrudgingly.

We know what that price will be. It will be full, impartial justice-justice done at every point and to every nation that the final settlement must affect, our enemies as well as our friends.

You catch, with me, the voices of humanity that are in the air. They grow daily more audible, more articulate, more persuasive, and they come from the hearts of men everywhere. They insist that the war shall not end in vindictive action of any kind; that no nation or people shall be robbed or punished because the irresponsible rulers of a single country have themselves done deep and abominable wrong. It is this thought that has been expressed in the formula, "No annexations, no contributions, no punitive indemnities."

Just because this crude formula expresses the instinctive judgment as to right of plain men everywhere, it has been made diligent use of by the masters of German intrigue to lead the people of Russia astray and the people of every other country their agents could reach-in order that a premature peace might be brought about before autocracy has been taught its final and convincing lesson and the people of the world put in control of their own destinies.

But the fact that a wrong use has been made of a just idea is no reason why a right use should not be made of it. It ought to be brought under the patronage of its real friends. Let it be said again that autocracy must first be shown the utter futility of its claim to power or leadership in the modern world. It is impossible to apply any standard of justice so long as such forces are unchecked and undefeated as the present masters of Germany command. Not until that has been done can right be set up as arbiter and peacemaker among the nations. But when that has been done-as, God willing, it assuredly will be-we shall at last be free to do an unprecedented thing, and this is the time to avow our purpose to do it. We shall be free to base peace on generosity and justice, to the exclusions of all selfish claims to advantage even on the part of the victors.

Let there be no misunderstanding. Our present and immediate task is to win the war and nothing shall turn us aside from it until it is accomplished. Every power and resource we possess, whether of men, of money, or of materials, is being devoted and will continue to be devoted to that purpose until it is achieved. Those who desire to bring peace about before that purpose is achieved I counsel to carry their advice elsewhere. We will not entertain it. We shall regard the war as won only when the German people say to us, through properly accredited representatives, that they are ready to agree to a settlement based upon justice and reparation of the wrongs their rulers have done. They have done a wrong to Belgium which must be repaired. They have established a power over other lands and peoples than their own--over the great empire of Austria-Hungary, over hitherto free Balkan states, over Turkey and within Asia-which must be relinquished.

Germany's success by skill, by industry, by knowledge, by enterprise we did not grudge or oppose, but admired, rather. She had built up for herself a real empire of trade and influence, secured by the peace of the world. We were content to abide by the rivalries of manufacture, science and commerce that were involved for us in her success, and stand or fall as we had or did not have the brains and the initiative to surpass her. But at the moment when she had conspicuously won her triumphs of peace she threw them away, to establish in their stead what the world will no longer permit to be established, military and political domination by arms, by which to oust where she could not excel the rivals she most feared and hated. The peace we make must remedy that wrong. It must deliver the once fair lands and happy peoples of Belgium and Northern France from the Prussian conquest and the Prussian menace, but it must deliver also the peoples of Austria-Hungary, the peoples of the Balkans and the peoples of Turkey, alike in Europe and Asia, from the impudent and alien dominion of the Prussian military and commercial autocracy.

We owe it, however, to ourselves, to say that we do not wish in any way to impair or to rearrange the Austro-Hungarian Empire. It is no affair of ours what they do with their own life, either industrially or politically. We do not purpose or desire to dictate to them in any way. We only desire to see that their affairs are left in their own hands, in all matters, great or small. We shall hope to secure for the peoples of the Balkan peninsula and for the people of the Turkish Empire the right and opportunity to make their own lives safe, their own fortunes secure against oppression or injustice and from the dictation of foreign courts or parties.

And our attitude and purpose with regard to Germany herself are of a like kind. We intend no wrong against the German Empire, no interference with her internal affairs. We should deem either the one or the other absolutely unjustifiable, absolutely contrary to the principles we have professed to live by and to hold most sacred throughout our life as a nation.

The people of Germany are being told by the men whom they now permit to deceive them and to act as their masters that they are fighting for the very life and existence of their empire, a war of desperate self-defense against deliberate aggression. Nothing could be more grossly or wantonly false, and we must seek by the utmost openness and candor as to our real aims to convince them of its falseness. We are in fact fighting for their emancipation from the fear, along with our own-from the fear as well as from the fact of unjust attack by neighbors or rivals or schemers after world empire. No one is threatening the existence or the independence of the peaceful enterprise of the German Empire.

The worst that can happen to the detriment the German people is this, that if they should still, after the war is over, continue to be obliged to live under ambitious and intriguing masters interested to disturb the peace of the world, men or classes of men whom the other peoples of the world could not trust, it might be impossible to admit them to the partnership of nations which must henceforth guarantee the world's peace. That partnership must be a partnership of peoples, not a mere partnership of governments. It might be impossible, also, in such untoward circumstances, to admit Germany to the free economic intercourse which must inevitably spring out of the other partnerships of a real peace. But there would be no aggression in that; and such a situation, inevitable, because of distrust, would in the very nature of things sooner or later cure itself, by processes which would assuredly set in.

The wrongs, the very deep wrongs, committed in this war will have to be righted. That, of course. But they cannot and must not be righted by the commission of similar wrongs against Germany and her allies. The world will not permit the commission of similar wrongs as a means of reparation and settlement. Statesmen must by this time have learned that the opinion of the world is everywhere wide awake and fully comprehends the issues involved. No representative of any self-governed nation will dare disregard it by attempting any such covenants of selfishness and compromise as were entered into at the Congress of Vienna. The thought of the plain people here and everywhere throughout the world, the people who enjoy no privilege and have very simple and unsophisticated standards of right and wrong, is the air all governments must henceforth breathe if they would live.

It is in the full disclosing light of that thought that all policies must be received and executed in this midday hour of the world's life. Ger. man rulers have been able to upset the peace of the world only because the German people were not suffered under their tutelage to share the comradeship of the other peoples of the world either in thought or in purpose. They were allowed to have no opinion of their own which might be set up as a rule of conduct for those who exercised authority over them. But the Congress that concludes this war will feel the full strength of the tides that run now in the hearts and consciences of free men everywhere. Its conclusions will run with those tides.

All those things have been true from the very beginning of this stupendous war; and I cannot help thinking that if they had been made plain at the very outset the sympathy and enthusiasm of the Russian people might have been once for all enlisted on the side of the Allies, suspicion and distrust swept away, and a real and lasting union of purpose effected. Had they believed these things at the very moment of their revolution, and had they been confirmed in that belief since, the sad reverses which have recently marked the progress of their affairs towards an ordered and stable government of free men might have been avoided. The Russian people have been poisoned by the very same falsehoods that have kept the German people in the dark, and the poison has been administered by the very same hand. The only possible antidote is the truth. It cannot be uttered too plainly or too often.

From every point of view, therefore, it has seemed to be my duty to speak these declarations of purpose, to add these specific interpretations to what I took the liberty of saying to the Senate in January. Our entrance into the war has not altered out attitude towards the settlement that must come when it is over.

When I said in January that the nations of the world were entitled not only to free pathways upon the sea, but also to assured and unmolested access to those pathways, I was thinking, and I am thinking now, not of the smaller and weaker nations alone which need our countenance and support, but also of the great and powerful nations and of our present enemies as well as our present associates in the war. I was thinking, and am thinking now, of Austria herself, among the rest, as well as of Serbia and of Poland.

Justice and equality of rights can be had only at a great price. We are seeking permanent, not temporary, foundations for the peace of the world, and must seek them candidly and fearlessly. As always, the right will prove to be the expedient.

What shall we do, then, to push this great war of freedom and justice to its righteous conclusion? We must clear away with a thorough hand all impediments to success, and we must make every adjustment of law that will facilitate the full and free use of our whole capacity and force as a fighting unit.

One very embarrassing obstacle that stands hi our way is that we are at war with Germany but not with her allies. I, therefore, very earnestly recommend that the Congress immediately declare the United States in a state of war with Austria-Hungary. Does it seem strange to you that this should be the conclusion of the argument I have just addressed to you? It is not. It is in fact the inevitable logic of what I have said. Austria-Hungary is for the time being not her own mistress but simply the vassal of the German Government.

We must face the facts as they are and act upon them without sentiment in this stern business. The Government of Austria and Hungary is not acting upon its own initiative or in response to the wishes and feelings of its own peoples, but as the instrument of another nation. We must meet its force with our own and regard the Central Powers as but one. The war can be successfully conducted in no other way.

The same logic would lead also to a declaration of war against Turkey and Bulgaria. They also are the tools of Germany, but they are mere tools and do not yet stand in the direct path of our necessary action. We shall go wherever the necessities of this war carry us, but it seems to me that we should go only where immediate and practical considerations lead us, and not heed any others.

The financial and military measures which must be adopted will suggest themselves as the war and its undertakings develop, but I will take the liberty of proposing to you certain other acts of legislation which seem to me to be needed for the support of the war and for the release of our whole force and energy.

It will be necessary to extend in certain particulars the legislation of the last session with regard to alien enemies, and also necessary, I believe, to create a very definite and particular control over the entrance and departure of all persons into and from the United States.

Legislation should be enacted defining as a criminal offense every wilful violation of the presidential proclamation relating to alien enemies promulgated under section 4067 of the revised statutes and providing appropriate punishments; and women, as well as men, should be included under the terms of the acts placing restraints upon alien enemies.

It is likely that as time goes on many alien enemies will be willing to be fed and housed at the expense of the Government in the detention camps, and it would be the purpose of the legislation I have suggested to confine offenders among them in the penitentiaries and other similar institutions where they could be made to work as other criminals do.

Recent experience has convinced me that the Congress must go further in authorizing the Government to set limits to prices. The law of supply and demand, I am sorry to say, has been replaced by the law of unrestrained selfishness. While we have eliminated profiteering in several branches of industry, it still runs impudently rampant in others. The farmers for example, complain with a great deal of justice that, while the regulation of food prices restricts their incomes, no restraints are placed upon the prices of most of the things they must themselves purchase; and similar inequities obtain on all sides.

It is imperatively necessary that the consideration of the full use of the water power of the country, and also of the consideration of the systematic and yet economical development of such of the natural resources of the country as are still under the control of the Federal Government should be immediately resumed and affirmatively and constructively dealt with at the earliest possible moment. The pressing need of such legislation is daily becoming more obvious.

The legislation proposed at the last session with regard to regulated combinations among our exporters in order to provide for our foreign trade a more effective organization and method of co-operation ought by all means to be completed at this session.

And I beg that the members of the House of Representatives will permit me to express the opinion that it will be impossible to deal in any but a very wasteful and extravagant fashion with the enormous appropriations of the public moneys which must continue to be made if the war is to be properly sustained, unless the House will consent to return to its former practice of initiating and preparing all appropriation bills through a single committee, in order that responsibility may be centered, expenditures standardized and made uniform, and waste and duplication as much as possible avoided.

Additional legislation may also become necessary before the present Congress again adjourns in order to effect the most efficient co-ordination and operation of the railways and other transportation systems of the country; but to that I shall, if circumstances should demand, call the attention of Congress upon another occasion.

If I have overlooked anything that ought to be done for the more effective conduct of the war, your own counsels will supply the omission. What I am perfectly clear about is that in the present session of the Congress our whole attention and energy should be concentrated on the vigorous, rapid and successful prosecution of the great task of winning the war.

We can do this with all the greater zeal and enthusiasm because we know that for us this is a war of high principle, debased by no selfish ambition of conquest or spoliation; because we know, and all the world knows, that we have been forced into it to save the very institutions we five under from corruption and destruction. The purpose of the Central Powers strikes straight at the very heart of everything we believe in; their methods of warfare outrage every principle of humanity and of knightly honor; their intrigue has corrupted the very thought and spirit of many of our people; their sinister and secret diplomacy has sought to take our very territory away from us and disrupt the union of the states. Our safety would be at an end, our honor forever sullied and brought into contempt, were we to permit their triumph. They are striking at the very existence of democracy and liberty.

It is because it is for us a war of high, disinterested purpose, in which all the free peoples of the world are banded together for the vindication of right, a war for the preservation of our nation, of all that it has held dear, of principle and of purpose, that we feel ourselves doubly constrained to propose for its outcome only that which is righteous and of irreproachable intention, for our foes as well as for our friends. The cause being just and holy, the settlement must be of like motive and equality. For this we can fight, but for nothing less noble or less worthy of our traditions. For this cause we entered the war and for this cause will we battle until the last gun is fired.

I have spoken plainly because this seems to me the time when it is most necessary to speak plainly, in order that all the world may know that, even in the heat and ardor of the struggle and when our whole thought is of carrying the war through to its end, we have not forgotten any ideal or principle for which the name of America has been held in honor among the nations and for which it has been our glory to contend in the great generations that went before us. A supreme moment of history has come. The eyes of the people have been opened and they see. The hand of God is laid upon the nations. He will show them favor, I devoutly believe, only if they rise to the clear heights of His own justice and mercy.

Sixth State of the Union address

Woodrow Wilson

December 2, 1918

GENTLEMEN OF THE CONGRESS:

The year that has elapsed since I last stood before you to fulfil my constitutional duty to give to the Congress from time to time information on the state of the Union has been so crowded with great events, great processes, and great results that I cannot hope to give you an adequate picture of its transactions or of the far-reaching changes which have been wrought of our nation and of the world. You have yourselves witnessed these things, as I have. It is too soon to assess them; and we who stand in the midst of them and are part of them are less qualified than men of another generation will be to say what they mean, or even what they have been. But some great outstanding facts are unmistakable and constitute, in a sense, part of the public business with which it is our duty to deal. To state them is to set the stage for the legislative and executive action which must grow out of them and which we have yet to shape and determine.

A year ago we had sent 145,918 men overseas. Since then we have sent 1,950,513, an average of 162,542 each month, the number in fact rising, in May last, to 245,951, in June to 278,760, in July to 307,182, and continuing to reach similar figures in August and September, in August 289,570 and in September 257,438. No such movement of troops ever took place before, across three thousand miles of sea, followed by adequate equipment and supplies, and carried safely through extraordinary dangers of attack,-dangers which were alike strange and infinitely difficult to guard against. In all this movement only seven hundred and fifty-eight men were lost by enemy attack, six hundred and thirty of whom were upon a single English transport which was sunk near the Orkney Islands.

I need not tell you what lay back of this great movement of men and material. It is not invidious to say that back of it lay a supporting organization of the industries of the country and of all its productive activities more complete, more thorough in method and effective in result, more spirited and unanimous in purpose and effort than any other great belligerent had been able to effect. We profited greatly by the experience of the nations which had already been engaged for nearly three years in the exigent and exacting business, their every resource and every executive proficiency taxed to the utmost. We were their pupils. But we learned quickly and acted with a promptness and a readiness of cooperation that justify our great pride that we were able to serve the world with unparalleled energy and quick accomplishment.

But it is not the physical scale and executive efficiency of preparation, supply, equipment and despatch that I would dwell upon, but the mettle and quality of the officers and men we sent over and of the sailors who kept the seas, and the spirit of the nation that stood behind them. No soldiers or sailors ever proved themselves more quickly ready for the test of battle or acquitted themselves with more splendid courage and achievement when put to the test. Those of us who played some part in directing the great processes by which the war was pushed irresistibly forward to the final triumph may now forget all that and delight our thoughts with the story of what our men did. Their officers understood the grim and exacting task they had undertaken and performed it with an audacity, efficiency, and unhesitating courage that touch the story of convoy and battle with imperishable distinction at every turn, whether the enterprise were great or small, from their great chiefs, Pershing and Sims, down to the youngest lieutenant; and their men were worthy of them,-such men as hardly need to be commanded, and go to their terrible adventure blithely and with the quick intelligence of those who know just what it is they would accomplish. I am proud to be the fellow-countryman of men of such stuff and valor. Those of us who stayed at home did our duty; the war could not have been won or the gallant men who fought it given their opportunity to win it otherwise; but for many a long day we shall think ourselves "accurs'd we were not there, and hold our manhoods cheap while any speaks that fought" with these at St. Mihiel or Thierry. The memory of those days of triumphant battle will go with these fortunate men to their graves; and each will have his favorite memory. "Old men forget; yet all shall be forgot, but hell remember with advantages what feats he did that day!"

What we all thank God for with deepest gratitude is that our men went in force into the line of battle just at the critical moment when the whole fate of the world seemed to hang in the balance and threw their fresh strength into the ranks of freedom in time to turn the whole tide and sweep of the fateful struggle,-turn it once for all, so that thenceforth it was back, back, back for their enemies, always back, never again forward! After that it was only a scant four months before the commanders of the Central Empires knew themselves beaten; and now their very empires are in liquidation!

And throughout it all how fine the spirit of the nation was: what unity of purpose, what untiring zeal! What elevation of purpose ran through all its splendid display of strength, its untiring accomplishment! I have said that those of us who stayed at home to do the work of organization and supply will always wish that we had been with the men whom we sustained by our labor; but we can never be ashamed. It has been an inspiring thing to be here in the midst of fine men who had turned aside from every private interest of their own and devoted the whole of their trained capacity to the tasks that supplied the sinews of the whole great undertaking! The patriotism, the unselfishness, the thoroughgoing devotion and distinguished capacity that marked their toilsome labors, day after day, month after month, have made them fit mates and comrades of the men in the trenches and on the sea. And not the men here in Washington only. They have but directed the vast achievement. Throughout innumerable factories, upon innumerable farms, in the depths of coal mines and iron mines and copper mines, wherever the stuffs of industry were to be obtained and prepared, in the shipyards, on the railways, at the docks, on the sea, in every labor that was needed to sustain the battle lines, men have vied with each other to do their part and do it well. They can look any man-at-arms in the face, and say, We also strove to win and gave the best that was in us to make our fleets and armies sure of their triumph!

And what shall we say of the women,-of their instant intelligence, quickening every task that they touched; their capacity for organization and cooperation, which gave their action discipline and enhanced the effectiveness of everything they attempted; their aptitude at tasks to which they had never before set their hands; their utter self-sacrifice alike in what they did and in what they gave? Their contribution to the great result is beyond appraisal. They have added a new lustre to the annals of American womanhood.

The least tribute we can pay them is to make them the equals of men in political rights as they have proved themselves their equals in every field of practical work they have entered, whether for themselves or for their country. These great days of completed achievement would be sadly marred were we to omit that act of justice. Besides the immense practical services they have rendered the women of the country have been the moving spirits in the systematic economies by which our people have voluntarily assisted to supply the suffering peoples of the world and the armies upon every front with food and everything else that we had that might serve the common cause. The details of such a story can never be fully written, but we carry them at our hearts and thank God that we can say that we are the kinsmen of such.

And now we are sure of the great triumph for which every sacrifice was made. It has come, come in its completeness, and with the pride and inspiration of these days of achievement quick within us, we turn to the tasks of peace again,-a peace secure against the violence of irresponsible monarchs and ambitious military coteries and made ready for a new order, for new foundations of justice and fair dealing.

We are about to give order and organization to this peace not only for ourselves but for the other peoples of the world as well, so far as they will suffer us to serve them. It is international justice that we seek, not domestic safety merely. Our thoughts have dwelt of late upon Europe, upon Asia, upon the near and the far East, very little upon the acts of peace and accommodation that wait to be performed at our own doors. While we are adjusting our relations with the rest of the world is it not of capital importance that we should clear away all grounds of misunderstanding with our immediate neighbors and give proof of the friendship we really feel? I hope that the members of the Senate will permit me to speak once more of the unratified treaty of friendship and adjustment with the Republic of Colombia. I very earnestly urge upon them an early and favorable action upon that vital matter. I believe that they will feel, with me, that the stage of affairs is now set for such action as will be not only just but generous and in the spirit of the new age upon which we have so happily entered.

So far as our domestic affairs are concerned the problem of our return to peace is a problem of economic and industrial readjustment. That problem is less serious for us than it may turn out too be for the nations which have suffered the disarrangements and the losses of war longer than we. Our people, moreover, do not wait to be coached and led. They know their own business, are quick and resourceful at every readjustment, definite in purpose, and self-reliant in action. Any leading strings we might seek to put them in would speedily become hopelessly tangled because they would pay no attention to them and go their own way. All that we can do as their legislative and executive servants is to mediate the process of change here, there, and elsewhere as we may. I have heard much counsel as to the plans that should be formed and personally conducted to a happy consummation, but from no quarter have I seen any general scheme of "reconstruction" emerge which I thought it likely we could force our spirited business men and self-reliant laborers to accept with due pliancy and obedience.

While the war lasted we set up many agencies by which to direct the industries of the country in the services it was necessary for them to render, by which to make sure of an abundant supply of the materials needed, by which to check undertakings that could for the time be dispensed with and stimulate those that were most serviceable in war, by which to gain for the purchasing departments of the Government a certain control over the prices of essential articles and materials, by which to restrain trade with alien enemies, make the most of the available shipping, and systematize financial transactions, both public and private, so that there would be no unnecessary conflict or confusion,-by which, in short, to put every material energy of the country in harness to draw the common load and make of us one team in the accomplishment of a great task. But the moment we knew the armistice to have been signed we took the harness off. Raw materials upon which the Government had kept its hand for fear there should not be enough for the industries that supplied the armies have been released and put into the general market again. Great industrial plants whose whole output and machinery had been taken over for the uses of the Government have been set free to return to the uses to which they were put before the war. It has not been possible to remove so readily or so quickly the control of foodstuffs and of shipping, because the world has still to be fed from our granaries and the ships are still needed to send supplies to our men overseas and to bring the men back as fast as the disturbed conditions on the other side of the water permit; but even there restraints are being relaxed as much as possible and more and more as the weeks go by.

Never before have there been agencies in existence in this country which knew so much of the field of supply, of labor, and of industry as the War Industries Board, the War Trade Board, the Labor Department, the Food Administration, and the Fuel Administration have known since their labors became thoroughly systematized; and they have not been isolated agencies; they have been directed by men who represented the permanent Departments of the Government and so have been the centres of unified and cooperative action. It has been the policy of the Executive, therefore, since the armistice was assured (which is in effect a complete submission of the enemy) to put the knowledge of these bodies at the disposal of the business men of the country and to offer their intelligent mediation at every point and in every matter where it was desired. It is surprising how fast the process of return to a peace footing has moved in the three weeks since the fighting stopped. It promises to outrun any inquiry that may be instituted and any aid that may be offered. It will not be easy to direct it any better than it will direct itself. The American business man is of quick initiative.

The ordinary and normal processes of private initiative will not, however, provide immediate employment for all of the men of our returning armies. Those who are of trained capacity, those who are skilled workmen, those who have acquired familiarity with established businesses, those who are ready and willing to go to the farms, all those whose aptitudes are known or will be sought out by employers will find no difficulty, it is safe to say, in finding place and employment. But there will be others who will be at a loss where to gain a livelihood unless pains are taken to guide them and put them in the way of work. There will be a large floating residuum of labor which should not be left wholly to shift for itself. It seems to me important, therefore, that the development of public works of every sort should be promptly resumed, in order that opportunities should be created for unskilled labor in particular, and that plans should be made for such developments of our unused lands and our natural resources as we have hitherto lacked stimulation to undertake.

I particularly direct your attention to the very practical plans which the Secretary of the Interior has developed in his annual report and before your Committees for the reclamation of arid, swamp, and cutover lands which might, if the States were willing and able to cooperate, redeem some three hundred million acres of land for cultivation. There are said to be fifteen or twenty million acres of land in the West, at present arid, for whose reclamation water is available, if properly conserved. There are about two hundred and thirty million acres from which the forests have been cut but which have never yet been cleared for the plow and which lie waste and desolate. These lie scattered all over the Union. And there are nearly eighty million acres of land that lie under swamps or subject to periodical overflow or too wet for anything but grazing, which it is perfectly feasible to drain and protect and redeem. The Congress can at once direct thousands of the returning soldiers to the reclamation of the arid lands which it has already undertaken, if it will but enlarge the plans and appropriations which it has entrusted to the Department of the Interior. It is possible in dealing with our unused land to effect a great rural and agricultural development which will afford the best sort of opportunity to men who want to help themselves and the Secretary of the Interior has thought the possible methods out in a way which is worthy of your most friendly attention.

I have spoken of the control which must yet for a while, perhaps for a long long while, be exercised over shipping because of the priority of service to which our forces overseas are entitled and which should also be accorded the shipments which are to save recently liberated peoples from starvation and many devastated regions from permanent ruin. May I not say a special word about the needs of Belgium and northern France? No sums of money paid by way of indemnity will serve of themselves to save them from hopeless disadvantage for years to come. Something more must be done than merely find the money. If they had money and raw materials in abundance to-morrow they could not resume their place in the industry of the world to-morrow,-the very important place they held before the flame of war swept across them. Many of their factories are razed to the ground. Much of their machinery is destroyed or has been taken away. Their people are scattered and many of their best workmen are dead. Their markets will be taken by others, if they are not in some special way assisted to rebuild their factories and replace their lost instruments of manufacture. They should not be left to the vicissitudes of the sharp competition for materials and for industrial facilities which is now to set in. I hope, therefore, that the Congress will not be unwilling, if it should become necessary, to grant to some such agency as the War Trade Board the right to establish priorities of export and supply for the benefit of these people whom we have been so happy to assist in saving from the German terror and whom we must not now thoughtlessly leave to shift for themselves in a pitiless competitive market.

For the steadying, and facilitation of our own domestic business readjustments nothing is more important than the immediate determination of the taxes that are to be levied for 1918, 1919, and 1920. As much of the burden of taxation must be lifted from business as sound methods of financing the Government will permit, and those who conduct the great essential industries of the country must be told as exactly as possible what obligations to the Government they will be expected to meet in the years immediately ahead of them. It will be of serious consequence to the country to delay removing all uncertainties in this matter a single day longer than the right processes of debate justify. It is idle to talk of successful and confident business reconstruction before those uncertainties are resolved.

If the war had continued it would have been necessary to raise at least eight billion dollars by taxation payable in the year 1919; but the war has ended and I agree with the Secretary of the Treasury that it will be safe to reduce the amount to six billions. An immediate rapid decline in the expenses of the Government is not to be looked for. Contracts made for war supplies will, indeed, be rapidly cancelled and liquidated, but their immediate liquidation will make heavy drains on the Treasury for the months just ahead of us. The maintenance of our forces on the other side of the sea is still necessary. A considerable proportion of those forces must remain in Europe during the period of occupation, and those which are brought home will be transported and demobilized at heavy expense for months to come. The interest on our war debt must of course be paid and provision made for the retirement of the obligations of the Government which represent it. But these demands will of course fall much below what a continuation of military operations would have entailed and six billions should suffice to supply a sound foundation for the financial operations of the year.

I entirely concur with the Secretary of the Treasury in recommending that the two billions needed in addition to the four billions provided by existing law be obtained from the profits which have accrued and shall accrue from war contracts and distinctively war business, but that these taxes be confined to the war profits accruing in 1918, or in 1919 from business originating in war contracts. I urge your acceptance of his recommendation that provision be made now, not subsequently, that the taxes to be paid in 1920 should be reduced from six to four billions. Any arrangements less definite than these would add elements of doubt and confusion to the critical period of industrial readjustment through which the country must now immediately pass, and which no true friend of the nation's essential business interests can afford to be responsible for creating or prolonging. Clearly determined conditions, clearly and simply charted, are indispensable to the economic revival and rapid industrial development which may confidently be expected if we act now and sweep all interrogation points away.

I take it for granted that the Congress will carry out the naval programme which was undertaken before we entered the war. The Secretary of the Navy has submitted to your Committees for authorization that part of the programme which covers the building plans of the next three years. These plans have been prepared along the lines and in accordance with the policy which the Congress established, not under the exceptional conditions of the war, but with the intention of adhering to a definite method of development for the navy. I earnestly recommend the uninterrupted pursuit of that policy. It would clearly be unwise for us to attempt to adjust our programmes to a future world policy as yet undetermined.

The question which causes me the greatest concern is the question of the policy to be adopted towards the railroads. I frankly turn to you for counsel upon it. I have no confident judgment of my own. I do not see how any thoughtful man can have who knows anything of the complexity of the problem. It is a problem which must be studied, studied immediately, and studied without bias or prejudice. Nothing can be gained by becoming partisans of any particular plan of settlement.

It was necessary that the administration of the railways should be taken over by the Government so long as the war lasted. It would have been impossible otherwise to establish and carry through under a single direction the necessary priorities of shipment. It would have been impossible otherwise to combine maximum production at the factories and mines and farms with the maximum possible car supply to take the products to the ports and markets; impossible to route troop shipments and freight shipments without regard to the advantage or-disadvantage of the roads employed; impossible to subordinate, when necessary, all questions of convenience to the public necessity; impossible to give the necessary financial support to the roads from the public treasury. But all these necessities have now been served, and the question is, What is best for the railroads and for the public in the future?

Exceptional circumstances and exceptional methods of administration were not needed to convince us that the railroads were not equal to the immense tasks of transportation imposed upon them by the rapid and continuous development of the industries of the country. We knew that already. And we knew that they were unequal to it partly because their full cooperation was rendered impossible by law and their competition made obligatory, so that it has been impossible to assign to them severally the traffic which could best be carried by their respective lines in the interest of expedition and national economy.

We may hope, I believe, for the formal conclusion of the war by treaty by the time Spring has come. The twenty-one months to which the present control of the railways is limited after formal proclamation of peace shall have been made will run at the farthest, I take it for granted, only to the January of 1921. The full equipment of the railways which the federal administration had planned could not be completed within any such period. The present law does not permit the use of the revenues of the several roads for the execution of such plans except by formal contract with their directors, some of whom will consent while some will not, and therefore does not afford sufficient authority to undertake improvements upon the scale upon which it would be necessary to undertake them. Every approach to this difficult subject-matter of decision brings us face to face, therefore, with this unanswered question: What is it right that we should do with the railroads, in the interest of the public and in fairness to their owners?

Let me say at once that I have no answer ready. The only thing that is perfectly clear to me is that it is not fair either to the public or to the owners of the railroads to leave the question unanswered and that it will presently become my duty to relinquish control of the roads, even before the expiration of the statutory period, unless there should appear some clear prospect in the meantime of a legislative solution. Their release would at least produce one element of a solution, namely certainty and a quick stimulation of private initiative.

I believe that it will be serviceable for me to set forth as explicitly as possible the alternative courses that lie open to our choice. We can simply release the roads and go back to the old conditions of private management, unrestricted competition, and multiform regulation by both state and federal authorities; or we can go to the opposite extreme and establish complete government control, accompanied, if necessary, by actual government ownership; or we can adopt an intermediate course of modified private control, under a more unified and affirmative public regulation and under such alterations of the law as will permit wasteful competition to be avoided and a considerable degree of unification of administration to be effected, as, for example, by regional corporations under which the railways of definable areas would be in effect combined in single systems.

The one conclusion that I am ready to state with confidence is that it would be a disservice alike to the country and to the owners of the railroads to return to the old conditions unmodified. Those are conditions of restraint without development. There is nothing affirmative or helpful about them. What the country chiefly needs is that all its means of transportation should be developed, its railways, its waterways, its highways, and its countryside roads. Some new element of policy, therefore, is absolutely necessary--necessary for the service of the public, necessary for the release of credit to those who are administering the railways, necessary for the protection of their security holders. The old policy may be changed much or little, but surely it cannot wisely be left as it was. I hope that the Con will have a complete and impartial study of the whole problem instituted at once and prosecuted as rapidly as possible. I stand ready and anxious to release the roads from the present control and I must do so at a very early date if by waiting until the statutory limit of time is reached I shall be merely prolonging the period of doubt and uncertainty which is hurtful to every interest concerned.

I welcome this occasion to announce to the Congress my purpose to join in Paris the representatives of the governments with which we have been associated in the war against the Central Empires for the purpose of discussing with them the main features of the treaty of peace. I realize the great inconveniences that will attend my leaving the country, particularly at this time, but the conclusion that it was my paramount duty to go has been forced upon me by considerations which I hope will seem as conclusive to you as they have seemed to me.

The Allied governments have accepted the bases of peace which I outlined to the Congress on the eighth of January last, as the Central Empires also have, and very reasonably desire my personal counsel in their interpretation and application, and it is highly desirable that I should give it in order that the sincere desire of our Government to contribute without selfish purpose of any kind to settlements that will be of common benefit to all the nations concerned may be made fully manifest. The peace settlements which are now to be agreed upon are of transcendent importance both to us and to the rest of the world, and I know of no business or interest which should take precedence of them. The gallant men of our armed forces on land and sea have consciously fought for the ideals which they knew to be the ideals of their country; I have sought to express those ideals; they have accepted my statements of them as the substance of their own thought and purpose, as the associated governments have accepted them; I owe it to them to see to it, so far as in me lies, that no false or mistaken interpretation is put upon them, and no possible effort omitted to realize them. It is now my duty to play my full part in making good what they offered their life's blood to obtain. I can think of no call to service which could transcend this.

I shall be in close touch with you and with affairs on this side the water, and you will know all that I do. At my request, the French and English governments have absolutely removed the censorship of cable news which until within a fortnight they had maintained and there is now no censorship whatever exercised at this end except upon attempted trade communications with enemy countries. It has been necessary to keep an open wire constantly available between Paris and the Department of State and another between France and the Department of War. In order that this might be done with the least possible interference with the other uses of the cables, I have temporarily taken over the control of both cables in order that they may be used as a single system. I did so at the advice of the most experienced cable officials, and I hope that the results will justify my hope that the news of the next few months may pass with the utmost freedom and with the least possible delay from each side of the sea to the other.

May I not hope, Gentlemen of the Congress, that in the delicate tasks I shall have to perform on the other side of the sea, in my efforts truly and faithfully to interpret the principles and purposes of the country we love, I may have the encouragement and the added strength of your united support? I realize the magnitude and difficulty of the duty I am undertaking; I am poignantly aware of its grave responsibilities. I am the servant of the nation. I can have no private thought or purpose of my own in performing such an errand. I go to give the best that is in me to the common settlements which I must now assist in arriving at in conference with the other working heads of the associated governments. I shall count upon your friendly countenance and encouragement. I shall not be inaccessible. The cables and the wireless will render me available for any counsel or service you may desire of me, and I shall be happy in the thought that I am constantly in touch with the weighty matters of domestic policy with which we shall have to deal. I shall make my absence as brief as possible and shall hope to return with the happy assurance that it has been possible to translate into action the great ideals for which America has striven.

Seventh State of the Union address

Woodrow Wilson

December 2, 1919

TO THE SENATE AND HOUSE OF REPRESENTATIVES:

I sincerely regret that I cannot be present at the opening of this session of the Congress. I am thus prevented from presenting in as direct a way as I could wish the many questions that are pressing for solution at this time. Happily, I have had the advantage of the advice of the heads of the several executive departments who have kept in close touch with affairs in their detail and whose thoughtful recommendations I earnestly second.

In the matter of the railroads and the readjustment of their affairs growing out of Federal control, I shall take the liberty at a later date of addressing you.

I hope that Congress will bring to a conclusion at this session legislation looking to the establishment of a budget system. That there should be one single authority responsible for the making of all appropriations and that appropriations should be made not independently of each other, but with reference to one single comprehensive plan of expenditure properly related to the nation's income, there can be no doubt I believe the burden of preparing the budget must, in the nature of the case, if the work is to be properly done and responsibility concentrated instead of divided, rest upon the executive. The budget so prepared should be submitted to and approved or amended by a single committee of each House of Congress and no single appropriation should be made by the Congress, except such as may have been included in the budget prepared by the executive or added by the particular committee of Congress charged with the budget legislation.

Another and not less important aspect of the problem is the ascertainment of the economy and efficiency with which the moneys appropriated are expended. Under existing law the only audit is for the purpose of ascertaining whether expenditures have been lawfully made within the appropriations. No one is authorized or equipped to ascertain whether the money has been spent wisely, economically and effectively. The auditors should be highly trained officials with permanent tenure in the Treasury Department, free of obligations to or motives of consideration for this or any subsequent administration, and authorized and empowered to examine into and make report upon the methods employed and the results obtained by the executive departments of the Government. Their reports should be made to the Congress and to the Secretary of the Treasury.

I trust that the Congress will give its immediate consideration to the problem of future taxation. Simplification of the income and profits taxes has become an immediate necessity. These taxes performed indispensable service during the war. They must, however, be simplified, not only to save the taxpayer inconvenience and expense, but in order that his liability may be made certain and definite.

With reference to the details of the Revenue Law, the Secretary of the Treasury and the Commissioner of Internal Revenue will lay before you for your consideration certain amendments necessary or desirable in connection with the administration of the law-recommendations which have my approval and support. It is of the utmost importance that in dealing with this matter the present law should not be disturbed so far as regards taxes for the calendar year 1920 payable in the calendar year 1921. The Congress might well consider whether the higher rates of income and profits taxes can in peace times be effectively productive of revenue, and whether they may not, on the contrary, be destructive of business activity and productive of waste and inefficiency. There is a point at which in peace times high rates of income and profits taxes discourage energy, remove the incentive to new enterprises, encourage extravagant expenditures and produce industrial stagnation with consequent unemployment and other attendant evils.

The problem is not an easy one. A fundamental change has taken place with reference to the position of America in the world's affairs. The prejudice and passions engendered by decades of controversy between two schools of political and economic thought,-the one believers in protection of American industries, the other believers in tariff for revenue only,-must be subordinated to the single consideration of the public interest in the light of utterly changed conditions. Before the war America was heavily the debtor of the rest of the world and the interest payments she had to make to foreign countries on American securities held abroad, the expenditures of American travelers abroad and the ocean freight charges she had to pay to others, about balanced the value of her pre-war favorable balance of trade. During the war America's exports have been greatly stimulated, and increased prices have increased their value. On the other hand, she has purchased a large proportion of the American securities previously held abroad, has loaned some $9,000,000,000 to foreign governments, and has built her own ships. Our favorable balance of trade has thus been greatly increased and Europe has been deprived of the means of meeting it heretofore existing. Europe can have only three ways of meeting the favorable balance of trade in peace times: by imports into this country of gold or of goods, or by establishing new credits. Europe is in no position at the present time to ship gold to us nor could we contemplate large further imports of gold into this country without concern. The time has nearly passed for international governmental loans and it will take time to develop in this country a market for foreign securities. Anything, therefore, which would tend to prevent foreign countries from settling for our exports by shipments of goods into this country could only have the effect of preventing them from paying for our exports and therefore of preventing the exports from being made. The productivity of the country, greatly stimulated by the war, must find an outlet by exports to foreign countries, and any measures taken to prevent imports will inevitably curtail exports, force curtailment of production, load the banking machinery of the country with credits to carry unsold products and produce industrial stagnation and unemployment. If we want to sell, we must be prepared to buy. Whatever, therefore, may have been our views during the period of growth of American business concerning tariff legislation, we must now adjust our own economic life to a changed condition growing out of the fact that American business is full grown and that America is the greatest capitalist in the world.

No policy of isolation will satisfy the growing needs and opportunities of America. The provincial standards and policies of the past, which have held American business as if in a straitjacket, must yield and give way to the needs and exigencies of the new day in which we live, a day full of hope and promise for American business, if we will but take advantage of the opportunities that are ours for the asking. The recent war has ended our isolation and thrown upon us a great duty and responsibility. The United States must share the expanding world market. The United States desires for itself only equal opportunity with the other nations of the world, and that through the process of friendly cooperation and fair competition the legitimate interests of the nations concerned may be successfully and equitably adjusted.

There are other matters of importance upon which I urged action at the last session of Congress which are still pressing for solution. I am sure it is not necessary for me again to remind you that there is one immediate and very practicable question resulting from the war which we should meet in the most liberal spirit. It is a matter of recognition and relief to our soldiers. I can do no better than to quote from my last message urging this very action:

"We must see to it that our returning soldiers are assisted in every practicable way to find the places for which they are fitted in the daily work of the country. This can be done by developing and maintaining upon an adequate scale the admirable organization created by the Department of Labor for placing men seeking work; and it can also be done, in at least one very great field, by creating new opportunities for individual enterprise. The Secretary of the Interior has pointed out the way by which returning soldiers may be helped to find and take up land in the hitherto undeveloped regions of the country which the Federal Government has already prepared, or can readily prepare, for cultivation and also on many of the cutover or neglected areas which lie within the limits of the older states; and I once more take the liberty of recommending very urgently that his plans shall receive the immediate and substantial support of the Congress."

In the matter of tariff legislation, I beg to call your attention to the statements contained in my last message urging legislation with reference to the establishment of the chemical and dyestuffs industry in America:

"Among the industries to which special consideration should be given is that of the manufacture of dyestuffs and related chemicals. Our complete dependence upon German supplies before the war made the interruption of trade a cause of exceptional economic disturbance. The close relation between the manufacture of dyestuffs, on the one hand, and of explosive and poisonous gases, on the other, moreover, has given the industry an exceptional significance and value. Although the United States will gladly and unhesitatingly join in the programme of international disarmament, it will, nevertheless, be a policy of obvious prudence to make certain of the successful maintenance of many strong and well-equipped chemical plants. The German chemical industry, with which we will be brought into competition, was and may well be again, a thoroughly knit monopoly capable of exercising a competition of a peculiarly insidious and dangerous kind."

During the war the farmer performed a vital and willing service to the nation. By materially increasing the production of his land, he supplied America and the Allies with the increased amounts of food necessary to keep their immense armies in the field. He indispensably helped to win the war. But there is now scarcely less need of increasing the production in food -and the necessaries of life. I ask the Congress to consider means of encouraging effort along these lines. The importance of doing everything possible to promote production along economical lines, to improve marketing, and to make rural life more attractive and healthful, is obvious. I would urge approval of the plans already proposed to the Congress by the Secretary of Agriculture, to secure the essential facts required for the proper study of this question, through the proposed enlarged programmes for farm management studies and crop estimates. I would urge, also, the continuance of Federal participation in the building of good roads, under the terms of existing law and under the direction of present agencies; the need of further action on the part of the States and the Federal Government to preserve and develop our forest resources, especially through the practice of better forestry methods on private holdings and the extension of the publicly owned forests; better support for country schools and the more definite direction of their courses of study along lines related to rural problems; and fuller provision for sanitation in rural districts and the building up of needed hospital and medical facilities in these localities. Perhaps the way might be cleared for many of these desirable reforms by a fresh, comprehensive survey made of rural conditions by a conference composed of representatives of the farmers and of the agricultural agencies responsible for leadership.

I would call your attention to the widespread condition of political restlessness in our body politic. The causes of this unrest, while various and complicated, are superficial rather than deep-seated. Broadly, they arise from or are connected with the failure on the part of our Government to arrive speedily at a just and permanent peace permitting return to normal conditions, from the transfusion of radical theories from seething European centers pending such delay, from heartless profiteering resulting in the increase of the cost of living, and lastly from the machinations of passionate and malevolent agitators. With the return to normal conditions, this unrest will rapidly disappear. In the meantime, it does much evil. It seems to me that in dealing with this situation Congress should not be impatient or drastic but should seek rather to remove the causes. It should endeavor to bring our country back speedily to a peace basis, with ameliorated living conditions under the minimum of restrictions upon personal liberty that is consistent with our reconstruction problems. And it should arm the Federal Government with power to deal in its criminal courts with those persons who by violent methods would abrogate our time-tested institutions. With the free expression of opinion and with the advocacy of orderly political change, however fundamental, there must be no interference, but towards passion and malevolence tending to incite crime and insurrection under guise of political evolution there should be no leniency. Legislation to this end has been recommended by the Attorney General and should be enacted. In this direct connection, I would call your attention to my recommendations on August 8th, pointing out legislative measures which would be effective in controlling and bringing down the present cost of living, which contributes so largely to this unrest. On only one of these recommendations has the Congress acted. If the Government's campaign is to be effective, it is necessary that the other steps suggested should be acted on at once.

I renew and strongly urge the necessity of the extension of the present Food Control Act as to the period of time in which it shall remain in operation. The Attorney General has submitted a bill providing for an extension of this Act for a period of six months. As it now stands, it is limited in operation to the period of the war and becomes inoperative upon the formal proclamation of peace. It is imperative that it should be extended at once. The Department of justice has built up extensive machinery for the purpose of enforcing its provisions; all of which must be abandoned upon the conclusion of peace unless the provisions of this Act are extended.

During this period the Congress will have an opportunity to make similar permanent provisions and regulations with regard to all goods destined for interstate commerce and to exclude them from interstate shipment, if the requirements of the law are not compiled with. Some such regulation is imperatively necessary. The abuses that have grown up in the manipulation of prices by the withholding of foodstuffs and other necessaries of life cannot otherwise be effectively prevented. There can be no doubt of either the necessity of the legitimacy of such measures.

As I pointed out in my last message, publicity can accomplish a great deal in this campaign. The aims of the Government must be clearly brought to the attention of the consuming public, civic organizations and state officials, who are in a position to lend their assistance to our efforts. You have made available funds with which to carry on this campaign, but there is no provision in the law authorizing their expenditure for the purpose of making the public fully informed about the efforts of the Government. Specific recommendation has been made by the Attorney General in this regard. I would strongly urge upon you its immediate adoption, as it constitutes one of the preliminary steps to this campaign.

I also renew my recommendation that the Congress pass a law regulating cold storage as it is regulated, for example, by the laws of the State of New Jersey, which limit the time during which goods may be kept in storage, prescribe the method of disposing of them if kept beyond the permitted period, and require that goods released from storage shall in all cases bear the date of their receipt. It would materially add to the serviceability of the law, for the purpose we now have in view, if it were also prescribed that all goods released from storage for interstate shipment should have plainly marked upon each package the selling or market price at which they went into storage. By this means the purchaser would always be able to learn what profits stood between him and the producer or the wholesale dealer.

I would also renew my recommendation that all goods destined for interstate commerce should in every case, where their form or package makes it possible, be plainly marked with the price at which they left the hands of the producer.

We should formulate a law requiring a Federal license of all corporations engaged in interstate commerce and embodying in the license or in the conditions under which it is to be issued, specific regulations designed to secure competitive selling and prevent unconscionable profits in the method of marketing. Such a law would afford a welcome opportunity to effect other much needed reforms in the business of interstate shipment and in the methods of corporations which are engaged in it; but for the moment I confine my recommendations to the object immediately in hand, which is to lower the cost of living.

No one who has observed the march of events in the last year can fail to note the absolute need of a definite programme to bring about an improvement in the conditions of labor. There can be no settled conditions leading to increased production and a reduction in the cost of living if labor and capital are to be antagonists instead of partners. Sound thinking and an honest desire to serve the interests of the whole nation, as distinguished from the interests of a class, must be applied to the solution of this great and pressing problem. The failure of other nations to consider this matter in a vigorous way has produced bitterness and jealousies and antagonisms, the food of radicalism. The only way to keep men from agitating against grievances is to remove the grievances. An unwillingness even to discuss these matters produces only dissatisfaction and gives comfort to the extreme elements in our country which endeavor to stir up disturbances in order to provoke governments to embark upon a course of retaliation and repression. The seed of revolution is repression. The remedy for these things must not be negative in character. It must be constructive. It must comprehend the general interest. The real antidote for the unrest which manifests itself is not suppression, but a deep consideration of the wrongs that beset our national life and the application of a remedy.

Congress has already shown its willingness to deal with these industrial wrongs by establishing the eight-hour day as the standard in every field of labor. It has sought to find a way to prevent child labor. It has served the whole country by leading the way in developing the means of preserving and safeguarding lives and health in dangerous industries. It must now help in the difficult task of finding a method that will bring about a genuine democratization of industry, based upon the full recognition of the right of those who work, in whatever rank, to participate in some organic way in every decision which directly affects their welfare. It is with this purpose in mind that I called a conference to meet in Washington on December 1st, to consider these problems in all their broad aspects, with the idea of bringing about a better understanding between these two interests.

The great unrest throughout the world, out of which has emerged a demand for an immediate consideration of the difficulties between capital and labor, bids us put our own house in order. Frankly, there can be no permanent and lasting settlements between capital and labor which do not recognize the fundamental concepts for which labor has been struggling through the years. The whole world gave its recognition and endorsement to these fundamental purposes in the League of Notions. The statesmen gathered at Versailles recognized the fact that world stability could not be had by reverting to industrial standards and conditions against which the average workman of the world had revolted. It is, therefore, the task of the states men of this new day of change and readjustment to recognize world conditions and to seek to bring about, through legislation, conditions that will mean the ending of age-long antagonisms between capital and labor and that will hopefully lead to the building up of a comradeship which will result not only in greater contentment among the mass of workmen but also bring about a greater production and a greater prosperity to business itself.

To analyze the particulars in the demands of labor is to admit the justice of their complaint in many matters that lie at their basis. The workman demands an adequate wage, sufficient to permit him to live in comfort, unhampered by the fear of poverty and want in his old age. He demands the right to live and the right to work amidst sanitary surroundings, both in home and in workshop, surroundings that develop and do not retard his own health and wellbeing; and the right to provide for his children's wants in the matter of health and education. In other words, it is his desire to make the conditions of his life and the lives of those dear to him tolerable and easy to bear.

The establishment of the principles regarding labor laid down ill the covenant of the League of Nations offers us the way to industrial peace and conciliation. No other road lies open to us. Not to pursue this one is longer to invite enmities, bitterness, and antagonisms which in the end only lead to industrial and social disaster. The unwilling workman is not a profitable servant. An employee whose industrial life is hedged about by hard and unjust conditions, which he did not create and over which he has no control, lacks that fine spirit of enthusiasm and volunteer effort which are the necessary ingredients of a great producing entity. Let us be frank about this solemn matter. The evidences of world-wide unrest which manifest themselves in violence throughout the world bid us pause and consider the means to be found to stop the spread of this contagious thing before it saps the very vitality of the nation itself. Do we gain strength by withholding the remedy? Or is it not the business of statesmen to treat these manifestations of unrest which meet us on every hand as evidences of an economic disorder and to apply constructive remedies wherever necessary, being sure that in the application of the remedy we touch not the vital tissues of our industrial and economic life? There can be no recession of the tide of unrest until constructive instrumentalities are set up to stem that tide.

Governments must recognize the right of men collectively to bargain for humane objects that have at their base the mutual protection and welfare of those engaged in all industries. Labor must not be longer treated as a commodity. It must be regarded as the activity of human beings, possessed of deep yearnings and desires. The business man gives his best thought to the repair and replenishment of his machinery, so that its usefulness will not be impaired and its power to produce may always be at its height and kept in full vigor and motion. No less regard ought to be paid to the human machine, which after all propels the machinery of the world and is the great dynamic force that lies back of all industry and progress. Return to the old standards of wage and industry in employment are unthinkable. The terrible tragedy of war which has just ended and which has brought the world to the verge of chaos and disaster would be in vain if there should ensue a return to the conditions of the past. Europe itself, whence has come the unrest which now holds the world at bay, is an example of standpatism in these vital human matters which America might well accept as an example, not to be followed but studiously to be avoided. Europe made labor the differential, and the price of it all is enmity and antagonism and prostrated industry, The right of labor to live in peace and comfort must be recognized by governments and America should be the first to lay the foundation stones upon which industrial peace shall be built.

Labor not only is entitled to an adequate wage, but capital should receive a reasonable return upon its investment and is entitled to protection at the hands of the Government in every emergency. No Government worthy of the name can "play" these elements against each other, for there is a mutuality of interest between them which the Government must seek to express and to safeguard at all cost.

The right of individuals to strike is inviolate and ought not to be interfered with by any process of Government, but there is a predominant right and that is the right of the Government to protect all of its people and to assert its power and majesty against the challenge of any class. The Government, when it asserts that right, seeks not to antagonize a class but simply to defend the right of the whole people as against the irreparable harm and injury that might be done by the attempt by any class to usurp a power that only Government itself has a right to exercise as a protection to all.

In the matter of international disputes which have led to war, statesmen have sought to set up as a remedy arbitration for war. Does this not point the way for the settlement of industrial disputes, by the establishment of a tribunal, fair and just alike to all, which will settle industrial disputes which in the past have led to war and disaster? America, witnessing the evil conse-quences which have followed out of such disputes between these contending forces, must not admit itself impotent to deal with these matters by means of peaceful processes. Surely, there must be some method of bringing together in a council of peace and amity these two great interests, out of which will come a happier day of peace and cooperation, a day that will make men more hopeful and enthusiastic in their various tasks, that will make for more comfort and happiness in living and a more tolerable condition among all classes of men. Certainly human intelligence can devise some acceptable tribunal for adjusting the differences between capital and labor.

This is the hour of test and trial for America. By her prowess and strength, and the in-domitable courage of her soldiers, she demonstrated her power to vindicate on foreign bat-tlefields her conceptions of liberty and justice. Let not her influence as a mediator between capital and labor be weakened and her own failure to settle matters of purely domestic concern be proclaimed to the world. There are those in this country who threaten direct action to force their will, upon a majority. Russia today, with its blood and terror, is a painful object lesson of the power of minorities. It makes little difference what minority it is; whether capital or labor, or any other class; no sort of privilege will ever be permitted to dominate this country. We are a partnership or nothing that is worth while. We are a democracy, where the majority are the masters, or all the hopes and purposes of the men who founded this government have been defeated and forgotten. In America there is but one way by which great reforms can be accomplished and the relief sought by classes obtained, and that is through the orderly processes of representative government. Those who would propose any other method of reform are enemies of this country. America will not be daunted by threats nor lose her composure or calmness in these distressing times. We can afford, in the midst of this day of passion and unrest, to be self-contained and sure. The instrument of all reform in America is the ballot. The road to economic and social reform in America is the straight road of justice to all classes and conditions of men. Men have but to follow this road to realize the full fruition of their objects and purposes. Let those beware who would take the shorter road of disorder and revolution. The right road is the road of justice and orderly process.

Eighth State of the Union address

Woodrow Wilson

December 7, 1920

GENTLEMEN OF THE CONGRESS:

When I addressed myself to performing the duty laid upon the President by the Constitution to present to you an annual report on the state of the Union, I found my thought dominated by an immortal sentence of Abraham Lincoln's--"Let us have faith that right makes might, and in that faith let us dare to do our duty as we understand it"--a sentence immortal because it embodies in a form of utter simplicity and purity the essential faith of the nation, the faith in which it was conceived, and the faith in which it has grown to glory and power. With that faith and the birth of a nation founded upon it came the hope into the world that a new order would prevail throughout the affairs of mankind, an order in which reason and right would take precedence over covetousness and force; and I believe that I express the wish and purpose of every thoughtful American when I say that this sentence marks for us in the plainest manner the part we should play alike in the arrangement of our domestic affairs and in our exercise of influence upon the affairs of the world.

By this faith, and by this faith alone, can the world be lifted out of its present confusion and despair. It was this faith which prevailed over the wicked force of Germany. You will remember that the beginning of the end of the war came when the German people found themselves face to face with the conscience of the world and realized that right was everywhere arrayed against the wrong that their government was attempting to perpetrate. I think, therefore, that it is true to say that this was the faith which won the war. Certainly this is the faith with which our gallant men went into the field and out upon the seas to make sure of victory.

This is the mission upon which Democracy came into the world. Democracy is an assertion of the right of the individual to live and to be treated justly as against any attempt on the part of any combination of individuals to make laws which will overburden him or which will destroy his equality among his fellows in the matter of right or privilege; and I think we all realize that the day has come when Democracy is being put upon its final test. The Old World is just now suffering from a wanton rejection of the principle of democracy and a substitution of the principle of autocracy as asserted in the name, but without the authority and sanction, of the multitude. This is the time of all others when Democracy should prove its purity and its spiritual power to prevail. It is surely the manifest destiny of the United States to lead in the attempt to make this spirit prevail.

There are two ways in which the United States can assist to accomplish this great object. First, by offering the example within her own borders of the will and power of Democracy to make and enforce laws which are unquestionably just and which are equal in their administration-laws which secure its full right to Labor and yet at the same time safeguard the integrity of property, and particularly of that property which is devoted to the development of industry and the increase of the necessary wealth of the world. Second, by standing for right and justice as toward individual nations. The law of Democracy is for the protection of the weak, and the influence of every democracy in the world should be for the protection of the weak nation, the nation which is struggling toward its right and toward its proper recognition and privilege in the family of nations.

The United States cannot refuse this role of champion without putting the stigma of rejection upon the great and devoted men who brought its government into existence and established it in the face of almost universal opposition and intrigue, even in the face of wanton force, as, for example, against the Orders in Council of Great Britain and the arbitrary Napoleonic decrees which involved us in what we know as the War of 1812.

I urge you to consider that the display of an immediate disposition on the part of the Congress to remedy any injustices or evils that may have shown themselves in our own national life will afford the most effectual offset to the forces of chaos and tyranny which are playing so disastrous a part in the fortunes of the free peoples of more than one part of the world. The United States is of necessity the sample democracy of the world, and the triumph of Democracy depends upon its success.

Recovery from the disturbing and sometimes disastrous effects of the late war has been exceedingly slow on the other side of the water, and has given promise, I venture to say, of early completion only in our own fortunate country; but even with us the recovery halts and is impeded at times, and there are immediately serviceable acts of legislation which it seems to me we ought to attempt, to assist that recovery and prove the indestructible recuperative force of a great government of the people. One of these is to prove that a great democracy can keep house as successfully and in as business-like a fashion as any other government. It seems to me that the first step toward providing this is to supply ourselves with a systematic method of handling our estimates and expenditures and bringing them to the point where they will not be an unnecessary strain upon our income or necessitate unreasonable taxation; in other words, a workable budget system. And I respectfully suggest that two elements are essential to such a system-namely, not only that the proposal of appropriations should be in the hands of a single body, such as a single appropriations committee in each house of the Congress, but also that this body should be brought into such cooperation with the Departments of the Government and with the Treasury of the United States as would enable it to act upon a complete conspectus of the needs of the Government and the resources from which it must draw its income.

I reluctantly vetoed the budget bill passed by the last session of the Congress because of a constitutional objection. The House of Representatives subsequently modified the bill in order to meet this objection. In the revised form, I believe that the bill, coupled with action already taken by the Congress to revise its rules and procedure, furnishes the foundation for an effective national budget system. I earnestly hope, therefore, that one of the first steps to be taken by the present session of the Congress will be to pass the budget bill.

The nation's finances have shown marked improvement during the last year. The total ordinary receipts of $6,694,000,000 for the fiscal year 1920 exceeded those for 1919 by $1,542,000,000, while the total net ordinary expenditures decreased from $18,514,000,000 to $6,403,000,000. The gross public debt, which reached its highest point on August 31, 1919, when it was $26,596,000,000, had dropped on November 30, 1920, to $24,175,000,000.

There has also been a marked decrease in holdings of government war securities by the banking institutions of the country, as well as in the amount of bills held by the Federal Reserve Banks secured by government war obligations. This fortunate result has relieved the banks and left them freer to finance the needs of Agriculture, Industry, and Commerce. It has been due in large part to the reduction of the public debt, especially of the floating debt, but more particularly to the improved distribution of government securities among permanent investors. The cessation of the Government's borrowings, except through short-term certificates of indebtedness, has been a matter of great consequence to the people of the country at large, as well as to the holders of Liberty Bonds and Victory Notes, and has had an important bearing on the matter of effective credit control.

The year has been characterized by the progressive withdrawal of the Treasury from the domestic credit market and from a position of dominant influence in that market. The future course will necessarily depend upon the extent to which economies are practiced and upon the burdens placed upon the Treasury, as well as upon industrial developments and the maintenance of tax receipts at a sufficiently high level. The fundamental fact which at present dominates the Government's financial situation is that seven and a half billions of its war indebtedness mature within the next two and a half years. Of this amount, two and a half billions are floating debt and five billions, Victory Notes and War. Savings Certificates. The fiscal program of the Government must be determined with reference to these maturities. Sound policy demands that Government expenditures be reduced to the lowest amount which will permit the various services to operate efficiently and that Government receipts from taxes and salvage be maintained sufficiently high to provide for current requirements, including interest and sinking fund charges on the public debt, and at the same time retire the floating debt and part of the Victory Loan before maturity.

With rigid economy, vigorous salvage operations, and adequate revenues from taxation, a surplus of current receipts over current expenditures can be realized and should be applied to the floating debt. All branches of the Government should cooperate to see that this program is realized. I cannot overemphasize the necessity of economy in Government appropriations and expenditures and the avoidance by the Congress of practices which take money from the Treasury by indefinite or revolving fund appropriations. The estimates for the present year show that over a billion dollars of expenditures were authorized by the last Congress in addition to the amounts shown in the usual compiled statements of appropriations. This strikingly illustrates the importance of making direct and specific appropriations. The relation between the current receipts and current expenditures of the Government during the present fiscal year, as well as during the last half of the last fiscal year, has been disturbed by the extraordinary burdens thrown upon the Treasury by the Transportation Act, in connection with the return of the railroads to private control. Over $600,000,000 has already been paid to the railroads under this act-$350,000,000 during the present fiscal year; and it is estimated that further payments aggregating possibly $650,000,000 must still be made to the railroads during the current year. It is obvious that these large payments have already seriously limited the Government's progress in retiring the floating debt.

Closely connected with this, it seems to me, is the necessity for an immediate consideration of the revision of our tax laws. Simplification of the income and profits taxes has become an immediate necessity. These taxes performed an indispensable service during the war. The need for their simplification, however, is very great, in order to save the taxpayer inconvenience and expense and in order to make his liability more certain and definite. Other and more detailed recommendations with regard to taxes will no doubt be laid before you by the Secretary of the Treasury and the Commissioner of Internal Revenue.

It is my privilege to draw to the attention of Congress for very sympathetic consideration the problem of providing adequate facilities for the care and treatment of former members of the military and naval forces who are sick and disabled as the result of their participation in the war. These heroic men can never be paid in money for the service they patriotically rendered the nation. Their reward will lie rather in realization of the fact that they vindicated the rights of their country and aided in safeguarding civilization. The nation's gratitude must be effectively revealed to them by the most ample provision for their medical care and treatment as well as for their vocational training and placement. The time has come when a more complete program can be formulated and more satisfactorily administered for their treatment and training, and I earnestly urge that the Congress give the matter its early consideration. The Secretary of the Treasury and the Board for Vocational Education will outline in their annual reports proposals covering medical care and rehabilitation which I am sure will engage your earnest study and commend your most generous support.

Permit me to emphasize once more the need for action upon certain matters upon which I dwelt at some length in my message to the second session of the Sixty-sixth Congress. The necessity, for example, of encouraging the manufacture of dyestuffs and related chemicals; the importance of doing everything possible to promote agricultural production along economic lines, to improve agricultural marketing, and to make rural life more attractive and healthful; the need for a law regulating cold storage in such a way as to limit the time during which goods may be kept in storage, prescribing the method of disposing of them if kept beyond the permitted period, and requiring goods released from storage in all cases to bear the date of their receipt. It would also be most serviceable if it were provided that all goods released from cold storage for interstate shipment should have plainly marked upon each package the selling or market price at which they went into storage, in order that the purchaser might be able to learn what profits stood between him and the producer or the wholesale dealer. Indeed, It would be very serviceable to the public if all goods destined for interstate commerce were made to carry upon every packing case whose form made it possible a plain statement of the price at which they left the hands of the producer. I respectfully call your attention also to the recommendations of the message referred to with regard to a federal license for all corporations engaged in interstate commerce.

In brief, the immediate legislative need of the time is the removal of all obstacles to the realization of the best ambitions of our people in their several classes of employment and the strengthening of all instrumentalities by. which difficulties are to be met and removed and justice dealt out, whether by law or by some form of mediation and conciliation. I do not feel it to be my privilege at present to, suggest the detailed and particular methods by which these objects may be attained, but I have faith that the inquiries of your several committees will discover the way and the method.

In response to what I believe to be the impulse of sympathy and opinion throughout the United States, I earnestly suggest that the Congress authorize the Treasury of the United States to make to the struggling government of Armenia such a loan as was made to several of the Allied governments during the war, and I would also suggest that it would be desirable to provide in the legislation itself that the expenditure of the money thus loaned should be under the supervision of a commission, or at least a commissioner, from the United States in order that revolutionary tendencies within Armenia itself might not be afforded by the loan a further tempting opportunity.

Allow me to call your attention to the fact that the people of the Philippine Islands have succeeded in maintaining a stable government since the last action of the Congress in their behalf, and have thus fulfilled the condition set by the Congress as precedent to a consideration of granting independence to the Islands. I respectfully submit that this condition precedent having been fulfilled, it is now our liberty and our duty to keep our promise to the people of those islands by granting them the independence which they so honorably covet.

I have not so much laid before you a series of recommendations, gentlemen, as sought to utter a confession of faith, of the faith in which I was bred and which it is my solemn purpose to stand by until my last fighting day. I believe this to be the faith of America, the faith of the future, and of all the victories which await national action in the days to come, whether in America or elsewhere.

Other Addresses

First Address to Congress

[Delivered at a joint session of the two Houses of Congress, at the beginning of the first session of the Sixty-third Congress, April 8, 1913.]

Mr. Speaker, Mr. President, Gentlemen of the Congress:

I am very glad indeed to have this opportunity to address the two Houses directly and to verify for myself the impression that the President of the United States is a person, not a mere department of the Government hailing Congress from some isolated island of jealous power, sending messages, not speaking naturally and with his own voice-that he is a human being trying to coöperate with other human beings in a common service. After this pleasant experience I shall feel quite normal in all our dealings with one another.[2]

I have called the Congress together in extraordinary session because a duty was laid upon the party now in power at the recent elections which it ought to perform promptly, in order that the burden carried by the people under existing law may be lightened as soon as possible and in order, also, that the business interests of the country may not be kept too long in suspense as to what the fiscal changes are to be to which they will be required to adjust themselves. It is clear to the whole country that the tariff duties must be altered. They must be changed to meet the radical alteration in the conditions of our economic life which the country has witnessed within the last generation. While the whole face and method of our industrial and commercial life were being changed beyond recognition the tariff schedules have remained what they were before the change began, or have moved in the direction they were given when no large circumstance of our industrial development was what it is to-day. Our task is to square them with the actual facts. The sooner that is done the sooner we shall escape from suffering from the facts and the sooner our men of business will be free to thrive by the law of nature (the nature of free business) instead of by the law of legislation and artificial arrangement.

We have seen tariff legislation wander very far afield in our day-very far indeed from the field in which our prosperity might have had a normal growth and stimulation. No one who looks the facts squarely in the face or knows anything that lies beneath the surface of action can fail to perceive the principles upon which recent tariff legislation has been based. We long ago passed beyond the modest notion of "protecting" the industries of the country and moved boldly forward to the idea that they were entitled to the direct patronage of the Government. For a long time —a time so long that the men now active in public policy hardly remember the conditions that preceded it-we have sought in our tariff schedules to give each group of manufacturers or producers what they themselves thought that they needed in order to maintain a practically exclusive market as against the rest of the world. Consciously or unconsciously, we have built up a set of privileges and exemptions from competition behind which it was easy by any, even the crudest, forms of combination to organize monopoly; until at last nothing is normal, nothing is obliged to stand the tests of efficiency and economy, in our world of big business, but everything thrives by concerted arrangement. Only new principles of action will save us from a final hard crystallization of monopoly and a complete loss of the influences that quicken enterprise and keep independent energy alive.

It is plain what those principles must be. We must abolish everything that bears even the semblance of privilege or of any kind of artificial advantage, and put our business men and producers under the stimulation of a constant necessity to be efficient, economical, and enterprising, masters of competitive supremacy, better workers and merchants than any in the world. Aside from the duties laid upon articles which we do not, and probably cannot, produce, therefore, and the duties laid upon luxuries and merely for the sake of the revenues they yield, the object of the tariff duties henceforth laid must be effective competition, the whetting of American wits by contest with the wits of the rest of the world.

It would be unwise to move toward this end headlong, with reckless haste, or with strokes that cut at the very roots of what has grown up amongst us by long process and at our own invitation. It does not alter a thing to upset it and break it and deprive it of a chance to change. It destroys it. We must make changes in our fiscal laws, in our fiscal system, whose object is development, a more free and wholesome development, not revolution or upset or confusion. We must build up trade, especially foreign trade. We need the outlet and the enlarged field of energy more than we ever did before. We must build up industry as well, and must adopt freedom in the place of artificial stimulation only so far as it will build, not pull down. In dealing with the tariff the method by which this may be done will be a matter of judgment, exercised item by item. To some not accustomed to the excitements and responsibilities of greater freedom our methods may in some respects and at some points seem heroic, but remedies may be heroic and yet be remedies. It is our business to make sure that they are genuine remedies. Our object is clear. If our motive is above just challenge and only an occasional error of judgment is chargeable against us, we shall be fortunate.

We are called upon to render the country a great service in more matters than one. Our responsibility should be met and our methods should be thorough, as thorough as moderate and well considered, based upon the facts as they are, and not worked out as if we were beginners. We are to deal with the facts of our own day, with the facts of no other, and to make laws which square with those facts. It is best, indeed it is necessary, to begin with the tariff. I will urge nothing upon you now at the opening of your session which can obscure that first object or divert our energies from that clearly defined duty. At a later time I may take the liberty of calling your attention to reforms which should press close upon the heels of the tariff changes, if not accompany them, of which the chief is the reform of our banking and currency laws; but just now I refrain. For the present, I put these matters on one side and think only of this one thing-of the changes in our fiscal system which may best serve to open once more the free channels of prosperity to a great people whom we would serve to the utmost and throughout both rank and file.

I thank you for your courtesy.

Address on the Banking System

[Delivered at a joint session of the two Houses of Congress, June 23, 1913.]

Mr. Speaker, Mr. President, Gentlemen of the Congress:

It is under the compulsion of what seems to me a clear and imperative duty that I have a second time this session sought the privilege of addressing you in person. I know, of course, that the heated season of the year is upon us, that work in these chambers and in the committee rooms is likely to become a burden as the season lengthens, and that every consideration of personal convenience and personal comfort, perhaps, in the cases of some of us, considerations of personal health even, dictate an early conclusion of the deliberations of the session; but there are occasions of public duty when these things which touch us privately seem very small, when the work to be done is so pressing and so fraught with big consequence that we know that we are not at liberty to weigh against it any point of personal sacrifice. We are now in the presence of such an occasion. It is absolutely imperative that we should give the business men of this country a banking and currency system by means of which they can make use of the freedom of enterprise and of individual initiative which we are about to bestow upon them.

We are about to set them free; we must not leave them without the tools of action when they are free. We are about to set them free by removing the trammels of the protective tariff. Ever since the Civil War they have waited for this emancipation and for the free opportunities it will bring with it. It has been reserved for us to give it to them. Some fell in love, indeed, with the slothful security of their dependence upon the Government; some took advantage of the shelter of the nursery to set up a mimic mastery of their own within its walls. Now both the tonic and the discipline of liberty and maturity are to ensue. There will be some readjustments of purpose and point of view. There will follow a period of expansion and new enterprise, freshly conceived. It is for us to determine now whether it shall be rapid and facile and of easy accomplishment. This it cannot be unless the resourceful business men who are to deal with the new circumstances are to have at hand and ready for use the instrumentalities and conveniences of free enterprise which independent men need when acting on their own initiative.

It is not enough to strike the shackles from business. The duty of statesmanship is not negative merely. It is constructive also. We must show that we understand what business needs and that we know how to supply it. No man, however casual and superficial his observation of the conditions now prevailing in the country, can fail to see that one of the chief things business needs now, and will need increasingly as it gains in scope and vigor in the years immediately ahead of us, is the proper means by which readily to vitalize its credit, corporate and individual, and its originative brains. What will it profit us to be free if we are not to have the best and most accessible instrumentalities of commerce and enterprise? What will it profit us to be quit of one kind of monopoly if we are to remain in the grip of another and more effective kind? How are we to gain and keep the confidence of the business community unless we show that we know how both to aid and to protect it? What shall we say if we make fresh enterprise necessary and also make it very difficult by leaving all else except the tariff just as we found it? The tyrannies of business, big and little, lie within the field of credit. We know that. Shall we not act upon the knowledge? Do we not know how to act upon it? If a man cannot make his assets available at pleasure, his assets of capacity and character and resource, what satisfaction is it to him to see opportunity beckoning to him on every hand, when others have the keys of credit in their pockets and treat them as all but their own private possession? It is perfectly clear that it is our duty to supply the new banking and currency system the country needs, and it will need it immediately more than it has ever needed it before.

The only question is, When shall we supply it—now, or later, after the demands shall have become reproaches that we were so dull and so slow? Shall we hasten to change the tariff laws and then be laggards about making it possible and easy for the country to take advantage of the change? There can be only one answer to that question. We must act now, at whatever sacrifice to ourselves. It is a duty which the circumstances forbid us to postpone. I should be recreant to my deepest convictions of public obligation did I not press it upon you with solemn and urgent insistence.

The principles upon which we should act are also clear. The country has sought and seen its path in this matter within the last few years-sees it more clearly now than it ever saw it before-much more clearly than when the last legislative proposals on the subject were made. We must have a currency, not rigid as now, but readily, elastically responsive to sound credit, the expanding and contracting credits of everyday transactions, the normal ebb and flow of personal and corporate dealings. Our banking laws must mobilize reserves; must not permit the concentration anywhere in a few hands of the monetary resources of the country or their use for speculative purposes in such volume as to hinder or impede or stand in the way of other more legitimate, more fruitful uses. And the control of the system of banking and of issue which our new laws are to set up must be public, not private, must be vested in the Government itself, so that the banks may be the instruments, not the masters, of business and of individual enterprise and initiative.

The committees of the Congress to which legislation of this character is referred have devoted careful and dispassionate study to the means of accomplishing these objects. They have honored me by consulting me. They are ready to suggest action. I have come to you, as the head of the Government and the responsible leader of the party in power, to urge action now, while there is time to serve the country deliberately and as we should, in a clear air of common counsel. I appeal to you with a deep conviction of duty. I believe that you share this conviction. I therefore appeal to you with confidence. I am at your service without reserve to play my part in any way you may call upon me to play it in this great enterprise of exigent reform which it will dignify and distinguish us to perform and discredit us to neglect.

Address at Gettysburg

[Delivered in the presence of Union and Confederate veterans, on the occasion of the fiftieth anniversary of the battle, July 4, 1913.]

Friends and Fellow Citizens:

I need not tell you what the Battle of Gettysburg meant. These gallant men in blue and gray sit all about us here.[3] Many of them met upon this ground in grim and deadly struggle. Upon these famous fields and hillsides their comrades died about them. In their presence it were an impertinence to discourse upon how the battle went, how it ended, what it signified! But fifty years have gone by since then, and I crave the privilege of speaking to you for a few minutes of what those fifty years have meant.

What *have* they meant? They have meant peace and union and vigor, and the maturity and might of a great nation. How wholesome and healing the peace has been! We have found one another again as brothers and comrades in arms, enemies no longer, generous friends rather, our battles long past, the quarrel forgotten-except that we shall not forget the splendid valor, the manly devotion of the men then arrayed against one another, now grasping hands and smiling into each other's eyes. How complete the union has become and how dear to all of us, how unquestioned, how benign and majestic, as State after State has been added to this our great family of free men! How handsome the vigor, the maturity, the might of the great Nation we love with undivided hearts; how full of large and confident promise that a life will be wrought out that will crown its strength with gracious justice and with a happy welfare that will touch all alike with deep contentment! We are debtors to those fifty crowded years; they have made us heirs to a mighty heritage.

But do we deem the Nation complete and finished? These venerable men crowding here to this famous field have set us a great example of devotion and utter sacrifice. They were willing to die that the people might live. But their task is done. Their day is turned into evening. They look to us to perfect what they established. Their work is handed on to us, to be done in another way, but not in another spirit. Our day is not over; it is upon us in full tide.

Have affairs paused? Does the Nation stand still? Is what the fifty years have wrought since those days of battle finished, rounded out, and completed? Here is a great people, great with every force that has ever beaten in the lifeblood of mankind. And it is secure. There is no one within its borders, there is no power among the nations of the earth, to make it afraid. But has it yet squared itself with its own great standards set up at its birth, when it made that first noble, naïve appeal to the moral judgment of mankind to take notice that a government had now at last been established which was to serve men, not masters? It is secure in everything except the satisfaction that its life is right, adjusted to the uttermost to the standards of righteousness and humanity. The days of sacrifice and cleansing are not closed. We have harder things to do than were done in the heroic days of war, because harder to see clearly, requiring more vision, more calm balance of judgment, a more candid searching of the very springs of right.

Look around you upon the field of Gettysburg! Picture the array, the fierce heats and agony of battle, column hurled against column, battery bellowing to battery! Valor? Yes! Greater no man shall see in war; and self-sacrifice, and loss to the uttermost; the high recklessness of exalted devotion which does not count the cost. We are made by these tragic, epic things to know what it costs to make a nation-the blood and sacrifice of multitudes of unknown men lifted to a great stature in the view of all generations by knowing no limit to their manly willingness to serve. In armies thus marshaled from the ranks of free men you will see, as it were, a nation embattled, the leaders and the led, and may know, if you will, how little except in form its action differs in days of peace from its action in days of war.

May we break camp now and be at ease? Are the forces that fight for the Nation dispersed, disbanded, gone to their homes forgetful of the common cause? Are our forces disorganized, without constituted leaders and the might of men consciously united because we contend, not with armies, but with principalities and powers and wickedness in high places? Are we content to lie still? Does our union mean sympathy, our peace contentment, our vigor right action, our maturity self-comprehension and a clear confidence in choosing what we shall do? War fitted us for action, and action never ceases.

I have been chosen the leader of the Nation. I cannot justify the choice by any qualities of my own, but so it has come about, and here I stand. Whom do I command? The ghostly hosts who fought upon these battlefields long ago and are gone? These gallant gentlemen stricken in years whose fighting days, are over, their glory won? What are the orders for them, and who rallies them? I have in my mind another host, whom these set free of civil strife in order that they might work out in days of peace and settled order the life of a great Nation. That host is the people themselves, the great and the small, without class or difference of kind or race or origin; and undivided in interest, if we have but the vision to guide and direct them and order their lives aright in what we do. Our constitutions are their articles of enlistment. The orders of the day are the laws upon our statute books. What we strive for is their freedom, their right to lift themselves from day to day and behold the things they have hoped for, and so make way for still better days for those whom they love who are to come after them. The recruits are the little children crowding in. The quartermaster's stores are in the mines and forests and fields, in the shops and factories. Every day something must be done to push the campaign forward; and it must be done by plan and with an eye to some great destiny.

How shall we hold such thoughts in our hearts and not be moved? I would not have you live even to-day wholly in the past, but would wish to stand with you in the light that streams upon us now out of that great day gone by. Here is the nation God has builded by our hands. What shall we do with it? Who stands ready to act again and always in the spirit of this day of reunion and hope and patriotic fervor? The day of our country's life has but broadened into morning. Do not put uniforms by. Put the harness of the present on. Lift your eyes to the great tracts of life yet to be conquered in the interest of righteous peace, of that prosperity which lies in a people's hearts and outlasts all wars and errors of men. Come, let us be comrades and soldiers yet to serve our fellow-men in quiet counsel, where the blare of trumpets is neither heard nor heeded and where the things are done which make blessed the nations of the world in peace and righteousness and love.

Address on Mexican Affairs

[Delivered at a joint session of the two Houses of Congress, August 27, 1913.]

Gentlemen of the Congress:

It is clearly my duty to lay before you, very fully and without reservation, the facts concerning our present relations with the Republic of Mexico. The deplorable posture of affairs in Mexico I need not describe,[4] but I deem it my duty to speak very frankly of what this Government has done and should seek to do in fulfillment of its obligation to Mexico herself, as a friend and neighbor, and to American citizens whose lives and vital interests are daily affected by the distressing conditions which now obtain beyond our southern border.

Those conditions touch us very nearly. Not merely because they lie at our very doors. That of course makes us more vividly and more constantly conscious of them, and every instinct of neighborly interest and sympathy is aroused and quickened by them; but that is only one element in the determination of our duty. We are glad to call ourselves the friends of Mexico, and we shall, I hope, have many an occasion, in happier times as well as in these days of trouble and confusion, to show that our friendship is genuine and disinterested, capable of sacrifice and every generous manifestation. The peace, prosperity, and contentment of Mexico mean more, much more, to us than merely an enlarged field for our commerce and enterprise. They mean an enlargement of the field of self-government and the realization of the hopes and rights of a nation with whose best aspirations, so long suppressed and disappointed, we deeply sympathize. We shall yet prove to the Mexican people that we know how to serve them without first thinking how we shall serve ourselves.

But we are not the only friends of Mexico. The whole world desires her peace and progress; and the whole world is interested as never before. Mexico lies at last where all the world looks on. Central America is about to be touched by the great routes of the world's trade and intercourse running free from ocean to ocean at the Isthmus. The future has much in store for Mexico, as for all the States of Central America; but the best gifts can come to her only if she be ready and free to receive them and to enjoy them honorably. America in particular-America north and south and upon both continents-waits upon the development of Mexico; and that development can be sound and lasting only if it be the product of a genuine freedom, a just and ordered government founded upon law. Only so can it be peaceful or fruitful of the benefits of peace. Mexico has a great and enviable future before her, if only she choose and attain the paths of honest constitutional government.

The present circumstances of the Republic, I deeply regret to say, do not seem to promise even the foundations of such a peace. We have waited many months, months full of peril and anxiety, for the conditions there to improve, and they have not improved. They have grown worse, rather. The territory in some sort controlled by the provisional authorities at Mexico City has grown smaller, not larger. The prospect of the pacification of the country, even by arms, has seemed to grow more and more remote; and its pacification by the authorities at the capital is evidently impossible by any other means than force. Difficulties more and more entangle those who claim to constitute the legitimate government of the Republic. They have not made good their claim in fact. Their successes in the field have proved only temporary. War and disorder, devastation and confusion, seem to threaten to become the settled fortune of the distracted country. As friends we could wait no longer for a solution which every week seemed further away. It was our duty at least to volunteer our good offices-to offer to assist, if we might, in effecting some arrangement which would bring relief and peace and set up a universally acknowledged political authority there.

Accordingly, I took the liberty of sending the Hon. John Lind, formerly governor of Minnesota, as my personal spokesman and representative, to the City of Mexico, with *the following instructions*:

Press very earnestly upon the attention of those who are now exercising authority or wielding influence in Mexico the following considerations and advice:

The Government of the United States does not feel at liberty any longer to stand inactively by while it becomes daily more and more evident that no real progress is being made towards the establishment of a government at the City of Mexico which the country will obey and respect.

The Government of the United States does not stand in the same case with the other great Governments of the world in respect of what is happening or what is likely to happen in Mexico. We offer our good offices, not only because of our genuine desire to play the part of a friend, but also because we are expected by the powers of the world to act as Mexico's nearest friend.

We wish to act in these circumstances in the spirit of the most earnest and disinterested friendship. It is our purpose in whatever we do or propose in this perplexing and distressing situation not only to pay the most scrupulous regard to the sovereignty and independence of Mexico-that we take as a matter of course to which we are bound by every obligation of right and honor-but also to give every possible evidence that we act in the interest of Mexico alone, and not in the interest of any person or body of persons who may have personal or property claims in Mexico which they may feel that they have the right to press. We are seeking to counsel Mexico for her own good and in the interest of her own peace, and not for any other purpose whatever. The Government of the United States would deem itself discredited if it had any selfish or ulterior purpose in transactions where the peace, happiness, and prosperity of a whole people are involved. It is acting as its friendship for Mexico, not as any selfish interest, dictates.

The present situation in Mexico is incompatible with the fulfillment of international obligations on the part of Mexico, with the civilized development of Mexico herself, and with the maintenance of tolerable political and economic conditions in Central America. It is upon no common occasion, therefore, that the United States offers her counsel and assistance. All America cries out for a settlement.

A satisfactory settlement seems to us to be conditioned on —

(a) An immediate cessation of fighting throughout Mexico, a definite armistice solemnly entered into and scrupulously observed;

(b) Security given for an early and free election in which all will agree to take part;

(c) The consent of Gen. Huerta to bind himself not to be a candidate for election as President of the Republic at this election; and

(d) The agreement of all parties to abide by the results of the election and coöperate in the most loyal way in organizing and supporting the new administration.

The Government of the United States will be glad to play any part in this settlement or in its carrying out which it can play honorably and consistently with international right. It pledges itself to recognize and in every way possible and proper to assist the administration chosen and set up in Mexico in the way and on the conditions suggested.

Taking all the existing conditions into consideration, the Government of the United States can conceive of no reasons sufficient to justify those who are now attempting to shape the policy or exercise the authority of Mexico in declining the offices of friendship thus offered. Can Mexico give the civilized world a satisfactory reason for rejecting our good offices? If Mexico can suggest any better way in which to show our friendship, serve the people of Mexico, and meet our international obligations, we are more than willing to consider the suggestion.

Mr. Lind executed his delicate and difficult mission with singular tact, firmness, and good judgment, and made clear to the authorities at the City of Mexico not only the purpose of his visit but also the spirit in which it had been undertaken. But the proposals he submitted were rejected, in a note the full text of which I take the liberty of laying before you.

I am led to believe that they were rejected partly because the authorities at Mexico City had been grossly misinformed and misled upon two points. They did not realize the spirit of the American people in this matter, their earnest friendliness and yet sober determination that some just solution be found for the Mexican difficulties; and they did not believe that the present administration spoke, through Mr. Lind, for the people of the United States. The effect of this unfortunate misunderstanding on their part is to leave them singularly isolated and without friends who can effectually aid them. So long as the misunderstanding continues we can only await the time of their awakening to a realization of the actual facts. We cannot thrust our good offices upon them. The situation must be given a little more time to work itself out in the new circumstances; and I believe that only a little while will be necessary. For the circumstances are new. The rejection of our friendship makes them new and will inevitably bring its own alterations in the whole aspect of affairs. The actual situation of the authorities at Mexico City will presently be revealed.

Meanwhile, what is it our duty to do? Clearly, everything that we do must be rooted in patience and done with calm and disinterested deliberation. Impatience on our part would be childish, and would be fraught with every risk of wrong and folly. We can afford to exercise the self-restraint of a really great nation which realizes its own strength and scorns to misuse it. It was our duty to offer our active assistance. It is now our duty to show what true neutrality will do to enable the people of Mexico to set their affairs in order again and wait for a further opportunity to offer our friendly counsels. The door is not closed against the resumption, either upon the initiative of Mexico or upon our own, of the effort to bring order out of the confusion by friendly coöperative action, should fortunate occasion offer.

While we wait the contest of the rival forces will undoubtedly for a little while be sharper than ever, just because it will be plain that an end must be made of the existing situation, and that very promptly; and with the increased activity of the contending factions will come, it is to be feared, increased danger to the non-combatants in Mexico as well as to those actually in the field of battle. The position of outsiders is always particularly trying and full of hazard where there is civil strife and a whole country is upset. We should earnestly urge all Americans to leave Mexico at once, and should assist them to get away in every way possible-not because we would mean to slacken in the least our efforts to safeguard their lives and their interests, but because it is imperative that they should take no unnecessary risks when it is physically possible for them to leave the country. We should let every one who assumes to exercise authority in any part of Mexico know in the most unequivocal way that we shall vigilantly watch the fortunes of those Americans who cannot get away, and shall hold those responsible for their sufferings and losses to a definite reckoning. That can be and will be made plain beyond the possibility of a misunderstanding.

For the rest, I deem it my duty to exercise the authority conferred upon me by the law of March 14, 1912, to see to it that neither side to the struggle now going on in Mexico receive any assistance from this side the border. I shall follow the best practice of nations in the matter of neutrality by forbidding the exportation of arms or munitions of war of any kind from the United States to any part of the Republic of Mexico —a policy suggested by several interesting precedents and certainly dictated by many manifest considerations of practical expediency. We cannot in the circumstances be the partisans of either party to the contest that now distracts Mexico, or constitute ourselves the virtual umpire between them.

I am happy to say that several of the great Governments of the world have given this Government their generous moral support in urging upon the provisional authorities at the City of Mexico the acceptance of our proffered good offices in the spirit in which they were made. We have not acted in this matter under the ordinary principles of international obligation. All the world expects us in such circumstances to act as Mexico's nearest friend and intimate adviser. This is our immemorial relation towards her. There is nowhere any serious question that we have the moral right in the case or that we are acting in the interest of a fair settlement and of good government, not for the promotion of some selfish interest of our own. If further motive were necessary than our own good will towards a sister Republic and our own deep concern to see peace and order prevail in Central America, this consent of mankind to what we are attempting, this attitude of the great nations of the world towards what we may attempt in dealing with this distressed people at our doors, should make us feel the more solemnly bound to go to the utmost length of patience and forbearance in this painful and anxious business. The steady pressure of moral force will before many days break the barriers of pride and prejudice down, and we shall triumph as Mexico's friends sooner than we could triumph as her enemies-and how much more handsomely, with how much higher and finer satisfactions of conscience and of honor!

Understanding America

[Delivered at Philadelphia, Pa., on the occasion of the rededication of Congress Hall, Oct. 25, 1913. The United States Congress met in this hall till 1800. Here Washington was inaugurated the second time, and here he made his farewell address to the American people. Here John Adams took the oath of office when he succeeded Washington. The hall, after being long disused, was now restored and reopened. Before Mr. Wilson spoke, Mr. Frank Miles Day, representing the committee of architects, had referred to the "delightful silence, order, gravity, and personal dignity of manner" observed by the Senators of the first Congress, and had said, "They all appeared every morning full powdered, and dressed, as age or fancy might suggest, in the richest material."]

Your Honor, Mr. Chairman, Ladies, and Gentlemen:

No American could stand in this place to-day and think of the circumstances which we are come together to celebrate without being most profoundly stirred. There has come over me since I sat down here a sense of deep solemnity, because it has seemed to me that I saw ghosts crowding—a great assemblage of spirits, no longer visible, but whose influence we still feel as we feel the molding power of history itself. The men who sat in this hall, to whom we now look back with a touch of deep sentiment, were men of flesh and blood, face to face with extremely difficult problems. The population of the United States then was hardly three times the present population of the city of Philadelphia, and yet that was a Nation as this is a Nation, and the men who spoke for it were setting their hands to a work which was to last, not only that their people might be happy, but that an example might be lifted up for the instruction of the rest of the world.

I like to read the quaint old accounts such as Mr. Day has read to us this afternoon. Strangers came then to America to see what the young people that had sprung up here were like, and they found men in counsel who knew how to construct governments. They found men deliberating here who had none of the appearance of novices, none of the hesitation of men who did not know whether the work they were doing was going to last or not; men who addressed themselves to a problem of construction as familiarly as we attempt to carry out the traditions of a Government established these 137 years.

I feel to-day the compulsion of these men, the compulsion of examples which were set up in this place. And of what do their examples remind us? They remind us not merely of public service but of public service shot through with principle and honor. They were not histrionic men. They did not say—

Look upon us as upon those who shall hereafter be illustrious.

They said:

Look upon us who are doing the first free work of constitutional liberty in the world, and who must do it in soberness and truth, or it will not last.

Politics, ladies and gentlemen, is made up in just about equal parts of comprehension and sympathy. No man ought to go into politics who does not comprehend the task that he is going to attack. He may comprehend it so completely that it daunts him, that he doubts whether his own spirit is stout enough and his own mind able enough to attempt its great undertakings, but unless he comprehend it he ought not to enter it. After he has comprehended it, there should come into his mind those profound impulses of sympathy which connect him with the rest of mankind, for politics is a business of interpretation, and no men are fit for it who do not see and seek more than their own advantage and interest.

We have stumbled upon many unhappy circumstances in the hundred years that have gone by since the event that we are celebrating. Almost all of them have come from self-centered men, men who saw in their own interest the interest of the country, and who did not have vision enough to read it in wider terms, in the universal terms of equity and justice and the rights of mankind. I hear a great many people at Fourth of July celebrations laud the Declaration of Independence who in between Julys shiver at the plain language of our bills of rights. The Declaration of Independence was, indeed, the first audible breath of liberty, but the substance of liberty is written in such documents as the declaration of rights attached, for example, to the first constitution of Virginia, which was a model for the similar documents read elsewhere into our great fundamental charters. That document speaks in very plain terms. The men of that generation did not hesitate to say that every people has a right to choose its own forms of government-not once, but as often as it pleases-and to accommodate those forms of government to its existing interests and circumstances. Not only to establish but to alter is the fundamental principle of self-government.

We are just as much under compulsion to study the particular circumstances of our own day as the gentlemen were who sat in this hall and set us precedents, not of what to do but of how to do it. Liberty inheres in the circumstances of the day. Human happiness consists in the life which human beings are leading at the time that they live. I can feed my memory as happily upon the circumstances of the revolutionary and constitutional period as you can, but I cannot feed all my purposes with them in Washington now. Every day problems arise which wear some new phase and aspect, and I must fall back, if I would serve my conscience, upon those things which are fundamental rather than upon those things which are superficial, and ask myself this question, How are you going to assist in some small part to give the American people and, by example, the peoples of the world more liberty, more happiness, more substantial prosperity; and how are you going to make that prosperity a common heritage instead of a selfish possession? I came here to-day partly in order to feed my own spirit. I did not come in compliment. When I was asked to come I knew immediately upon the utterance of the invitation that I had to come, that to be absent would be as if I refused to drink once more at the original fountains of inspiration for our own Government.

The men of the day which we now celebrate had a very great advantage over us, ladies and gentlemen, in this one particular: Life was simple in America then. All men shared the same circumstances in almost equal degree. We think of Washington, for example, as an aristocrat, as a man separated by training, separated by family and neighborhood tradition, from the ordinary people of the rank and file of the country. Have you forgotten the personal history of George Washington? Do you not know that he struggled as poor boys now struggle for a meager and imperfect education; that he worked at his surveyor's tasks in the lonely forests; that he knew all the roughness, all the hardships, all the adventure, all the variety of the common life of that day; and that if he stood a little stiffly in this place, if he looked a little aloof, it was because life had dealt hardly with him? All his sinews had been stiffened by the rough work of making America. He was a man of the people, whose touch had been with them since the day he saw the light first in the old Dominion of Virginia. And the men who came after him, men, some of whom had drunk deep at the sources of philosophy and of study, were, nevertheless, also men who on this side of the water knew no complicated life but the simple life of primitive neighborhoods. Our task is very much more difficult. That sympathy which alone interprets public duty is more difficult for a public man to acquire now than it was then, because we live in the midst of circumstances and conditions infinitely complex.

No man can boast that he understands America. No man can boast that he has lived the life of America, as almost every man who sat in this hall in those days could boast. No man can pretend that except by common counsel he can gather into his consciousness what the varied life of this people is. The duty that we have to keep open eyes and open hearts and accessible understandings is a very much more difficult duty to perform than it was in their day. Yet how much more important that it should be performed, for fear we make infinite and irreparable blunders. The city of Washington is in some respects self-contained, and it is easy there to forget what the rest of the United States is thinking about. I count it a fortunate circumstance that almost all the windows of the White House and its offices open upon unoccupied spaces that stretch to the banks of the Potomac and then out into Virginia and on to the heavens themselves, and that as I sit there I can constantly forget Washington and remember the United States. Not that I would intimate that all of the United States lies south of Washington, but there is a serious thing back of my thought. If you think too much about being reëlected, it is very difficult to be worth reëlecting. You are so apt to forget that the comparatively small number of persons, numerous as they seem to be when they swarm, who come to Washington to ask for things, do not constitute an important proportion of the population of the country, that it is constantly necessary to come away from Washington and renew one's contact with the people who do not swarm there, who do not ask for anything, but who do trust you without their personal counsel to do your duty. Unless a man gets these contacts he grows weaker and weaker. He needs them as Hercules needed the touch of mother earth. If you lift him up too high or he lifts himself too high, he loses the contact and therefore loses the inspiration.

I love to think of those plain men, however far from plain their dress sometimes was, who assembled in this hall. One is startled to think of the variety of costume and color which would now occur if we were let loose upon the fashions of that age. Men's lack of taste is largely concealed now by the limitations of fashion. Yet these men, who sometimes dressed like the peacock, were, nevertheless, of the ordinary flight of their time. They were birds of a feather; they were birds come from a very simple breeding; they were much in the open heaven. They were beginning, when there was so little to distract their attention, to show that they could live upon fundamental principles of government. We talk those principles, but we have not time to absorb them. We have not time to let them into our blood, and thence have them translated into the plain mandates of action.

The very smallness of this room, the very simplicity of it all, all the suggestions which come from its restoration, are reassuring things-things which it becomes a man to realize. Therefore my theme here to-day, my only thought, is a very simple one. Do not let us go back to the annals of those sessions of Congress to find out what to do, because we live in another age and the circumstances are absolutely different; but let us be men of that kind; let us feel at every turn the compulsions of principle and of honor which thy felt; let us free our vision from temporary circumstances and look abroad at the horizon and take into our lungs the great air of freedom which has blown through this country and stolen across the seas and blessed people everywhere; and, looking east and west and north and south, let us remind ourselves that we are the custodians, in some degree, of the principles which have made men free and governments just.

Address Before the Southern Commercial Congress

[Delivered at Mobile, Alabama, October 27, 1913.]

Your Excellency, Mr. Chairman:

It is with unaffected pleasure that I find myself here to-day. I once before had the pleasure, in another southern city, of addressing the Southern Commercial Congress. I then spoke of what the future seemed to hold in store for this region, which so many of us love and toward the future of which we all look forward with so much confidence and hope. But another theme directed me here this time. I do not need to speak of the South. She has, perhaps, acquired the gift of speaking for herself. I come because I want to speak of our present and prospective relations with our neighbors to the south. I deemed it a public duty, as well as a personal pleasure, to be here to express for myself and for the Government I represent the welcome we all feel to those who represent the Latin-American States.

The future, ladies and gentlemen, is going to be very different for this hemisphere from the past. These States lying to the south of us, which have always been our neighbors, will now be drawn closer to us by innumerable ties, and, I hope, chief of all by the tie of a common understanding of each other. Interest does not tie nations together; it sometimes separates them. But sympathy and understanding does unite them, and I believe that by the new route that is just about to be opened, while we physically cut two continents asunder, we spiritually unite them. It is a spiritual union which we seek.

I wonder if you realize, I wonder if your imaginations have been filled with the significance of the tides of commerce. Your Governor alluded in very fit and striking terms to the voyage of Columbus, but Columbus took his voyage under compulsion of circumstances. Constantinople had been captured by the Turks, and all the routes of trade with the East had been suddenly closed. If there was not a way across the Atlantic to open those routes again, they were closed forever; and Columbus set out not to discover America, for he did not know that it existed, but to discover the eastern shores of Asia. He set sail for Cathay and stumbled upon America. With that change in the outlook of the world, what happened? England, that had been at the back of Europe with an unknown sea behind her, found that all things had turned as if upon a pivot and she was at the front of Europe; and since then all the tides of energy and enterprise that have issued out of Europe have seemed to be turned westward across the Atlantic. But you will notice that they have turned westward chiefly north of the Equator, and that it is the northern half of the globe that has seemed to be filled with the media of intercourse and of sympathy and of common understanding.

Do you not see now what is about to happen? These great tides which have been running along parallels of latitude will now swing southward athwart parallels of latitude, and that opening gate at the Isthmus of Panama will open the world to a commerce that she has not known before, a commerce of intelligence, of thought, and sympathy between North and South. The Latin-American States which, to their disadvantage, have been off the main lines will now be on the main lines. I feel that these gentlemen honoring us with their presence to-day will presently find that some part, at any rate, of the center of gravity of the world has shifted. Do you realize that New York, for example, will be nearer the western coast of South America than she is now to the eastern coast of South America? Do you realize that a line drawn northward parallel with the greater part of the western coast of South America will run only about one hundred and fifty miles west of New York? The great bulk of South America, if you will look at your globes (not at your Mercator's projection), lies eastward of the continent of North America. You will realize that when you realize that the canal will run southeast, not southwest, and that when you get into the Pacific you will be farther east then you were when you left the Gulf of

Mexico. These things are significant, therefore, of this, that we are closing one chapter in the history of the world and are opening another of great, unimaginable significance.

There is one peculiarity about the history of the Latin-American States which I am sure they are keenly aware of. You hear of "concessions" to foreign capitalists in Latin America. You do not hear of concessions to foreign capitalists in the United States. They are not granted concessions. They are invited to make investments. The work is ours, though they are welcome to invest in it. We do not ask them to supply the capital and do the work. It is an invitation, not a privilege; and States that are obliged, because their territory does not lie within the main field of modern enterprise and action, to grant concessions are in this condition, that foreign interests are apt to dominate their domestic affairs, a condition of affairs always dangerous and apt to become intolerable. What these States are going to see, therefore, is an emancipation from the subordination, which has been inevitable, to foreign enterprise and an assertion of the splendid character which, in spite of these difficulties, they have again and again been able to demonstrate. The dignity, the courage, the self-possession, the self-respect of the Latin-American States, their achievements in the face of all these adverse circumstances, deserve nothing but the admiration and applause of the world. They have had harder bargains driven with them in the matter of loans than any other peoples in the world. Interest has been exacted of them that was not exacted of anybody else, because the risk was said to be greater; and then securities were taken that destroyed the risk-an admirable arrangement for those who were forcing the terms! I rejoice in nothing so much as in the prospect that they will now be emancipated from these conditions; and we ought to be the first to take part in assisting in that emancipation. I think some of these gentlemen have already had occasion to bear witness that the Department of State in recent months has tried to serve them in that wise. In the future they will draw closer and closer to us because of circumstances of which I wish to speak with moderation and, I hope, without indiscretion.

We must prove ourselves their friends and champions upon terms of equality and honor. You cannot be friends upon any other terms than upon the terms of equality. You cannot be friends at all except upon the terms of honor. We must show ourselves friends by comprehending their interest whether it squares with our own interest or not. It is a very perilous thing to determine the foreign policy of a nation in the terms of material interest. It not only is unfair to those with whom you are dealing, but it is degrading as regards your own actions.

Comprehension must be the soil in which shall grow all the fruits of friendship, and there is a reason and a compulsion lying behind all this which is dearer than anything else to the thoughtful men of America. I mean the development of constitutional liberty in the world. Human rights, national integrity, and opportunity as against material interests-that, ladies and gentlemen, is the issue which we now have to face. I want to take this occasion to say that the United States will never again seek one additional foot of territory by conquest. She will devote herself to showing that she knows how to make honorable and fruitful use of the territory she has, and she must regard it as one of the duties of friendship to see that from no quarter are material interests made superior to human liberty and national opportunity. I say this, not with a single thought that anyone will gainsay it, but merely to fix in our consciousness what our real relationship with the rest of America is. It is the relationship of a family of mankind devoted to the development of true constitutional liberty. We know that that is the soil out of which the best enterprise springs. We know that this is a cause which we are making in common with our neighbors, because we have had to make it for ourselves.

Reference has been made here to-day to some of the national problems which confront us as a nation. What is at the heart of all our national problems? It is that we have seen the hand of material interest sometimes about to close upon our dearest rights and possessions. We have seen material interests threaten constitutional freedom in the United States. Therefore we will now know how to sympathize with those in the rest of America who have to contend with such powers, not only within their borders but from outside their borders also.

I know what the response of the thought and heart of America will be to the program I have outlined, because America was created to realize a program like that. This is not America because it is rich. This is not America because it has set up for a great population great opportunities of material prosperity. America is a name which sounds in the ears of men everywhere as a synonym with individual opportunity because a synonym of individual liberty. I would rather belong to a poor nation that was free than to a rich nation that had ceased to be in love with liberty. But we shall not be poor if we love liberty, because the nation that loves liberty truly sets every man free to do his best and be his best, and that means the release of all the splendid energies of a great people who think for themselves. A nation of employees cannot be free any more than a nation of employers can be.

In emphasizing the points which must unite us in sympathy and in spiritual interest with the Latin-American peoples we are only emphasizing the points of our own life, and we should prove ourselves untrue to our own traditions if we proved ourselves untrue friends to them. Do not think, therefore, gentlemen, that the questions of the day are mere questions of policy and diplomacy. They are shot through with the principles of life. We dare not turn from the principle that morality and not expediency is the thing that must guide us and that we will never condone iniquity because it is most convenient to do so. It seems to me that this is a day of infinite hope, of confidence in a future greater than the past has been, for I am fain to believe that in spite of all the things that we wish to correct the nineteenth century that now lies behind us has brought us a long stage toward the time when, slowly ascending the tedious climb that leads to the final uplands, we shall get our ultimate view of the duties of mankind. We have breasted a considerable part of that climb and shall presently-it may be in a generation or two-come out upon those great heights where there shines unobstructed the light of the justice of God.

Trusts and Monopolies

[Address delivered at a joint session of the two Houses of Congress, January 20, 1914.]

Gentlemen of the Congress:

In my report "on the state of the Union," which I had the privilege of reading to you on the 2d of December last, I ventured to reserve for discussion at a later date the subject of additional legislation regarding the very difficult and intricate matter of trusts and monopolies. The time now seems opportune to turn to that great question; not only because the currency legislation, which absorbed your attention and the attention of the country in December, is now disposed of, but also because opinion seems to be clearing about us with singular rapidity in this other great field of action. In the matter of the currency it cleared suddenly and very happily after the much-debated Act was passed; in respect of the monopolies which have multiplied about us and in regard to the various means by which they have been organized and maintained it seems to be coming to a clear and all but universal agreement in anticipation of our action, as if by way of preparation, making the way easier to see and easier to set out upon with confidence and without confusion of counsel.

Legislation has its atmosphere like everything else, and the atmosphere of accommodation and mutual understanding which we now breathe with so much refreshment is matter of sincere congratulation. It ought to make our task very much less difficult and embarrassing than it would have been had we been obliged to continue to act amidst the atmosphere of suspicion and antagonism which has so long made it impossible to approach such questions with dispassionate fairness. Constructive legislation, when successful, is always the embodiment of convincing experience, and of the mature public opinion which finally springs out of that experience. Legislation is a business of interpretation, not of origination; and it is now plain what the opinion is to which we must give effect in this matter. It is not recent or hasty opinion. It springs out of the experience of a whole generation. It has clarified itself by long contest, and those who for a long time battled with it and sought to change it are now frankly and honorably yielding to it and seeking to conform their actions to it.

The great business men who organized and financed monopoly and those who administered it in actual everyday transactions have year after year, until now, either denied its existence or justified it as necessary for the effective maintenance and development of the vast business processes of the country in the modern circumstances of trade and manufacture and finance; but all the while opinion has made head against them. The average business man is convinced that the ways of liberty are also the ways of peace and the ways of success as well; and at last the masters of business on the great scale have begun to yield their preference and purpose, perhaps their judgment also, in honorable surrender.

What we are purposing to do, therefore, is, happily, not to hamper or interfere with business as enlightened business men prefer to do it, or in any sense to put it under the ban. The antagonism between business and government is over. We are now about to give expression to the best business judgment of America, to what we know to be the business conscience and honor of the land. The Government and business men are ready to meet each other half-way in a common effort to square business methods with both public opinion and the law. The best informed men of the business world condemn the methods and processes and consequences of monopoly as we condemn them; and the instinctive judgment of the vast majority of business men everywhere goes with them. We shall now be their spokesmen. That is the strength of our position and the sure prophecy of what will ensue when our reasonable work is done.

When serious contest ends, when men unite in opinion and purpose, those who are to change their ways of business joining with those who ask for the change, it is possible to effect it in the way in which prudent and thoughtful and patriotic men would wish to see it brought about with as few, as slight, as easy and simple business readjustments as possible in the circumstances, nothing essential disturbed, nothing torn up by the roots, no parts rent asunder which can be left in wholesome combination. Fortunately, no measures of sweeping or novel change are necessary. It will be understood that our object is *not* to unsettle business or anywhere seriously to break its established courses athwart. On the contrary, we desire the laws we are now about to pass to be the bulwarks and safeguards of industry against the forces that have disturbed it. What we have to do can be done in a new spirit, in thoughtful moderation, without revolution of any untoward kind.

We are all agreed that "private monopoly is indefensible and intolerable," and our program is founded upon that conviction. It will be a comprehensive but not a radical or unacceptable program and these are its items, the changes which opinion deliberately sanctions and for which business waits:

It waits with acquiescence, in the first place, for laws which will effectually prohibit and prevent such interlockings of the *personnel* of the directorates of great corporations-banks and railroads, industrial, commercial, and public service bodies-as in effect result in making those who borrow and those who lend practically one and the same, those who sell and those who buy but the same persons trading with one another under different names and in different combinations, and those who affect to compete in fact partners and masters of some whole field of business. Sufficient time should be allowed, of course, in which to effect these changes of organization without inconvenience or confusion.

Such a prohibition will work much more than a mere negative good by correcting the serious evils which have arisen because, for example, the men who have been the directing spirits of the great investment banks have usurped the place which belongs to independent industrial management working in its own behoof. It will bring new men, new energies, a new spirit of initiative, new blood, into the management of our great business enterprises. It will open the field of industrial development and origination to scores of men who have been obliged to serve when their abilities entitled them to direct. It will immensely hearten the young men coming on and will greatly enrich the business activities of the whole country.

In the second place, business men as well as those who direct public affairs now recognize, and recognize with painful clearness, the great harm and injustice which has been done to many, if not all, of the great railroad systems of the country by the way in which they have been financed and their own distinctive interests subordinated to the interests of the men who financed them and of other business enterprises which those men wished to promote. The country is ready, therefore, to accept, and accept with relief as well as approval, a law which will confer upon the Interstate Commerce Commission the power to superintend and regulate the financial operations by which the railroads are henceforth to be supplied with the money they need for their proper development to meet the rapidly growing requirements of the country for increased and improved facilities of transportation. We cannot postpone action in this matter without leaving the railroads exposed to many serious handicaps and hazards; and the prosperity of the railroads and the prosperity of the country are inseparably connected. Upon this question those who are chiefly responsible for the actual management and operation of the railroads have spoken very plainly and very earnestly, with a purpose we ought to be quick to accept. It will be one step, and a very important one, toward the necessary separation of the business of production from the business of transportation.

The business of the country awaits also, has long awaited and has suffered because it could not obtain, further and more explicit legislative definition of the policy and meaning of the existing antitrust law. Nothing hampers business like uncertainty. Nothing daunts or discourages it like the necessity to take chances, to run the risk of falling under the condemnation of the law before it can make sure just what the law is. Surely we are sufficiently familiar with the actual processes and methods of monopoly and of the many hurtful restraints of trade to make definition possible, at any rate up to the limits of what experience has disclosed. These practices, being now abundantly disclosed, can be explicitly and item by item forbidden by statute in such terms as will practically eliminate uncertainty, the law itself and the penalty being made equally plain.

And the business men of the country desire something more than that the menace of legal process in these matters be made explicit and intelligible. They desire the advice, the definite guidance and information which can be supplied by an administrative body, an interstate trade commission.

The opinion of the country would instantly approve of such a commission. It would not wish to see it empowered to make terms with monopoly or in any sort to assume control of business, as if the Government made itself responsible. It demands such a commission only as an indispensable instrument of information and publicity, as a clearing house for the facts by which both the public mind and the managers of great business undertakings should be guided, and as an instrumentality for doing justice to business where the processes of the courts or the natural forces of correction outside the courts are inadequate to adjust the remedy to the wrong in a way that will meet all the equities and circumstances of the case.

Producing industries, for example, which have passed the point up to which combination may be consistent with the public interest and the freedom of trade, cannot always be dissected into their component units as readily as railroad companies or similar organizations can be. Their dissolution by ordinary legal process may oftentimes involve financial consequences likely to overwhelm the security market and bring upon it breakdown and confusion. There ought to be an administrative commission capable of directing and shaping such corrective processes, not only in aid of the courts but also by independent suggestion, if necessary.

Inasmuch as our object and the spirit of our action in these matters is to meet business half-way in its processes of self-correction and disturb its legitimate course as little as possible, we ought to see to it, and the judgment of practical and sagacious men of affairs everywhere would applaud us if we did see to it, that penalties and punishments should fall, not upon business itself, to its confusion and interruption, but upon the individuals who use the instrumentalities of business to do things which public policy and sound business practice condemn. Every act of business is done at the command or upon the initiative of some ascertainable person or group of persons. These should be held individually responsible and the punishment should fall upon them, not upon the business organization of which they make illegal use. It should be one of the main objects of our legislation to divest such persons of their corporate cloak and deal with them as with those who do not represent their corporations, but merely by deliberate intention break the law. Business men the country through would, I am sure, applaud us if we were to take effectual steps to see that the officers and directors of great business bodies were prevented from bringing them and the business of the country into disrepute and danger.

Other questions remain which will need very thoughtful and practical treatment. Enterprises, in these modern days of great individual fortunes, are oftentimes interlocked, not by being under the control of the same directors, but by the fact that the greater part of their corporate stock is owned by a single person or group of persons who are in some way ultimately related in interest. We are agreed, I take it, that holding *companies* should be prohibited, but what of the controlling private ownership of individuals or actually coöperative groups of individuals? Shall the private owners of capital stock be suffered to be themselves in effect holding companies? We do not wish, I suppose, to forbid the purchase of stocks by any person who pleases to buy them in such quantities as he can afford, or in any way arbitrarily to limit the sale of stocks to bona fide purchasers. Shall we require the owners of stock, when their voting power in several companies which ought to be independent of one another would constitute actual control, to make election in which of them they will exercise their right to vote? This question I venture for your consideration.

There is another matter in which imperative considerations of justice and fair play suggest thoughtful remedial action. Not only do many of the combinations effected or sought to be effected in the industrial world work an injustice upon the public in general; they also directly and seriously injure the individuals who are put out of business in one unfair way or another by the many dislodging and exterminating forces of combination. I hope that we shall agree in giving private individuals who claim to have been injured by these processes the right to found their suits for redress upon the facts and judgments proved and entered in suits by the Government where the Government has upon its own initiative sued the combinations complained of and won its suit, and that the statute of limitations shall be suffered to run against such litigants only from the date of the conclusion of the Government's action. It is not fair that the private litigant should be obliged to set up and establish again the facts which the Government has proved. He cannot afford, he has not the power, to make use of such processes of inquiry as the Government has command of. Thus shall individual justice be done while the processes of business are rectified and squared with the general conscience.

I have laid the case before you, no doubt as it lies in your own mind, as it lies in the thought of the country. What must every candid man say of the suggestions I have laid before you, of the plain obligations of which I have reminded you? That these are new things for which the country is not prepared? No; but that they are old things, now familiar, and must of course be undertaken if we are to square our laws with the thought and desire of the country. Until these things are done, conscientious business men the country over will be unsatisfied. They are in these things our mentors and colleagues. We are now about to write the additional articles of our constitution of peace, the peace that is honor and freedom and prosperity.

Panama Canal Tolls

[Address delivered at a joint session of the two Houses of Congress, March 5, 1914.]

Gentlemen of the Congress:

I have come to you upon an errand which can be very briefly performed, but I beg that you will not measure its importance by the number of sentences in which I state it. No communication I have addressed to the Congress carried with it graver or more far-reaching implications as to the interest of the country, and I come now to speak upon a matter with regard to which I am charged in a peculiar degree, by the Constitution itself, with personal responsibility.

I have come to ask you for the repeal of that provision of the Panama Canal Act of August 24, 1912, which exempts vessels engaged in the coastwise trade of the United States from payment of tolls, and to urge upon you the justice, the wisdom, and the large policy of such a repeal with the utmost earnestness of which I am capable.

In my own judgment, very fully considered and maturely formed, that exemption constitutes a mistaken economic policy from every point of view, and is, moreover, in plain contravention of the treaty with Great Britain concerning the canal concluded on November 18, 1901. But I have not come to urge upon you my personal views. I have come to state to you a fact and a situation. Whatever may be our own differences of opinion concerning this much debated measure, its meaning is not debated outside the United States. Everywhere else the language of the treaty is given but one interpretation, and that interpretation precludes the exemption I am asking you to repeal. We consented to the treaty; its language we accepted, if we did not originate it; and we are too big, too powerful, too self-respecting a nation to interpret with a too strained or refined reading the words of our own promises just because we have power enough to give us leave to read them as we please. The large thing to do is the only thing we can afford to do, a voluntary withdrawal from a position everywhere questioned and misunderstood. We ought to reverse our action without raising the question whether we were right or wrong, and so once more deserve our reputation for generosity and for the redemption of every obligation without quibble or hesitation.

I ask this of you in support of the foreign policy of the administration. I shall not know how to deal with other matters of even greater delicacy and nearer consequence if you do not grant it to me in ungrudging measure.

The Tampico Incident

[Address delivered at a joint session of the two Houses of Congress, April 20, 1914.]

Gentlemen of the Congress:

It is my duty to call your attention to a situation which has arisen in our dealings with General Victoriano Huerta at Mexico City which calls for action, and to ask your advice and coöperation in acting upon it. On the 9th of April a paymaster of the U.S.S. *Dolphin* landed at the Iturbide Bridge landing at Tampico with a whaleboat and boat's crew to take off certain supplies needed by his ship, and while engaged in loading the boat was arrested by an officer and squad of men of the army of General Huerta. Neither the paymaster nor anyone of the boat's crew was armed. Two of the men were in the boat when the arrest took place and were obliged to leave it and submit to be taken into custody, notwithstanding the fact that the boat carried, both at her bow and at her stern, the flag of the United States. The officer who made the arrest was proceeding up one of the streets of the town with his prisoners when met by an officer of higher authority, who ordered him to return to the landing and await orders; and within an hour and a half from the time of the arrest orders were received from the commander of the Huertista forces at Tampico for the release of the paymaster and his men. The release was followed by apologies from the commander and later by an expression of regret by General Huerta himself. General Huerta urged that martial law obtained at the time at Tampico; that orders had been issued that no one should be allowed to land at the Iturbide Bridge; and that our sailors had no right to land there. Our naval commanders at the port had not been notified of any such prohibition; and, even if they had been, the only justifiable course open to the local authorities would have been to request the paymaster and his crew to withdraw and to lodge a protest with the commanding officer of the fleet. Admiral Mayo regarded the arrest as so serious an affront that he was not satisfied with the apologies offered, but demanded that the flag of the United States be saluted with special ceremony by the military commander of the port.

The incident cannot be regarded as a trivial one, especially as two of the men arrested were taken from the boat itself-that is to say, from the territory of the United States-but had it stood by itself it might have been attributed to the ignorance or arrogance of a single officer. Unfortunately, it was not an isolated case. A series of incidents have recently occurred which cannot but create the impression that the representatives of General Huerta were willing to go out of their way to show disregard for the dignity and rights of this Government and felt perfectly safe in doing what they pleased, making free to show in many ways their irritation and contempt. A few days after the incident at Tampico an orderly from the U.S.S. *Minnesota* was arrested at Vera Cruz while ashore in uniform to obtain the ship's mail, and was for a time thrown into jail. An official dispatch from this Government to its embassy at Mexico City was withheld by the authorities of the telegraphic service until peremptorily demanded by our chargé d'affaires in person. So far as I can learn, such wrongs and annoyances have been suffered to occur only against representatives of the United States. I have heard of no complaints from other Governments of similar treatment. Subsequent explanations and formal apologies did not and could not alter the popular impression, which it is possible it had been the object of the Huertista authorities to create, that the Government of the United States was being singled out, and might be singled out with impunity, for slights and affronts in retaliation for its refusal to recognize the pretensions of General Huerta to be regarded as the constitutional provisional President of the Republic of Mexico.

The manifest danger of such a situation was that such offenses might grow from bad to worse until something happened of so gross and intolerable a sort as to lead directly and inevitably to armed conflict. It was necessary that the apologies of General Huerta and his representatives should go much further, that they should be such as to attract the attention of the whole population to their significance, and such as to impress upon General Huerta himself the necessity of seeing to it that no further occasion for explanations and professed regrets should arise. I, therefore, felt it my duty to sustain Admiral Mayo in the whole of his demand and to insist that the flag of the United States should be saluted in such a way as to indicate a new spirit and attitude on the part of the Huertistas.

Such a salute General Huerta has refused, and I have come to ask your approval and support in the course I now purpose to pursue.

This Government can, I earnestly hope, in no circumstances be forced into war with the people of Mexico. Mexico is torn by civil strife. If we are to accept the tests of its own constitution, it has no government. General Huerta has set his power up in the City of Mexico, such as it is, without right and by methods for which there can be no justification. Only part of the country is under his control. If armed conflict should unhappily come as a result of his attitude of personal resentment toward this Government, we should be fighting only General Huerta and those who adhere to him and give him their support, and our object would be only to restore to the people of the distracted Republic the opportunity to set up again their own laws and their own government.

But I earnestly hope that war is not now in question. I believe that I speak for the American people when I say that we do not desire to control in any degree the affairs of our sister Republic. Our feeling for the people of Mexico is one of deep and genuine friendship, and everything that we have so far done or refrained from doing has proceeded from our desire to help them, not to hinder or embarrass them. We would not wish even to exercise the good offices of friendship without their welcome and consent. The people of Mexico are entitled to settle their own domestic affairs in their own way, and we sincerely desire to respect their right. The present situation need have none of the grave implications of interference if we deal with it promptly, firmly, and wisely.

No doubt I could do what is necessary in the circumstances to enforce respect for our Government without recourse to the Congress, and yet not exceed my constitutional powers as President; but I do not wish to act in a matter possibly of so grave consequence except in close conference and coöperation with both the Senate and House. I, therefore, come to ask your approval that I should use the armed forces of the United States in such ways and to such an extent as may be necessary to obtain from General Huerta and his adherents the fullest recognition of the rights and dignity of the United States, even amidst the distressing conditions now unhappily obtaining in Mexico.

There can in what we do be no thought of aggression or of selfish aggrandizement. We seek to maintain the dignity and authority of the United States only because we wish always to keep our great influence unimpaired for the uses of liberty, both in the United States and wherever else it may be employed for the benefit of mankind.

In the Firmament of Memory

[Address at the Services in Memory of those who lost their lives at Vera Cruz, Mexico, delivered at the Brooklyn Navy Yard, May 11, 1914. The roster, of fifteen sailors and four marines, was presented by the Secretary of the Navy, Mr. Daniels.]

Mr. Secretary:

I know that the feelings which characterize all who stand about me and the whole Nation at this hour are not feelings which can be suitably expressed in terms of attempted oratory or eloquence. They are things too deep for ordinary speech. For my own part, I have a singular mixture of feelings. The feeling that is uppermost is one of profound grief that these lads should have had to go to their death; and yet there is mixed with that grief a profound pride that they should have gone as they did, and, if I may say it out of my heart, a touch of envy of those who were permitted so quietly, so nobly, to do their duty. Have you thought of it, men? Here is the roster of the Navy-the list of the men, officers and enlisted men and marines-and suddenly there swim nineteen stars out of the list-men who have suddenly been lifted into a firmament of memory where we shall always see their names shine, not because they called upon us to admire them, but because they served us, without asking any questions and in the performance of a duty which is laid upon us as well as upon them.

Duty is not an uncommon thing, gentlemen. Men are performing it in the ordinary walks of life all around us all the time, and they are making great sacrifices to perform it. What gives men like these peculiar distinction is not merely that they did their duty, but that their duty had nothing to do with them or their own personal and peculiar interests. They did not give their lives for themselves. They gave their lives for us, because we called upon them as a Nation to perform an unexpected duty. That is the way in which men grow distinguished, and that is the only way, by serving somebody else than themselves. And what greater thing could you serve than a Nation such as this we love and are proud of? Are you sorry for these lads? Are you sorry for the way they will be remembered? Does it not quicken your pulses to think of the list of them? I hope to God none of you may join the list, but if you do you will join an immortal company.

So, while we are profoundly sorrowful, and while there goes out of our hearts a very deep and affectionate sympathy for the friends and relatives of these lads who for the rest of their lives shall mourn them, though with a touch of pride, we know why we do not go away from this occasion cast down, but with our heads lifted and our eyes on the future of this country, with absolute confidence of how it will be worked out. Not only upon the mere vague future of this country, but upon the immediate future. We have gone down to Mexico to serve mankind if we can find out the way. We do not want to fight the Mexicans. We want to serve the Mexicans if we can, because we know how we would like to be free, and how we would like to be served if there were friends standing by in such case ready to serve us. A war of aggression is not a war in which it is a proud thing to die, but a war of service is a thing in which it is a proud thing to die.

Notice how truly these men were of our blood. I mean of our American blood, which is not drawn from any one country, which is not drawn from any one stock, which is not drawn from any one language of the modern world; but free men everywhere have sent their sons and their brothers and their daughters to this country in order to make that great compounded Nation which consists of all the sturdy elements and of all the best elements of the whole globe. I listened again to this list of the dead with a profound interest because of the mixture of the names, for the names bear the marks of the several national stocks from which these men came. But they are not Irishmen or Germans or Frenchmen or Hebrews or Italians any more. They were not when they went to Vera Cruz; they were Americans, every one of them, and with no difference in their Americanism because of the stock from which they came. They were in a peculiar sense of our blood, and they proved it by showing that they were of our spirit-that no matter what their derivation, no matter where their people came from, they thought and wished and did the things that were American; and the flag under which they served was a flag in which all the blood of mankind is united to make a free Nation.

War, gentlemen, is only a sort of dramatic representation, a sort of dramatic symbol, of a thousand forms of duty. I never went into battle; I never was under fire; but I fancy that there are some things just as hard to do as to go under fire. I fancy that it is just as hard to do your duty when men are sneering at you as when they are shooting at you. When they shoot at you, they can only take your natural life; when they sneer at you, they can wound your living heart, and men who are brave enough, steadfast enough, steady in their principles enough, to go about their duty with regard to their fellow-men, no matter whether there are hisses or cheers, men who can do what Rudyard Kipling in one of his poems wrote, "Meet with triumph and disaster and treat those two impostors just the same," are men for a nation to be proud of. Morally speaking, disaster and triumph are impostors. The cheers of the moment are not what a man ought to think about, but the verdict of his conscience and of the consciences of mankind.

When I look at you, I feel as if I also and we all were enlisted men. Not enlisted in your particular branch of the service, but enlisted to serve the country, no matter what may come, even though we may sacrifice our lives in the arduous endeavor. We are expected to put the utmost energy of every power that we have into the service of our fellow-men, never sparing ourselves, not condescending to think of what is going to happen to ourselves, but ready, if need be, to go to the utter length of complete self-sacrifice.

As I stand and look at you to-day and think of these spirits that have gone from us, I know that the road is clearer for the future. These boys have shown us the way, and it is easier to walk on it because they have gone before and shown us how. May God grant to all of us that vision of patriotic service which here in solemnity and grief and pride is borne in upon our hearts and consciences!

Memorial Day Address at Arlington

[Delivered at the National Cemetery, Arlington, Va., May 30, 1914.]

Ladies and Gentlemen:

I have not come here to-day with a prepared address. The committee in charge of the exercises of the day have graciously excused me on the grounds of public obligations from preparing such an address, but I will not deny myself the privilege of joining with you in an expression of gratitude and admiration for the men who perished for the sake of the Union. They do not need our praise. They do not need that our admiration should sustain them. There is no immortality that is safer than theirs. We come not for their sakes but for our own, in order that we may drink at the same springs of inspiration from which they themselves selves drank.

A peculiar privilege came to the men who fought for the Union. There is no other civil war in history, ladies and gentlemen, the stings of which were removed before the men who did the fighting passed from the stage of life. So that we owe these men something more than a legal reëstablishment of the Union. We owe them the spiritual reëstablishment of the Union as well; for they not only reunited States, they reunited the spirits of men. That is their unique achievement, unexampled anywhere else in the annals of mankind, that the very men whom they overcame in battle join in praise and gratitude that the Union was saved. There is something peculiarly beautiful and peculiarly touching about that. Whenever a man who is still trying to devote himself to the service of the Nation comes into a presence like this, or into a place like this, his spirit must be peculiarly moved. A mandate is laid upon him which seems to speak from the very graves themselves. Those who serve this Nation, whether in peace or in war, should serve it without thought of themselves. I can never speak in praise of war, ladies and gentlemen; you would not desire me to do so. But there is this peculiar distinction belonging to the soldier, that he goes into an enterprise out of which he himself cannot get anything at all. He is giving everything that he hath, even his life, in order that others may live, not in order that he himself may obtain gain and prosperity. And just so soon as the tasks of peace are performed in the same spirit of self-sacrifice and devotion, peace societies will not be necessary. The very organization and spirit of society will be a guaranty of peace.

Therefore this peculiar thing comes about, that we can stand here and praise the memory of these soldiers in the interest of peace. They set us the example of self-sacrifice, which if followed in peace will make it unnecessary that men should follow war any more.

We are reputed to be somewhat careless in our discrimination between words in the use of the English language, and yet it is interesting to note that there are some words about which we are very careful. We bestow the adjective "great" somewhat indiscriminately. A man who has made conquest of his fellow-men for his own gain may display such genius in war, such uncommon qualities of organization and leadership that we may call him "great," but there is a word which we reserve for men of another kind and about which we are very careful; that is the word "noble." We never call a man "noble" who serves only himself; and if you will look about through all the nations of the world upon the statues that men have erected-upon the inscribed tablets where they have wished to keep alive the memory of the citizens whom they desire most to honor-you will find that almost without exception they have erected the statue to those who had a splendid surplus of energy and devotion to spend upon their fellow-men. Nobility exists in America without patent. We have no House of Lords, but we have a house of fame to which we elevate those who are the noble men of our race, who, forgetful of themselves, study and serve the public interest, who have the courage to face any number and any kind of adversary, to speak what in their hearts they believe to be the truth.

We admire physical courage, but we admire above all things else moral courage. I believe that soldiers will bear me out in saying that both come in time of battle. I take it that the moral courage comes in going into the battle, and the physical courage in staying in. There are battles which are just as hard to go into and just as hard to stay in as the battles of arms, and if the man will but stay and think never of himself there will come a time of grateful recollection when men will speak of him not only with admiration but with that which goes deeper, with affection and with reverence.

So that this flag calls upon us daily for service, and the more quiet and self-denying the service the greater the glory of the flag. We are dedicated to freedom, and that freedom means the freedom of the human spirit. All free spirits ought to congregate on an occasion like this to do homage to the greatness of America as illustrated by the greatness of her sons.

It has been a privilege, ladies and gentlemen, to come and say these simple words, which I am sure are merely putting your thought into language. I thank you for the opportunity to lay this little wreath of mine upon these consecrated graves.

Closing a Chapter

[Address in which President Wilson accepted the Monument in Memory of the Confederate Dead, at Arlington National Cemetery, June 4, 1914.].

Mr. Chairman, Mrs. McLaurin Stevens, Ladies and Gentlemen:

I assure you that I am profoundly aware of the solemn significance of the thing that has now taken place. The Daughters of the Confederacy have presented a memorial of their dead to the Government of the United States. I hope that you have noted the history of the conception of this idea. It was suggested by a President of the United States who had himself been a distinguished officer in the Union Army. It was authorized by an act of Congress of the United States. The corner-stone of the monument was laid by a President of the United States elevated to his position by the votes of the party which had chiefly prided itself upon sustaining the war for the Union, and who, while Secretary of War, had himself given authority to erect it. And, now, it has fallen to my lot to accept in the name of the great Government, which I am privileged for the time to represent, this emblem of a reunited people. I am not so much happy as proud to participate in this capacity on such an occasion, —proud that I should represent such a people. Am I mistaken, ladies and gentlemen, in supposing that nothing of this sort could have occurred in anything but a democracy? The people of a democracy are not related to their rulers as subjects are related to a government. They are themselves the sovereign authority, and as they are neighbors of each other, quickened by the same influences and moved by the same motives, they can understand each other. They are shot through with some of the deepest and profoundest instincts of human sympathy. They choose their governments; they select their rulers; they live their own life, and they will not have that life disturbed and discolored by fraternal misunderstandings. I know that a reuniting of spirits like this can take place more quickly in our time than in any other because men are now united by an easier transmission of those influences which make up the foundations of peace and of mutual understanding, but no process can work these effects unless there is a conducting medium. The conducting medium in this instance is the united heart of a great people. I am not going to detain you by trying to repeat any of the eloquent thoughts which have moved us this afternoon, for I rejoice in the simplicity of the task which is assigned to me. My privilege is this, ladies and gentlemen: To declare this chapter in the history of the United States closed and ended, and I bid you turn with me with your faces to the future, quickened by the memories of the past, but with nothing to do with the contests of the past, knowing, as we have shed our blood upon opposite sides, we now face and admire one another. I do not know how many years ago it was that the *Century Dictionary* was published, but I remember one day in the *Century Cyclopedia of Names* I had occasion to turn to the name of Robert E. Lee, and I found him there in that book published in New York City simply described as a great American general. The generosity of our judgments did not begin to-day. The generosity of our judgment was made up soon after this great struggle was over. Men came and sat together again in the Congress and united in all the efforts of peace and of government, and our solemn duty is to see that each one of us is in his own consciousness and in his own conduct a replica of this great reunited people. It is our duty and our privilege to be like the country we represent and, speaking no word of malice, no word of criticism even, stand shoulder to shoulder to lift the burdens of mankind in the future and show the paths of freedom to all the world.

Annapolis Commencement Address

[Delivered before the Graduating Class of the United States Naval Academy, Annapolis, Maryland, June 5, 1914.]

Mr. Superintendent, Young Gentlemen, Ladies and Gentlemen:

During the greater part of my life I have been associated with young men, and on occasions it seems to me without number have faced bodies of youngsters going out to take part in the activities of the world, but I have a consciousness of a different significance in this occasion from that which I have felt on other similar occasions. When I have faced the graduating classes at universities I have felt that I was facing a great conjecture. They were going out into all sorts of pursuits and with every degree of preparation for the particular thing they were expecting to do; some without any preparation at all, for they did not know what they expected to do. But in facing you I am facing men who are trained for a special thing. You know what you are going to do, and you are under the eye of the whole Nation in doing it. For you, gentlemen, are to be part of the power of the Government of the United States. There is a very deep and solemn significance in that fact, and I am sure that every one of you feels it. The moral is perfectly obvious. Be ready and fit for anything that you have to do. And keep ready and fit. Do not grow slack. Do not suppose that your education is over because you have received your diplomas from the academy. Your education has just begun. Moreover, you are to have a very peculiar privilege which not many of your predecessors have had. You are yourselves going to become teachers. You are going to teach those 50,000 fellow-countrymen of yours who are the enlisted men of the Navy. You are going to make them fitter to obey your orders and to serve the country. You are going to make them fitter to see what the orders mean in their outlook upon life and upon the service; and that is a great privilege, for out of you is going the energy and intelligence which are going to quicken the whole body of the United States Navy.

I congratulate you upon that prospect, but I want to ask you not to get the professional point of view. I would ask it of you if you were lawyers; I would ask it of you if you were merchants; I would ask it of you whatever you expected to be. Do not get the professional point of view. There is nothing narrower or more unserviceable than the professional point of view, to have the attitude toward life that it centers in your profession. It does not. Your profession is only one of the many activities which are meant to keep the world straight, and to keep the energy in its blood and in its muscle. We are all of us in this world, as I understand it, to set forward the affairs of the whole world, though we play a special part in that great function. The Navy goes all over the world, and I think it is to be congratulated upon having that sort of illustration of what the world is and what it contains; and inasmuch as you are going all over the world you ought to be the better able to see the relation that your country bears to the rest of the world.

It ought to be one of your thoughts all the time that you are sample Americans-not merely sample Navy men, not merely sample soldiers, but sample Americans-and that you have the point of view of America with regard to her Navy and her Army; that she is using them as the instruments of civilization, not as the instruments of aggression. The idea of America is to serve humanity, and every time you let the Stars and Stripes free to the wind you ought to realize that that is in itself a message that you are on an errand which other navies have sometimes tunes forgotten; not an errand of conquest, but an errand of service. I always have the same thought when I look at the flag of the United States, for I know something of the history of the struggle of mankind for liberty. When I look at that flag it seems to me as if the white stripes were strips of parchment upon which are written the rights of man, and the red stripes the streams of blood by which those rights have been made good. Then in the little blue firmament in the corner have swung out the stars of the States of the American Union. So it is, as it were, a sort of floating charter that has come down to us from Runnymede, when men said, "We will not have masters; we will be a people, and we will seek our own liberty."

You are not serving a government, gentlemen; you are serving a people. For we who for the time being constitute the Government are merely instruments for a little while in the hands of a great Nation which chooses whom it will to carry out its decrees and who invariably rejects the man who forgets the ideals which it intended him to serve. So that I hope that wherever you go you will have a generous, comprehending love of the people you come into contact with, and will come back and tell us, if you can, what service the United States can render to the remotest parts of the world; tell us where you see men suffering; tell us where you think advice will lift them up; tell us where you think that the counsel of statesmen may better the fortunes of unfortunate men; always having it in mind that you are champions of what is right and fair all 'round for the public welfare, no matter where you are, and that it is that you are ready to fight for and not merely on the drop of a hat or upon some slight punctilio, but that you are champions of your fellow-men, particularly of that great body one hundred million strong whom you represent in the United States.

What do you think is the most lasting impression that those boys down at Vera Cruz are going to leave? They have had to use some force —I pray God it may not be necessary for them to use any more-but do you think that the way they fought is going to be the most lasting impression? Have men not fought ever since the world began? Is there anything new in using force? The new things in the world are the things that are divorced from force. The things that show the moral compulsions of the human conscience, those are the things by which we have been building up civilization, not by force. And the lasting impression that those boys are going to leave is this, that they exercise self-control; that they are ready and diligent to make the place where they went fitter to live in than they found it; that they regarded other people's rights; that they did not strut and bluster, but went quietly, like self-respecting gentlemen, about their legitimate work. And the people of Vera Cruz, who feared the Americans and despised the Americans, are going to get a very different taste in their mouths about the whole thing when the boys of the Navy and the Army come away. Is that not something to be proud of, that you know how to use force like men of conscience and like gentlemen, serving your fellow-men and not trying to overcome them? Like that gallant gentleman who has so long borne the heats and perplexities and distresses of the situation in Vera Cruz-Admiral Fletcher. I mention him, because his service there has been longer and so much of the early perplexities fell upon him. I have been in almost daily communication with Admiral Fletcher, and I have tested his temper. I have tested his discretion. I know that he is a man with a touch of statesmanship about him, and he has grown bigger in my eye each day as I have read his dispatches, for he has sought always to serve the thing he was trying to do in the temper that we all recognize and love to believe is typically American.

I challenge you youngsters to go out with these conceptions, knowing that you are part of the Government and force of the United States and that men will judge us by you. I am not afraid of the verdict. I cannot look in your faces and doubt what it will be, but I want you to take these great engines of force out onto the seas like adventurers enlisted for the elevation of the spirit of the human race. For that is the only distinction that America has. Other nations have been strong, other nations have piled wealth as high as the sky, but they have come into disgrace because they used their force and their wealth for the oppression of mankind and their own aggrandizement; and America will not bring glory to herself, but disgrace, by following the beaten paths of history. We must strike out upon new paths, and we must count upon you gentlemen to be the explorers who will carry this spirit and spread this message all over the seas and in every port of the civilized world.

You see, therefore, why I said that when I faced you I felt there was a special significance. I am not present on an occasion when you are about to scatter on various errands. You are all going on the same errand, and I like to feel bound with you in one common organization for the glory of America. And her glory goes deeper than all the tinsel, goes deeper than the sound of guns and the clash of sabers; it goes down to the very foundations of those things that have made the spirit of men free and happy and content.

The Meaning of Liberty

[Address at Independence Hall, Philadelphia, July 4, 1914.]

Mr. Chairman and Fellow-Citizens:

We are assembled to celebrate the one hundred and thirty-eighth anniversary of the birth of the United States. I suppose that we can more vividly realize the circumstances of that birth standing on this historic spot than it would be possible to realize them anywhere else. The Declaration of Independence was written in Philadelphia; it was adopted in this historic building by which we stand. I have just had the privilege of sitting in the chair of the great man who presided over the deliberations of those who gave the declaration to the world. My hand rests at this moment upon the table upon which the declaration was signed. We can feel that we are almost in the visible and tangible presence of a great historic transaction.

Have you ever read the Declaration of Independence or attended with close comprehension to the real character of it when you have heard it read? If you have, you will know that it is not a Fourth of July oration. The Declaration of Independence was a document preliminary to war. It was a vital piece of practical business, not a piece of rhetoric; and if you will pass beyond those preliminary passages which we are accustomed to quote about the rights of men and read into the heart of the document you will see that it is very express and detailed, that it consists of a series of definite specifications concerning actual public business of the day. Not the business of our day, for the matter with which it deals is past, but the business of that first revolution by which the Nation was set up, the business of 1776. Its general statements, its general declarations cannot mean anything to us unless we append to it a similar specific body of particulars as to what we consider the essential business of our own day.

Liberty does not consist, my fellow-citizens, in mere general declarations of the rights of man. It consists in the translation of those declarations into definite action. Therefore, standing here where the declaration was adopted, reading its businesslike sentences, we ought to ask ourselves what there is in it for us. There is nothing in it for us unless we can translate it into the terms of our own conditions and of our own lives. We must reduce it to what the lawyers call a bill of particulars. It contains a bill of particulars, but the bill of particulars of 1776. If we would keep it alive, we must fill it with a bill of particulars of the year 1914.

The task to which we have constantly to readdress ourselves is the task of proving that we are worthy of the men who drew this great declaration and know what they would have done in our circumstances. Patriotism consists in some very practical things-practical in that they belong to the life of every day, that they wear no extraordinary distinction about them, that they are connected with commonplace duty. The way to be patriotic in America is not only to love America but to love the duty that lies nearest to our hand and know that in performing it we are serving our country. There are some gentlemen in Washington, for example, at this very moment who are showing themselves very patriotic in a way which does not attract wide attention but seems to belong to mere everyday obligations. The Members of the House and Senate who stay in hot Washington to maintain a quorum of the Houses and transact the all-important business of the Nation are doing an act of patriotism. I honor them for it, and I am glad to stay there and stick by them until the work is done.

It is patriotic, also, to learn what the facts of our national life are and to face them with candor. I have heard a great many facts stated about the present business condition of this country, for example —a great many allegations of fact, at any rate, but the allegations do not tally with one another. And yet I know that truth always matches with truth and when I find some insisting that everything is going wrong and others insisting that everything is going right, and when I know from a wide observation of the general circumstances of the country taken as a whole that things are going extremely well, I wonder what those who are crying out that things are wrong are trying to do. Are they trying to serve the country, or are they trying to serve something smaller than the country? Are they trying to put hope into the hearts of the men who work and toil every day, or are they trying to plant discouragement and despair in those hearts? And why do they cry that everything is wrong and yet do nothing to set it right? If they love America and anything is wrong amongst us, it is their business to put their hand with ours to the task of setting it right. When the facts are known and acknowledged, the duty of all patriotic men is to accept them in candor and to address themselves hopefully and confidently to the common counsel which is necessary to act upon them wisely and in universal concert.

I have had some experiences in the last fourteen months which have not been entirely reassuring. It was universally admitted, for example, my fellow-citizens, that the banking system of this country needed reorganization. We set the best minds that we could find to the task of discovering the best method of reorganization. But we met with hardly anything but criticism from the bankers of the country; we met with hardly anything but resistance from the majority of those at least who spoke at all concerning the matter. And yet so soon as that act was passed there was a universal chorus of applause, and the very men who had opposed the measure joined in that applause. If it was wrong the day before it was passed, why was it right the day after it was passed? Where had been the candor of criticism not only, but the concert of counsel which makes legislative action vigorous and safe and successful?

It is not patriotic to concert measures against one another; it is patriotic to concert measures for one another.

In one sense the Declaration of Independence has lost its significance. It has lost its significance as a declaration of national independence. Nobody outside of America believed when it was uttered that we could make good our independence; now nobody anywhere would dare to doubt that we are independent and can maintain our independence. As a declaration of independence, therefore, it is a mere historic document. Our independence is a fact so stupendous that it can be measured only by the size and energy and variety and wealth and power of one of the greatest nations in the world. But it is one thing to be independent and it is another thing to know what to do with your independence. It is one thing to come to your majority and another thing to know what you are going to do with your life and your energies; and one of the most serious questions for sober-minded men to address themselves to in the United States is this: What are we going to do with the influence and power of this great Nation? Are we going to play the old role of using that power for our aggrandizement and material benefit only? You know what that may mean. It may upon occasion mean that we shall use it to make the peoples of other nations suffer in the way in which we said it was intolerable to suffer when we uttered our Declaration of Independence.

The Department of State at Washington is constantly called upon to back up the commercial enterprises and the industrial enterprises of the United States in foreign countries, and it at one time went so far in that direction that all its diplomacy came to be designated as "dollar diplomacy." It was called upon to support every man who wanted to earn anything anywhere if he was an American. But there ought to be a limit to that. There is no man who is more interested than I am in carrying the enterprise of American business men to every quarter of the globe. I was interested in it long before I was suspected of being a politician. I have been preaching it year after year as the great thing that lay in the future for the United States, to show her wit and skill and enterprise and influence in every country in the world. But observe the limit to all that which is laid upon us perhaps more than upon any other nation in the world. We set this Nation up, at any rate we professed to set it up, to vindicate the rights of men. We did not name any differences between one race and another. We did not set up any barriers against any particular people. We opened our gates to all the world and said, "Let all men who wish to be free come to us and they will be welcome." We said, "This independence of ours is not a selfish thing for our own exclusive private use. It is for everybody to whom we can find the means of extending it." We cannot with that oath taken in our youth, we cannot with that great ideal set before us when we were a young people and numbered only a scant

3,000,000, take upon ourselves, now that we are 100,000,000 strong, any other conception of duty than we then entertained. If American enterprise in foreign countries, particularly in those foreign countries which are not strong enough to resist us, takes the shape of imposing upon and exploiting the mass of the people of that country it ought to be checked and not encouraged. I am willing to get anything for an American that money and enterprise can obtain except the suppression of the rights of other men. I will not help any man buy a power which he ought not to exercise over his fellow-beings.

You know, my fellow-countrymen, what a big question there is in Mexico. Eighty-five per cent of the Mexican people have never been allowed to have any genuine participation in their own Government or to exercise any substantial rights with regard to the very land they live upon. All the rights that men most desire have been exercised by the other fifteen per cent. Do you suppose that that circumstance is not sometimes in my thought? I know that the American people have a heart that will beat just as strong for those millions in Mexico as it will beat, or has beaten, for any other millions elsewhere in the world, and that when once they conceive what is at stake in Mexico they will know what ought to be done in Mexico. I hear a great deal said about the loss of property in Mexico and the loss of the lives of foreigners, and I deplore these things with all my heart. Undoubtedly, upon the conclusion of the present disturbed conditions in Mexico those who have been unjustly deprived of their property or in any wise unjustly put upon ought to be compensated. Men's individual rights have no doubt been invaded, and the invasion of those rights has been attended by many deplorable circumstances which ought sometime, in the proper way, to be accounted for. But back of it all is the struggle of a people to come into its own, and while we look upon the incidents in the foreground let us not forget the great tragic reality in the background which towers above the whole picture.

A patriotic American is a man who is not niggardly and selfish in the things that he enjoys that make for human liberty and the rights of man. He wants to share them with the whole world, and he is never so proud of the great flag under which he lives as when it comes to mean to other people as well as to himself a symbol of hope and liberty. I would be ashamed of this flag if it ever did anything outside America that we would not permit it to do inside of America.

The world is becoming more complicated every day, my fellow-citizens. No man ought to be foolish enough to think that he understands it all. And, therefore, I am glad that there are some simple things in the world. One of the simple things is principle. Honesty is a perfectly simple thing. It is hard for me to believe that in most circumstances when a man has a choice of ways he does not know which is the right way and which is the wrong way. No man who has chosen the wrong way ought even to come into Independence Square; it is holy ground which he ought not to tread upon. He ought not to come where immortal voices have uttered the great sentences of such a document as this Declaration of Independence upon which rests the liberty of a whole nation.

And so I say that it is patriotic sometimes to prefer the honor of the country to its material interest. Would you rather be deemed by all the nations of the world incapable of keeping your treaty obligations in order that you might have free tolls for American ships? The treaty under which we gave up that right may have been a mistaken treaty, but there was no mistake about its meaning.

When I have made a promise as a man I try to keep it, and I know of no other rule permissible to a nation. The most distinguished nation in the world is the nation that can and will keep its promises even to its own hurt. And I want to say parenthetically that I do not think anybody was hurt. I cannot be enthusiastic for subsidies to a monopoly, but let those who are enthusiastic for subsidies ask themselves whether they prefer subsidies to unsullied honor.

The most patriotic man, ladies and gentlemen, is sometimes the man who goes in the direction that he thinks right even when he sees half the world against him. It is the dictate of patriotism to sacrifice yourself if you think that that is the path of honor and of duty. Do not blame others if they do not agree with you. Do not die with bitterness in your heart because you did not convince the rest of the world, but die happy because you believe that you tried to serve your country by not selling your soul. Those were grim days, the days of 1776. Those gentlemen did not attach their names to the Declaration of Independence on this table expecting a holiday on the next day, and that 4th of July was not itself a holiday. They attached their signatures to that significant document knowing that if they failed it was certain that every one of them would hang for the failure. They were committing treason in the interest of the liberty of 3,000,000 people in America. All the rest of the world was against them and smiled with cynical incredulity at the audacious undertaking. Do you think that if they could see this great Nation now they would regret anything that they then did to draw the gaze of a hostile world upon them? Every idea must be started by somebody, and it is a lonely thing to start anything. Yet if it is in you, you must start it if you have a man's blood in you and if you love the country that you profess to be working for.

I am sometimes very much interested when I see gentlemen supposing that popularity is the way to success in America. The way to success in this great country, with its fair judgments, is to show that you are not afraid of anybody except God and his final verdict. If I did not believe that, I would not believe in democracy. If I did not believe that, I would not believe that people can govern themselves. If I did not believe that the moral judgment would be the last judgment, the final judgment, in the minds of men as well as the tribunal of God, I could not believe in popular government. But I do believe these things, and, therefore, I earnestly believe in the democracy not only of America but of every awakened people that wishes and intends to govern and control its own affairs.

It is very inspiring, my friends, to come to this that may be called the original fountain of independence and liberty in American and here drink draughts of patriotic feeling which seem to renew the very blood in one's veins. Down in Washington sometimes when the days are hot and the business presses intolerably and there are so many things to do that it does not seem possible to do anything in the way it ought to be done, it is always possible to lift one's thought above the task of the moment and, as it were, to realize that great thing of which we are all parts, the great body of American feeling and American principle. No man could do the work that has to be done in Washington if he allowed himself to be separated from that body of principle. He must make himself feel that he is a part of the people of the United States, that he is trying to think not only for them, but with them, and then he cannot feel lonely. He not only cannot feel lonely but he cannot feel afraid of anything.

My dream is that as the years go on and the world knows more and more of America it will also drink at these fountains of youth and renewal; that it also will turn to America for those moral inspirations which lie at the basis of all freedom; that the world will never fear America unless it feels that it is engaged in some enterprise which is inconsistent with the rights of humanity; and that America will come into the full light of the day when all shall know that she puts human rights above all other rights and that her flag is the flag not only of America but of humanity.

What other great people has devoted itself to this exalted ideal? To what other nation in the world can all eyes look for an instant sympathy that thrills the whole body politic when men anywhere are fighting for their rights? I do not know that there will ever be a declaration of independence and of grievances for mankind, but I believe that if any such document is ever drawn it will be drawn in the spirit of the American Declaration of Independence, and that America has lifted high the light which will shine unto all generations and guide the feet of mankind to the goal of justice and liberty and peace.

American Neutrality

[An appeal to the citizens of the Republic, requesting their assistance in maintaining a state of neutrality during the European War, August 20, 1914.]

My Fellow-Countrymen:

I suppose that every thoughtful man in America has asked himself, during these last troubled weeks, what influence the European war may exert upon the United States, and I take the liberty of addressing a few words to you in order to point out that it is entirely within our own choice what its effects upon us will be and to urge very earnestly upon you the sort of speech and conduct which will best safeguard the Nation against distress and disaster.

The effect of the war upon the United States will depend upon what American citizens say and do. Every man who really loves America will act and speak in the true spirit of neutrality, which is the spirit of impartiality and fairness and friendliness to all concerned. The spirit of the Nation in this critical matter will be determined largely by what individuals and society and those gathered in public meetings do and say, upon what newspapers and magazines contain, upon what ministers utter in their pulpits, and men proclaim as their opinions on the street.

The people of the United States are drawn from many nations, and chiefly from the nations now at war. It is natural and inevitable that there should be the utmost variety of sympathy and desire among them with regard to the issues and circumstances of the conflict. Some will wish one nation, others another, to succeed in the momentous struggle. It will be easy to excite passion and difficult to allay it. Those responsible for exciting it will assume a heavy responsibility, responsibility for no less a thing than that the people of the United States, whose love of their country and whose loyalty to its Government should unite them as Americans all, bound in honor and affection to think first of her and her interests, may be divided in camps of hostile opinion, hot against each other, involved in the war itself in impulse and opinion if not in action.

Such divisions among us would be fatal to our peace of mind and might seriously stand in the way of the proper performance of our duty as the one great nation at peace, the one people holding itself ready to play a part of impartial mediation and speak the counsels of peace and accommodation, not as a partisan, but as a friend.

I venture, therefore, my fellow countrymen, to speak a solemn word of warning to you against that deepest, most subtle, most essential breach of neutrality which may spring out of partisanship, out of passionately taking sides. The United States must be neutral in fact as well as in name during these days that are to try men's souls. We must be impartial in thought as well as in action, must put a curb upon our sentiments as well as upon every transaction that might be construed as a preference of one party to the struggle before another.

My thought is of America. I am speaking, I feel sure, the earnest wish and purpose of every thoughtful American that this great country of ours, which is, of course, the first in our thoughts and in our hearts, should show herself in this time of peculiar trial a Nation fit beyond others to exhibit the fine poise of undisturbed judgment, the dignity of self-control, the efficiency of dispassionate action; a Nation that neither sits in judgment upon others nor is disturbed in her own counsels and which keeps herself fit and free to do what is honest and disinterested and truly serviceable for the peace of the world.

Shall we not resolve to put upon ourselves the restraints which will bring to our people the happiness and the great and lasting influence for peace we covet for them?

Appeal for Additional Revenue

[Address delivered at a joint session of the two Houses of Congress, September 4, 1914.]

Gentlemen of the Congress:

I come to you to-day to discharge a duty which I wish with all my heart I might have been spared; but it is a very clear duty, and therefore I perform it without hesitation or apology. I come to ask very earnestly that additional revenue be provided for the Government.

During the month of August there was, as compared with the corresponding month of last year, a falling off of $10,629,538 in the revenues collected from customs. A continuation of this decrease in the same proportion throughout the current fiscal year would probably mean a loss of customs revenues of from sixty to one hundred millions. I need not tell you to what this falling off is due. It is due, in chief part, not to the reductions recently made in the customs duties, but to the great decrease in importations; and that is due to the extraordinary extent of the industrial area affected by the present war in Europe. Conditions have arisen which no man foresaw; they affect the whole world of commerce and economic production; and they must be faced and dealt with.

It would be very unwise to postpone dealing with them. Delay in such a matter and in the particular circumstances in which we now find ourselves as a nation might involve consequences of the most embarrassing and deplorable sort, for which I, for one, would not care to be responsible. It would be very dangerous in the present circumstances to create a moment's doubt as to the strength and sufficiency of the Treasury of the United States, its ability to assist, to steady, and sustain the financial operations of the country's business. If the Treasury is known, or even thought, to be weak, where will be our peace of mind? The whole industrial activity of the country would be chilled and demoralized. Just now the peculiarly difficult financial problems of the moment are being successfully dealt with, with great self-possession and good sense and very sound judgment; but they are only in process of being worked out. If the process of solution is to be completed, no one must be given reason to doubt the solidity and adequacy of the Treasury of the Government which stands behind the whole method by which our difficulties are being met and handled.

The Treasury itself could get along for a considerable period, no doubt, without immediate resort to new sources of taxation. But at what cost to the business of the community? Approximately $75,000,000, a large part of the present Treasury balance, is now on deposit with national banks distributed throughout the country. It is deposited, of course, on call. I need not point out to you what the probable consequences of inconvenience and distress and confusion would be if the diminishing income of the Treasury should make it necessary rapidly to withdraw these deposits. And yet without additional revenue that plainly might become necessary, and the time when it became necessary could not be controlled or determined by the convenience of the business of the country. It would have to be determined by the operations and necessities of the Treasury itself. Such risks are not necessary and ought not to be run. We cannot too scrupulously or carefully safeguard a financial situation which is at best, while war continues in Europe, difficult and abnormal. Hesitation and delay are the worst forms of bad policy under such conditions.

And we ought not to borrow. We ought to resort to taxation, however we may regret the necessity of putting additional temporary burdens on our people. To sell bonds would be to make a most untimely and unjustifiable demand on the money market; untimely, because this is manifestly not the time to withdraw working capital from other uses to pay the Government's bills; unjustifiable, because unnecessary. The country is able to pay any just and reasonable taxes without distress. And to every other form of borrowing, whether for long periods or, for short, there is the same objection. These are not the circumstances, this is at this particular moment and in this particular exigency not the market, to borrow large sums of money. What we are seeking is to ease and assist every financial transaction, not to add a single additional embarrassment to the situation. The people of this country are both intelligent and profoundly patriotic. They are ready to meet the present conditions in the right way and to support the Government with generous self-denial. They know and understand, and will be intolerant only of those who dodge responsibility or are not frank with them.

The occasion is not of our own making. We had no part in making it. But it is here. It affects us as directly and palpably almost as if we were participants in the circumstances which gave rise to it. We must accept the inevitable with calm judgment and unruffled spirits, like men accustomed to deal with the unexpected, habituated to take care of themselves, masters of their own affairs and their own fortunes. We shall pay the bill, though we did not deliberately incur it.

In order to meet every demand upon the Treasury without delay or peradventure and in order to keep the Treasury strong, unquestionably strong, and strong throughout the present anxieties, I respectfully urge that an additional revenue of $100,000,000 be raised through internal taxes devised in your wisdom to meet the emergency. The only suggestion I take the liberty of making is that such sources of revenue be chosen as will begin to yield at once and yield with a certain and constant flow.

I cannot close without expressing the confidence with which I approach a Congress, with regard to this or any other matter, which has shown so untiring a devotion to public duty, which has responded to the needs of the Nation throughout a long season despite inevitable fatigue and personal sacrifice, and so large a proportion of whose Members have devoted their whole time and energy to the business of the country.

The Opinion of the World

[Address before the American Bar Association, in Continental Hall, October 20, 1914.]

Mr. President, Gentlemen of the American Bar Association:

I am very deeply gratified by the greeting that your president has given me and by your response to it. My only strength lies in your confidence.

We stand now in a peculiar case. Our first thought, I suppose, as lawyers, is of international law, of those bonds of right and principle which draw the nations together and hold the community of the world to some standards of action. We know that we see in international law, as it were, the moral processes by which law itself came into existence. I know that as a lawyer I have myself at times felt that there was no real comparison between the law of a nation and the law of nations, because the latter lacked the sanction that gave the former strength and validity. And yet, if you look into the matter more closely, you will find that the two have the same foundations, and that those foundations are more evident and conspicuous in our day than they have ever been before.

The opinion of the world is the mistress of the world; and the processes of international law are the slow processes by which opinion works its will. What impresses me is the constant thought that that is the tribunal at the bar of which we all sit. I would call your attention, incidentally, to the circumstance that it does not observe the ordinary rules of evidence; which has sometimes suggested to me that the ordinary rules of evidence had shown some signs of growing antique. Everything, rumor included, is heard in this court, and the standard of judgment is not so much the character of the testimony as the character of the witness. The motives are disclosed, the purposes are conjectured, and that opinion is finally accepted which seems to be, not the best founded in law, perhaps, but the best founded in integrity of character and of morals. That is the process which is slowly working its will upon the world; and what we should be watchful of is not so much jealous interests as sound principles of action. The disinterested course is always the biggest course to pursue not only, but it is in the long run the most profitable course to pursue. If you can establish your character, you can establish your credit.

What I wanted to suggest to this association, in bidding them very hearty welcome to the city, is whether we sufficiently apply these same ideas to the body of municipal law which we seek to administer. Citations seem to play so much larger a role now than principle. There was a time when the thoughtful eye of the judge rested upon the changes of social circumstances and almost palpably saw the law arise out of human life. Have we got to a time when the only way to change law is by statute? The changing of law by statute seems to me like mending a garment with a patch, whereas law should grow by the life that is in it, not by the life that is outside of it.

I once said to a lawyer with whom I was discussing some question of precedent, and in whose presence I was venturing to doubt the rational validity, at any rate, of the particular precedents he cited, "After all, isn't our object justice?" And he said, "God forbid! We should be very much confused if we made that our standard. Our standard is to find out what the rule has been and how the rule that has been applies to the case that is." I should hate to think that the law was based entirely upon "has beens." I should hate to think that the law did not derive its impulse from looking forward rather than from looking backward, or, rather, that it did not derive its instruction from looking about and seeing what the circumstances of man actually are and what the impulses of justice necessarily are.

Understand me, gentlemen, I am not venturing in this presence to impeach the law. For the present, by the force of circumstances, I am in part the embodiment of the law, and it would be very awkward to disavow myself. But I do wish to make this intimation, that in this time of world change, in this time when we are going to find out just how, in what particulars, and to what extent the real facts of human life and the real moral judgments of mankind prevail, it is worth while looking inside our municipal law and seeing whether the judgments of the law are made square with the moral judgments of mankind. For I believe that we are custodians, not of commands, but of a spirit. We are custodians of the spirit of righteousness, of the spirit of equal-handed justice, of the spirit of hope which believes in the perfectibility of the law with the perfectibility of human life itself.

Public life, like private life, would be very dull and dry if it were not for this belief in the essential beauty of the human spirit and the belief that the human spirit could be translated into action and into ordinance. Not entire. You cannot go any faster than you can advance the average moral judgments of the mass, but you can go at least as fast as that, and you can see to it that you do not lag behind the average moral judgments of the mass. I have in my life dealt with all sorts and conditions of men, and I have found that the flame of moral judgment burned just as bright in the man of humble life and limited experience as in the scholar and the man of affairs. And I would like his voice always to be heard, not as a witness, not as speaking in his own case, but as if he were the voice of men in general, in our courts of justice, as well as the voice of the lawyers, remembering what the law has been. My hope is that, being stirred to the depths by the extraordinary circumstances of the time in which we live, we may recover from those depths something of a renewal of that vision of the law with which men may be supposed to have started out in the old days of the oracles, who communed with the intimations of divinity.

The Power of Christian Young Men

[Address at the Young Men's Christian Association's Celebration, Pittsburgh, October 24, 1914.]

Mr. President, Mr. Porter, Ladies and Gentlemen:

I feel almost as if I were a truant, being away from Washington to-day, but I thought that perhaps if I were absent the Congress would have the more leisure to adjourn. I do not ordinarily open my office at Washington on Saturday. Being a schoolmaster, I am accustomed to a Saturday holiday, and I thought I could not better spend a holiday than by showing at least something of the true direction of my affections; for by long association with the men who have worked for this organization I can say that it has enlisted my deep affection.

I am interested in it for various reasons. First of all, because it is an association of young men. I have had a good deal to do with young men in my time, and I have formed an impression of them which I believe to be contrary to the general impression. They are generally thought to be arch radicals. As a matter of fact, they are the most conservative people I have ever dealt with. Go to a college community and try to change the least custom of that little world and find how the conservatives will rush at you. Moreover, young men are embarrassed by having inherited their fathers' opinions. I have often said that the use of a university is to make young gentlemen as unlike their fathers as possible. I do not say that with the least disrespect for the fathers; but every man who is old enough to have a son in college is old enough to have become very seriously immersed in some particular business and is almost certain to have caught the point of view of that particular business. And it is very useful to his son to be taken out of that narrow circle, conducted to some high place where he may see the general map of the world and of the interests of mankind, and there shown how big the world is and how much of it his father may happen to have forgotten. It would be worth while for men, middle-aged and old, to detach themselves more frequently from the things that command their daily attention and to think of the sweeping tides of humanity.

Therefore I am interested in this association, because it is intended to bring young men together before any crust has formed over them, before they have been hardened to any particular occupation, before they have caught an inveterate point of view; while they still have a searchlight that they can swing and see what it reveals of all the circumstances of the hidden world.

I am the more interested in it because it is an association of young men who are Christians. I wonder if we attach sufficient importance to Christianity as a mere instrumentality in the life of mankind. For one, I am not fond of thinking of Christianity as the means of saving *individual* souls. I have always been very impatient of processes and institutions which said that their purpose was to put every man in the way of developing his character. My advice is: Do not think about your character. If you will think about what you ought to do for other people, your character will take care of itself. Character is a by-product, and any man who devotes himself to its cultivation in his own case will become a selfish prig. The only way your powers can become great is by exerting them outside the circle of your own narrow, special, selfish interests. And that is the reason of Christianity. Christ came into the world to save others, not to save himself; and no man is a true Christian who does not think constantly of how he can lift his brother, how he can assist his friend, how he can enlighten mankind, how he can make virtue the rule of conduct in the circle in which he lives. An association merely of young men might be an association that had its energies put forth in every direction, but an association of Christian young men is an association meant to put its shoulders under the world and lift it, so that other men may feel that they have companions in bearing the weight and heat of the day; that other men may know that there are those who care for them, who would go into places of difficulty and danger to rescue them, who regard themselves as their brother's keeper.

And, then, I am glad that it is an association. Every word of its title means an element of strength. Young men are strong. Christian young men are the strongest kind of young men, and when they associate themselves together they have the incomparable strength of organization. The Young Men's Christian Association once excited, perhaps it is not too much to say, the hostility of the organized churches of the Christian world, because the movement looked as if it were so non-sectarian, as if it were so outside the ecclesiastical field, that perhaps it was an effort to draw young men away from the churches and to substitute this organization for the great bodies of Christian people who joined themselves in the Christian denominations. But after a while it appeared that it was a great instrumentality that belonged to all the churches; that it was a common instrument for sending the light of Christianity out into the world in its most practical form, drawing young men who were strangers into places where they could have companionship that stimulated them and suggestions that kept them straight and occupations that amused them without vicious practice; and then, by surrounding themselves with an atmosphere of purity and of simplicity of life, catch something of a glimpse of the great ideal which Christ lifted when He was elevated upon the cross.

I remember hearing a very wise man say once, a man grown old in the service of a great church, that he had never taught his son religion dogmatically at any time; that he and the boy's mother had agreed that if the atmosphere of that home did not make a Christian of the boy, nothing that they could say would make a Christian of him. They knew that Christianity was catching, and if they did not have it, it would not be communicated. If they did have it, it would penetrate while the boy slept, almost; while he was unconscious of the sweet influences that were about him, while he reckoned nothing of instruction, but merely breathed into his lungs the wholesome air of a Christian home. That is the principle of the Young Men's Christian Association-to make a place where the atmosphere makes great ideals contagious. That is the reason that I said, though I had forgotten that I said it, what is quoted on the outer page of the program-that you can test a modern community by the degree of its interest in its Young Men's Christian Association. You can test whether it knows what road it wants to travel or not. You can test whether it is deeply interested in the spiritual and essential prosperity of its rising generation. I know of no test that can be more conclusively put to a community than that.

I want to suggest to the young men of this association that it is the duty of young men not only to combine for the things that are good, but to combine in a militant spirit. There is a fine passage in one of Milton's prose writings which I am sorry to say I cannot quote, but the meaning of which I can give you, and it is worth hearing.[5] He says that he has no patience with a cloistered virtue that does not go out and seek its adversary. Ah, how tired I am of the men who are merely on the defensive, who hedge themselves in, who perhaps enlarge the hedge enough to include their little family circle and ward off all the evil influences of the world from that loved and hallowed group. How tired I am of the men whose virtue is selfish because it is merely self-protective! And how much I wish that men by the hundred thousand might volunteer to go out and seek an adversary and subdue him!

I have had the fortune to take part in affairs of a considerable variety of sorts, and I have tried to hate as few persons as possible, but there is an exquisite combination of contempt and hate that I have for a particular kind of person, and that is the moral coward. I wish we could give all our cowards a perpetual vacation. Let them go off and sit on the side lines and see us play the game; and put them off the field if they interfere with the game. They do nothing but harm, and they do it by that most subtle and fatal thing of all, that of taking the momentum and the spirit and the forward dash out of things. A man who is virtuous and a coward has no marketable virtue about him. The virtue, I repeat, which is merely self-defensive is not serviceable even, I suspect, to himself. For how a man can swallow and not taste bad when he is a coward and thinking only of himself I cannot imagine.

Be militant! Be an organization that is going to do things! If you can find older men who will give you countenance and acceptable leadership, follow them; but if you cannot, organize separately and dispense with them. There are only two sorts of men worth associating with when something is to be done. Those are young men and men who never grow old. Now, if you find men who have grown old, about whom the crust has hardened, whose hinges are stiff, whose minds always have their eye over the shoulder thinking of things as they *were* done, do not have anything to do with them. It would not be Christian to exclude them from your organization, but merely use them to pad the roll. If you can find older men who will lead you acceptably and keep you in countenance, I am bound as an older man to advise you to follow them. But suit yourselves. Do not follow people that stand still. Just remind them that this is not a statical proposition; it is a movement, and if they cannot get a move on them they are not serviceable.

Life, gentlemen-the life of society, the life of the world-has constantly to be fed from the bottom. It has to be fed by those great sources of strength which are constantly rising in new generations. Red blood has to be pumped into it. New fiber has to be supplied. That is the reason I have always said that I believed in popular institutions. If you can guess beforehand whom your rulers are going to be, you can guess with a very great certainty that most of them will not be fit to rule. The beauty of popular institutions is that you do not know where the man is going to come from, and you do not care so he is the right man. You do not know whether he will come from the avenue or from the alley. You do not know whether he will come from the city or the farm. You do not know whether you will ever have heard that name before or not. Therefore you do not limit at any point your supply of new strength. You do not say it has got to come through the blood of a particular family or through the processes of a particular training, or by anything except the native impulse and genius of the man himself. The humblest hovel, therefore, may produce you your greatest man. A very humble hovel did produce you one of your greatest men. That is the process of life, this constant surging up of the new strength of unnamed, unrecognized, uncatalogued men who are just getting into the running, who are just coming up from the masses of the unrecognized multitude. You do not know when you will see above the level masses of the crowd some great stature lifted head and shoulders above the rest, shouldering its way, not violently but gently, to the front and saying, "Here am I; follow me." And his voice will be your voice, his thought will be your thought, and you will follow him as if you were following the best things in yourselves.

When I think of an association of Christian young men I wonder that it has not already turned the world upside down. I wonder, not that it has done so much, for it has done a great deal, but that it has done so little; and I can only conjecture that it does not realize its own strength. I can only imagine that it has not yet got its pace. I wish I could believe, and I do believe, that at seventy it is just reaching its majority, and that from this time on a dream greater even than George Williams[6] ever dreamed will be realized in the great accumulating momentum of Christian men throughout the world. For, gentlemen, this is an age in which the principles of men who utter public opinion dominate the world. It makes no difference what is done for the time being. After the struggle is over the jury will sit, and nobody can corrupt that jury.

At one time I tried to write history. I did not know enough to write it, but I knew from experience how hard it was to find an historian out, and I trusted I would not be found out. I used to have this comfortable thought as I saw men struggling in the public arena. I used to think to myself, "This is all very well and very interesting. You probably assess yourself in such and such a way. Those who are your partisans assess you thus and so. Those who are your opponents urge a different verdict. But it does not make very much difference, because after you are dead and gone some quiet historian will sit in a secluded room and tell mankind for the rest of time just what to think about you, and his verdict, not the verdict of your partisans and not the verdict of your opponents, will be the verdict of posterity." I say that I used to say that to myself. It very largely was not so. And yet it was true in this sense: If the historian really speaks the judgment of the succeeding generation, then he really speaks the judgment also of the generations that succeed it, and his assessment, made without the passion of the time, made without partisan feeling in the matter-in other circumstances, when the air is cool-is the judgment of mankind upon your actions.

Now, is it not very important that we who shall constitute a portion of the jury should get our best judgments to work and base them upon Christian forbearance and Christian principles, upon the idea that it is impossible by sophistication to establish that a thing that is wrong is right? And yet, while we are going to judge with the absolute standard of righteousness, we are going to judge with Christian feeling, being men of a like sort ourselves, suffering the same temptations, having the same weaknesses, knowing the same passions; and while we do not condemn, we are going to seek to say and to live the truth. What I am hoping for is that these seventy years have just been a running start, and that now there will be a great rush of Christian principle upon the strongholds of evil and of wrong in the world. Those strongholds are not as strong as they look. Almost every vicious man is afraid of society, and if you once open the door where he is, he will run. All you have to do is to fight, not with cannon but with light.

May I illustrate it in this way? The Government of the United States has just succeeded in concluding a large number of treaties with the leading nations of the world, the sum and substance of which is this, that whenever any trouble arises the light shall shine on it for a year before anything is done; and my prediction is that after the light has shone on it for a year it will not be necessary to do anything; that after we know what happened, then we will know who was right and who was wrong. I believe that light is the greatest sanitary influence in the world. That, I suppose, is scientific commonplace, because if you want to make a place wholesome the best instrument you can use is the sun; to let his rays in, let him search out all the miasma that may lurk there. So with moral light: It is the most wholesome and rectifying, as well as the most revealing, thing in the world, provided it be genuine moral light; not the light of inquisitiveness, not the light of the man who likes to turn up ugly things, not the light of the man who disturbs what is corrupt for the mere sake of the sensation that he creates by disturbing it, but the moral light, the light of the man who discloses it in order that all the sweet influences of the world may go in and make it better.

That, in my judgment, is what the Young Men's Christian Association can do. It can point out to its members the things that are wrong. It can guide the feet of those who are going astray; and when its members have realized the power of the Christian principle, then they will not be men if they do not unite to see that the rest of the world experiences the same emancipation and reaches the same happiness of release.

I believe in the Young Men's Christian Association because I believe in the progress of moral ideas in the world; and I do not know that I am sure of anything else. When you are after something and have formulated it and have done the very best thing you know how to do you have got to be sure for the time being that that is the thing to do. But you are a fool if in the back of your head you do not know it is possible that you are mistaken. All that you can claim is that that is the thing as you see it now and that you cannot stand still; that you must push forward the things that are right. It may turn out that you made mistakes, but what you do know is your direction, and you are sure you are moving in that way. I was once a college reformer, until discouraged, and I remember a classmate of mine saying, "Why, man, can't you let anything alone?" I said, "I let everything alone that you can show me is not itself moving in the wrong direction, but I am not going to let those things alone that I see are going downhill"; and I borrowed this illustration from an ingenious writer. He says, "If you have a post that is painted white and want to keep it white, you cannot let it alone; and if anybody says to you, 'Why don't you let that post alone,' you will say, 'Because I want it to stay white, and therefore I have got to paint it at least every second year.'" There isn't anything in this world that will not change if you absolutely let it alone, and therefore you have constantly to be attending to it to see that it is being taken care of in the right way and that, if it is part of the motive force of the world, it is moving in the right direction.

That means that eternal vigilance is the price, not only of liberty, but of a great many other things. It is the price of everything that is good. It is the price of one's own soul. It is the price of the souls of the people you love; and when it comes down to the final reckoning you have a standard that is immutable. What shall a man give in exchange for his own soul? Will he sell that? Will he consent to see another man sell his soul? Will he consent to see the conditions of his community such that men's souls are debauched and trodden underfoot in the mire? What shall he give in exchange for his own soul, or any other man's soul? And since the world, the world of affairs, the world of society, is nothing less and nothing more than all of us put together, it is a great enterprise for the salvation of the soul in this world as well as in the next. There is a text in Scripture that has always interested me profoundly. It says godliness is profitable in this life as well as in the life that is to come; and if you do not start it in this life, it will not reach the life that is to come. Your measurements, your directions, your whole momentum, have to be established before you reach the next world. This world is intended as the place in which we shall show that we know how to grow in the stature of manliness and of righteousness.

I have come here to bid Godspeed to the great work of the Young Men's Christian Association. I love to think of the gathering force of such things as this in the generations to come. If a man had to measure the accomplishments of society, the progress of reform, the speed of the world's betterment, by the few little things that happened in his own life, by the trifling things that he can contribute to accomplish, he would indeed feel that the cost was much greater than the result. But no man can look at the past of the history of this world without seeing a vision of the future of the history of this world; and when you think of the accumulated moral forces that have made one age better than another age in the progress of mankind, then you can open your eyes to the vision. You can see that age by age, though with a blind struggle in the dust of the road, though often mistaking the path and losing its way in the mire, mankind is yet-sometimes with bloody hands and battered knees-nevertheless struggling step after step up the slow stages to the day when he shall live in the full light which shines upon the uplands, where all the light that illumines mankind shines direct from the face of God.

A Message

[Returning to the House of Representatives without approval an act to regulate the immigration of aliens to and the residence of aliens in the United States.]

To the House of Representatives:

It is with unaffected regret that I find myself constrained by clear conviction to return this bill (H.R. 6060, "An act to regulate the immigration of aliens to and the residence of aliens in the United States") without my signature. Not only do I feel it to be a very serious matter to exercise the power of veto in any case, because it involves opposing the single judgment of the President to the judgment of a majority of both the Houses of the Congress, a step which no man who realizes his own liability to error can take without great hesitation, but also because this particular bill is in so many important respects admirable, well conceived, and desirable. Its enactment into law would undoubtedly enhance the efficiency and improve the methods of handling the important branch of the public service to which it relates. But candor and a sense of duty with regard to the responsibility so clearly imposed upon me by the Constitution in matters of legislation leave me no choice but to dissent.

In two particulars of vital consequence this bill embodies a radical departure from the traditional and long-established policy of this country, a policy in which our people have conceived the very character of their Government to be expressed, the very mission and spirit of the Nation in respect of its relations to the peoples of the world outside their borders. It seeks to all but close entirely the gates of asylum which have always been open to those who could find nowhere else the right and opportunity of constitutional agitation for what they conceived to be the natural and inalienable rights of men; and it excludes those to whom the opportunities of elementary education have been denied, without regard to their character, their purposes, or their natural capacity.

Restrictions like these, adopted earlier in our history as a Nation, would very materially have altered the course and cooled the humane ardors of our politics. The right of political asylum has brought to this country many a man of noble character and elevated purpose who was marked as an outlaw in his own less fortunate land, and who has yet become an ornament to our citizenship and to our public councils. The children and the compatriots of these illustrious Americans must stand amazed to see the representatives of their Nation now resolved, in the fullness of our national strength and at the maturity of our great institutions, to risk turning such men back from our shores without test of quality or purpose. It is difficult for me to believe that the full effect of this feature of the bill was realized when it was framed and adopted, and it is impossible for me to assent to it in the form in which it is here cast.

The literacy test and the tests and restrictions which accompany it constitute an even more radical change in the policy of the Nation. Hitherto we have generously kept our doors open to all who were not unfitted by reason of disease or incapacity for self-support or such personal records and antecedents as were likely to make them a menace to our peace and order or to the wholesome and essential relationships of life. In this bill it is proposed to turn away from tests of character and of quality and impose tests which exclude and restrict; for the new tests here embodied are not tests of quality or of character or of personal fitness, but tests of opportunity. Those who come seeking opportunity are not to be admitted unless they have already had one of the chief of the opportunities they seek, the opportunity of education. The object of such provisions is restriction, not selection.

If the people of this country have made up their minds to limit the number of immigrants by arbitrary tests and so reverse the policy of all the generations of Americans that have gone before them, it is their right to do so. I am their servant and have no license to stand in their way. But I do not believe that they have. I respectfully submit that no one can quote their mandate to that effect. Has any political party ever avowed a policy of restriction in this fundamental matter, gone to the country on it, and been commissioned to control its legislation? Does this bill rest upon the conscious and universal assent and desire of the American people? I doubt it. It is because I doubt it that I make bold to dissent from it. I am willing to abide by the verdict, but not until it has been rendered. Let the platforms of parties speak out upon this policy and the people pronounce their wish. The matter is too fundamental to be settled otherwise.

I have no pride of opinion in this question. I am not foolish enough to profess to know the wishes and ideals of America better than the body of her chosen representatives know them. I only want instruction direct from those whose fortunes, with ours and all men's, are involved.

Woodrow Wilson.
The White House, *28 January, 1915.*

Address Before the United States Chamber of Commerce

[Delivered in Washington, February 3, 1915.]

Mr. President, Ladies and Gentlemen:

I feel that it is hardly fair to you for me to come in in this casual fashion among a body of men who have been seriously discussing great questions, and it is hardly fair to me, because I come in cold, not having had the advantage of sharing the atmosphere of your deliberations and catching the feeling of your conference. Moreover, I hardly know just how to express my interest in the things you are undertaking. When a man stands outside an organization and speaks to it he is too apt to have the tone of outside commendation, as who should say, "I would desire to pat you on the back and say 'Good boys; you are doing well!'" I would a great deal rather have you receive me as if for the time being I were one of your own number.

Because the longer I occupy the office that I now occupy the more I regret any lines of separation; the more I deplore any feeling that one set of men has one set of interests and another set of men another set of interests; the more I feel the solidarity of the Nation-the impossibility of separating one interest from another without misconceiving it; the necessity that we should all understand one another, in order that we may understand ourselves.

There is an illustration which I have used a great many times. I will use it again, because it is the most serviceable to my own mind. We often speak of a man who cannot find his way in some jungle or some desert as having "lost himself." Did you never reflect that that is the only thing he has not lost? *He is there.* He has lost the rest of the world. He has no fixed point by which to steer. He does not know which is north, which is south, which is east, which is west; and if he did know, he is so confused that he would not know in which of those directions his goal lay. Therefore, following his heart, he walks in a great circle from right to left and comes back to where he started-to himself again. To my mind that is a picture of the world. If you have lost sight of other interests and do not know the relation of your own interests to those other interests, then you do not understand your own interests, and have lost yourself. What you want is orientation, relationship to the points of the compass; relationship to the other people in the world; vital connections which you have for the time being severed.

I am particularly glad to express my admiration for the kind of organization which you have drawn together. I have attended banquets of chambers of commerce in various parts of the country and have got the impression at each of those banquets that there was only one city in the country. It has seemed to me that those associations were meant in order to destroy men's perspective, in order to destroy their sense of relative proportions. Worst of all, if I may be permitted to say so, they were intended to boost something in particular. Boosting is a very unhandsome thing. Advancing enterprise is a very handsome thing, but to exaggerate local merits in order to create disproportion in the general development is not a particularly handsome thing or a particularly intelligent thing. A city cannot grow on the face of a great state like a mushroom on that one spot. Its roots are throughout the state, and unless the state it is in, or the region it draws from, can itself thrive and pulse with life as a whole, the city can have no healthy growth. You forget the wide rootages of everything when you boost some particular region. There are dangers which probably you all understand in the mere practice of advertisement. When a man begins to advertise himself there are certain points that are somewhat exaggerated, and I have noticed that men who exaggerate most, most quickly lose any proper conception of what their own proportions are. Therefore, these local centers of enthusiasm may be local centers of mistake if they are not very wisely guided and if they do not themselves realize their relations to the other centers of enthusiasm and of advancement.

The advantage about a Chamber of Commerce of the United States is that there is only one way to boost the United States, and that is by seeing to it that the conditions under which business is done throughout the whole country are the best possible conditions. There cannot be any disproportion about that. If you draw your sap and your vitality from all quarters, then the more sap and vitality there is in you the more there is in the commonwealth as a whole, and every time you lift at all you lift the whole level of manufacturing and mercantile enterprise. Moreover, the advantage of it is that you cannot boost the United States in that way without understanding the United States. You learn a great deal. I agreed with a colleague of mine in the Cabinet the other day that we had never attended in our lives before a school to compare with that we were now attending for the purpose of gaining a liberal education.

Of course, I learn a great many things that are not so, but the interesting thing about that is this: Things that are not so do not match. If you hear enough of them, you see there is no pattern whatever; it is a crazy quilt. Whereas, the truth always matches, piece by piece, with other parts of the truth. No man can lie consistently, and he cannot lie about everything if he talks to you long. I would guarantee that if enough liars talked to you, you would get the truth; because the parts that they did not invent would match one another, and the parts that they did invent would *not* match one another. Talk long enough, therefore, and see the connections clearly enough, and you can patch together the case as a whole. I had somewhat that experience about Mexico, and that was about the only way in which I learned anything that was true about it. For there had been vivid imaginations and many special interests which depicted things as they wished me to believe them to be.

Seriously, the task of this body is to match all the facts of business throughout the country and to see the vast and consistent pattern of it. That is the reason I think you are to be congratulated upon the fact that you cannot do this thing without common counsel. There isn't any man who knows enough to comprehend the United States. It is coöperative effort, necessarily. You cannot perform the functions of this Chamber of Commerce without drawing in not only a vast number of men, but men, and a number of men, from every region and section of the country. The minute this association falls into the hands, if it ever should, of men from a single section or men with a single set of interests most at heart, it will go to seed and die. Its strength must come from the uttermost parts of the land and must be compounded of brains and comprehensions of every sort. It is a very noble and handsome picture for the imagination, and I have asked myself before I came here to-day, what relation you could bear to the Government of the United States and what relation the Government could bear to you?

There are two aspects and activities of the Government with which you will naturally come into most direct contact. The first is the Government's power of inquiry, systematic and disinterested inquiry, and its power of scientific assistance. You get an illustration of the latter, for example, in the Department of Agriculture. Has it occurred to you, I wonder, that we are just upon the eve of a time when our Department of Agriculture will be of infinite importance to the whole world? There is a shortage of food in the world now. That shortage will be much more serious a few months from now than it is now. It is necessary that we should plant a great deal more; it is necessary that our lands should yield more per acre than they do now; it is necessary that there should not be a plow or a spade idle in this country if the world is to be fed. And the methods of our farmers must feed upon the scientific information to be derived from the State departments of agriculture, and from that taproot of all, the United States Department of Agriculture. The object and use of that department is to inform men of the latest developments and disclosures of science with regard to all the processes by which soils can be put to their proper use and their fertility made the greatest possible. Similarly with the Bureau of Standards. It is ready to supply those things by which you can set norms, you can set bases, for all the scientific processes of business.

I have a great admiration for the scientific parts of the Government of the United States, and it has amazed me that so few men have discovered them. Here in these departments are quiet men, trained to the highest degree of skill, serving for a petty remuneration along lines that are infinitely useful to mankind; and yet in some cases they waited to be discovered until this Chamber of Commerce of the United States was established. Coming to this city, officers of that association found that there were here things that were infinitely useful to them and with which the whole United States ought to be put into communication.

The Government of the United States is very properly a great instrumentality of inquiry and information. One thing we are just beginning to do that we ought to have done long ago: We ought long ago to have had our Bureau of Foreign and Domestic Commerce. We ought long ago to have sent the best eyes of the Government out into the world to see where the opportunities and openings of American commerce and American genius were to be found-men who were not sent out as the commercial agents of any particular set of business men in the United States, but who were eyes for the whole business community. I have been reading consular reports for twenty years. In what I came to regard as an evil day the Congressman from my district began to send me the consular reports, and they ate up more and more of my time. They are very interesting, but they are a good deal like what the old lady said of the dictionary, that it was very interesting but a little disconnected. You get a picture of the world as if a spotlight were being dotted about over the surface of it. Here you see a glimpse of this, and here you see a glimpse of that, and through the medium of some consuls you do not see anything at all. Because the consul has to have eyes and the consul has to know what he is looking for. A literary friend of mine said that he used to believe in the maxim that "everything comes to the man who waits," but he discovered after awhile by practical experience that it needed an additional clause, "provided he knows what he is waiting for." Unless you know what you are looking for and have trained eyes to see it when it comes your way, it may pass you unnoticed. We are just beginning to do, systematically and scientifically, what we ought long ago to have done, to employ the Government of the United States to survey the world in order that American commerce might be guided.

But there are other ways of using the Government of the United States, ways that have long been tried, though not always with conspicuous success or fortunate results. You can use the Government of the United States by influencing its legislation. That has been a very active industry, but it has not always been managed in the interest of the whole people. It is very instructive and useful for the Government of the United States to have such means as you are ready to supply for getting a sort of consensus of opinion which proceeds from no particular quarter and originates with no particular interest. Information is the very foundation of all right action in legislation.

I remember once, a good many years ago, I was attending one of the local chambers of commerce of the United States at a time when everybody was complaining that Congress was interfering with business. If you have heard that complaint recently and supposed that it was original with the men who made it, you have not lived as long as I have. It has been going on ever since I can remember. The complaint came most vigorously from men who were interested in large corporate development. I took the liberty to say to that body of men, whom I did not know, that I took it for granted that there were a great many lawyers among them, and that it was likely that the more prominent of those lawyers were the intimate advisors of the corporations of that region. I said that I had met a great many lawyers from whom the complaint had come most vigorously, not only that there was too much legislation with regard to corporations, but that it was ignorant legislation. I said, "Now, the responsibility is with you. If the legislation is mistaken, you are on the inside and know where the mistakes are being made. You know not only the innocent and right things that your corporations are doing, but you know the other things, too. Knowing how they are done, you can be expert advisors as to how the wrong things can be prevented. If, therefore, this thing is handled ignorantly, there is nobody to blame but yourselves." If we on the outside cannot understand the thing and cannot get advice from the inside, then we will have to do it with the flat hand and not with the touch of skill and discrimination. Isn't that true? Men on the inside of business know how business is conducted and they cannot complain if men on the outside make mistakes about business if they do not come from the inside and give the kind of advice which is necessary.

The trouble has been that when they came in the past-for I think the thing is changing very rapidly-they came with all their bristles out; they came on the defensive; they came to see, not what they could accomplish, but what they could prevent. They did not come to guide; they came to block. That is of no use whatever to the general body politic. What has got to pervade us like a great motive power is that we cannot, and must not, separate our interests from one another, but must pool our interests. A man who is trying to fight for his single hand is fighting against the community and not fighting with it. There are a great many dreadful things about war, as nobody needs to be told in this day of distress and of terror, but there is one thing about war which has a very splendid side, and that is the consciousness that a whole nation gets that they must all act as a unit for a common end. And when peace is as handsome as war there will be no war. When men, I mean, engage in the pursuits of peace in the same spirit of self-sacrifice and of conscious service of the community with which, at any rate, the common soldier engages in war, then shall there be wars no more. You have moved the vanguard for the United States in the purposes of this association just a little nearer that ideal. That is the reason I am here, because I believe it.

There is a specific matter about which I, for one, want your advice. Let me say, if I may say it without disrespect, that I do not think you are prepared to give it right away. You will have to make some rather extended inquiries before you are ready to give it. What I am thinking of is competition in foreign markets as between the merchants of different nations.

I speak of the subject with a certain degree of hesitation, because the thing farthest from my thought is taking advantage of nations now disabled from playing their full part in that competition, and seeking a sudden selfish advantage because they are for the time being disabled. Pray believe me that we ought to eliminate all that thought from our minds and consider this matter as if we and the other nations now at war were in the normal circumstances of commerce.

There is a normal circumstance of commerce in which we are apparently at a disadvantage. Our anti-trust laws are thought by some to make it illegal for merchants in the United States to form combinations for the purpose of strengthening themselves in taking advantage of the opportunities of foreign trade. That is a very serious matter for this reason: There are some corporations, and some firms for all I know, whose business is great enough and whose resources are abundant enough to enable them to establish selling agencies in foreign countries; to enable them to extend the long credits which in some cases are necessary in order to keep the trade they desire; to enable them, in other words, to organize their business in foreign territory in a way which the smaller man cannot afford to do. His business has not grown big enough to permit him to establish selling agencies. The export commission merchant, perhaps, taxes him a little too highly to make that an available competitive means of conducting and extending his business.

The question arises, therefore, how are the smaller merchants, how are the younger and weaker corporations going to get a foothold as against the combinations which are permitted and even encouraged by foreign governments in this field of competition? There are governments which, as you know, distinctly encourage the formation of great combinations in each particular field of commerce in order to maintain selling agencies and to extend long credits, and to use and maintain the machinery which is necessary for the extension of business; and American merchants feel that they are at a very considerable disadvantage in contending against that. The matter has been many times brought to my attention, and I have each time suspended judgment. I want to be shown this: I want to be shown how such a combination can be made and conducted in a way which will not close it against the use of everybody who wants to use it. A combination has a tendency to exclude new members. When a group of men get control of a good thing, they do not see any particular point in letting other people into the good thing. What I would like very much to be shown, therefore, is a method of coöperation which is not a method of combination. Not that the two words are mutually exclusive, but we have come to have a special meaning attached to the word "combination." Most of our combinations have a safety lock, and you have to know the combination to get in. I want to know how these coöperative methods can be adopted for the benefit of everybody who wants to use them, and I say frankly if I can be shown that, I am for them. If I cannot be shown that, I am against them. I hasten to add that I hopefully expect I *can* be shown that.

You, as I have just now intimated, probably cannot show it to me offhand, but by the methods which you have the means of using you certainly ought to be able to throw a vast deal of light on the subject. Because the minute you ask the small merchant, the small banker, the country man, how he looks upon these things and how he thinks they ought to be arranged in order that he can use them, if he is like some of the men in country districts whom I know, he will turn out to have had a good deal of thought upon that subject and to be able to make some very interesting suggestions whose intelligence and comprehensiveness will surprise some city gentlemen who think that only the cities understand the business of the country. As a matter of fact, you do not have time to think in a city. It takes time to think. You can get what you call opinions by contagion in a city and get them very quickly, but you do not always know where the germ came from. And you have no scientific laboratory method by which to determine whether it is a good germ or a bad germ.

There are thinking spaces in this country, and some of the thinking done is very solid thinking indeed, the thinking of the sort of men that we all love best, who think for themselves, who do not see things as they are told to see them, but look at them and see them independently; who, if they are told they are white when they are black, plainly say that they are black-men with eyes and with a courage back of those eyes to tell what they see. The country is full of those men. They have been singularly reticent sometimes, singularly silent, but the country is full of them. And what I rejoice in is that you have called them into the ranks. For your methods are bound to be democratic in spite of you. I do not mean democratic with a big "D," though I have a private conviction that you cannot be democratic with a small "d" long without becoming democratic with a big "D." Still that is just between ourselves. The point is that when we have a *consensus* of opinion, when we have this common counsel, then the legislative processes of this Government will be infinitely illuminated.

I used to wonder when I was Governor of one of the States of this great country where all the bills came from. Some of them had a very private complexion. I found upon inquiry-it was easy to find-that practically nine-tenths of the bills that were introduced had been handed to the members who introduced them by some constituent of theirs, had been drawn up by some lawyer whom they might or might not know, and were intended to do something that would be beneficial to a particular set of persons. I do not mean, necessarily, beneficial in a way that would be hurtful to the rest; they may have been perfectly honest, but they came out of cubby-holes all over the State. They did not come out of public places where men had got together and compared views. They were not the products of common counsel, but the products of private counsel, a very necessary process if there is no other, but a process which it would be a very happy thing to dispense with if we could get another. And the only other process is the process of common counsel.

Some of the happiest experiences of my life have been like this. We had once when I was president of a university to revise the whole course of study.[7] Courses of study are chronically in need of revision. A committee of, I believe, fourteen men was directed by the faculty of the university to report a revised curriculum. Naturally, the men who had the most ideas on the subject were picked out and, naturally, each man came with a very definite notion of the kind of revision he wanted, and one of the first discoveries we made was that no two of us wanted exactly the same revision. I went in there with all my war paint on to get the revision I wanted, and I dare say, though it was perhaps more skillfully concealed, the other men had their war paint on, too. We discussed the matter for six months. The result was a report which no one of us had conceived or foreseen, but with which we were all absolutely satisfied. There was not a man who had not learned in that committee more than he had ever known before about the subject, and who had not willingly revised his prepossessions; who was not proud to be a participant in a genuine piece of common counsel. I have had several experiences of that sort, and it has led me, whenever I confer, to hold my particular opinion provisionally, as my contribution to go into the final result but not to dominate the final result.

That is the ideal of a government like ours, and an interesting thing is that if you only talk about an idea that will not work long enough, everybody will see perfectly plainly that it will not work; whereas, if you do not talk about it, and do not have a great many people talk about it, you are in danger of having the people who handle it think that it will work. Many minds are necessary to compound a workable method of life in a various and populous country; and as I think about the whole thing and picture the purposes, the infinitely difficult and complex purposes which we must conceive and carry out, not only does it minister to my own modesty, I hope, of opinion, but it also fills me with a very great enthusiasm. It is a splendid thing to be part of a great wide-awake Nation. It is a splendid thing to know that your own strength is infinitely multiplied by the strength of other men who love the country as you do. It is a splendid thing to feel that the wholesome blood of a great country can be united in common purposes, and that by frankly looking one another in the face and taking counsel with one another, prejudices will drop away, handsome understandings will arise, a universal spirit of service will be engendered, and that with this increased sense of community of purpose will come a vastly enhanced individual power of achievement; for we will be lifted by the whole mass of which we constitute a part.

Have you never heard a great chorus of trained voices lift the voice of the prima donna as if it soared with easy grace above the whole melodious sound? It does not seem to come from the single throat that produces it. It seems as if it were the perfect accent and crown of the great chorus. So it ought to be with the statesman. So it ought to be with every man who tries to guide the counsels of a great nation. He should feel that his voice is lifted upon the chorus and that it is only the crown of the common theme.

To Naturalized Citizens

[Address delivered at Convention Hall, Philadelphia, May 10, 1915. The audience included four thousand newly naturalized citizens. This speech attracted great attention because in it no reference was made to the sinking of the "Lusitania," three days before.]

Mr. Mayor, Fellow-Citizens:

It warms my heart that you should give me such a reception; but it is not of myself that I wish to think to-night, but of those who have just become citizens of the United States.

This is the only country in the world which experiences this constant and repeated rebirth. Other countries depend upon the multiplication of their own native people. This country is constantly drinking strength out of new sources by the voluntary association with it of great bodies of strong men and forward-looking women out of other lands. And so by the gift of the free will of independent people it is being constantly renewed from generation to generation by the same process by which it was originally created. It is as if humanity had determined to see to it that this great Nation, founded for the benefit of humanity, should not lack for the allegiance of the people of the world.

You have just taken an oath of allegiance to the United States. Of allegiance to whom? Of allegiance to no one, unless it be God-certainly not of allegiance to those who temporarily represent this great Government. You have taken an oath of allegiance to a great ideal, to a great body of principles, to a great hope of the human race. You have said, "We are going to America not only to earn a living, not only to seek the things which it was more difficult to obtain where we were born, but to help forward the great enterprises of the human spirit-to let men know that everywhere in the world there are men who will cross strange oceans and go where a speech is spoken which is alien to them if they can but satisfy their quest for what their spirits crave; knowing that whatever the speech there is but one longing and utterance of the human heart, and that is for liberty and justice." And while you bring all countries with you, you come with a purpose of leaving all other countries behind you-bringing what is best of their spirit, but not looking over your shoulders and seeking to perpetuate what you intended to leave behind in them. I certainly would not be one even to suggest that a man cease to love the home of his birth and the nation of his origin-these things are very sacred and ought not to be put out of our hearts-but it is one thing to love the place where you were born and it is another thing to dedicate yourself to the place to which you go. You cannot dedicate yourself to America unless you become in every respect and with every purpose of your will thorough Americans. You cannot become thorough Americans if you think of yourselves in groups. America does not consist of groups. A man who thinks of himself as belonging to a particular national group in America has not yet become an American, and the man who goes among you to trade upon your nationality is no worthy son to live under the Stars and Stripes.

My urgent advice to you would be, not only always to think first of America, but always, also, to think first of humanity. You do not love humanity if you seek to divide humanity into jealous camps. Humanity can be welded together only by love, by sympathy, by justice, not by jealousy and hatred. I am sorry for the man who seeks to make personal capital out of the passions of his fellow-men. He has lost the touch and ideal of America, for America was created to unite mankind by those passions which lift and not by the passions which separate and debase. We came to America, either ourselves or in the persons of our ancestors, to better the ideals of men, to make them see finer things than they had seen before, to get rid of the things that divide and to make sure of the things that unite. It was but an historical accident no doubt that this great country was called the "United States"; yet I am very thankful that it has that word "United" in its title, and the man who seeks to divide man from man, group from group, interest from interest in this great Union is striking at its very heart.

It is a very interesting circumstance to me, in thinking of those of you who have just sworn allegiance to this great Government, that you were drawn across the ocean by some beckoning finger of hope, by some belief, by some vision of a new kind of justice, by some expectation of a better kind of life. No doubt you have been disappointed in some of us. Some of us are very disappointing. No doubt you have found that justice in the United States goes only with a pure heart and a right purpose as it does everywhere else in the world. No doubt what you found here did not seem touched for you, after all, with the complete beauty of the ideal which you had conceived beforehand. But remember this: If we had grown at all poor in the ideal, you brought some of it with you. A man does not go out to seek the thing that is not in him. A man does not hope for the thing that he does not believe in, and if some of us have forgotten what America believed in, you, at any rate, imported in your own hearts a renewal of the belief. That is the reason that I, for one, make you welcome. If I have in any degree forgotten what America was intended for, I will thank God if you will remind me. I was born in America. You dreamed dreams of what America was to be, and I hope you brought the dreams with you. No man that does not see visions will ever realize any high hope or undertake any high enterprise. Just because you brought dreams with you, America is more likely to realize dreams such as you brought. You are enriching us if you came expecting us to be better than we are.

See, my friends, what that means. It means that Americans must have a consciousness different from the consciousness of every other nation in the world. I am not saying this with even the slightest thought of criticism of other nations. You know how it is with a family. A family gets centered on itself if it is not careful and is less interested in the neighbors than it is in its own members. So a nation that is not constantly renewed out of new sources is apt to have the narrowness and prejudice of a family; whereas, America must have this consciousness, that on all sides it touches elbows and touches hearts with all the nations of mankind. The example of America must be a special example. The example of America must be the example not merely of peace because it will not fight, but of peace because peace is the healing and elevating influence of the world and strife is not. There is such a thing as a man being too proud to fight. There is such a thing as a nation being so right that it does not need to convince others by force that it is right.

You have come into this great Nation voluntarily seeking something that we have to give, and all that we have to give is this: We cannot exempt you from work. No man is exempt from work anywhere in the world. We cannot exempt you from the strife and the heartbreaking burden of the struggle of the day-that is common to mankind everywhere; we cannot exempt you from the loads that you must carry. We can only make them light by the spirit in which they are carried. That is the spirit of hope, it is the spirit of liberty, it is the spirit of justice.

When I was asked, therefore, by the Mayor and the committee that accompanied him to come up from Washington to meet this great company of newly admitted citizens, I could not decline the invitation. I ought not to be away from Washington, and yet I feel that it has renewed my spirit as an American to be here. In Washington men tell you so many things every day that are not so, and I like to come and stand in the presence of a great body of my fellow-citizens, whether they have been fellow-citizens a long time or a short time, and drink, as it were, out of the common fountains with them and go back feeling what you have so generously given me-the sense of your support and of the living vitality in your hearts of the great ideals which have made America the hope of the world.

Address at Milwaukee

[Between January 27 and February 3, 1916, President Wilson made a series of speeches in New York, Pittsburgh, Cleveland, Milwaukee, Chicago, Des Moines, Topeka, Kansas City, and St. Louis. The address made at Milwaukee, on January 31, has been chosen as representing the general tenor and spirit of the whole series.]

Mr. Chairman And Fellow-Citizens:

I need not inquire whether the citizens of Milwaukee and Wisconsin are interested in the subject of my errand. The presence of this great body in this vast hall sufficiently attests your interest, but I want at the outset to remove a misapprehension that I fear may exist in your mind. There is no sudden crisis; nothing new has happened; I am not out upon this errand because of any unexpected situation. I have come to confer with you upon a matter upon which it would, in any circumstances, be necessary for us to confer when all the rest of the world is on fire and our own house is not fireproof. Everywhere the atmosphere of the world is thrilling with the passion of a disturbance such as the world has never seen before, and it is wise, in the words just uttered by your chairman, that we should see that our own house is set in order and that everything is done to make certain that we shall not suffer by the general conflagration.

There were some dangers to which this Nation seemed at the outset of the war to be exposed, which, I think I can say with confidence, are now passed and overcome. America has drawn her blood and her strength out of almost all the nations of the world. It is true of a great many of us that there lies deep in our hearts the recollection of an origin which is not American. We are aware that our roots, our traditions, run back into other national soils. There are songs that stir us; there are some far-away historical recollections which engage our affections and stir our memories. We cannot forget our forbears; we cannot altogether ignore the fact of our essential blood relationship; and at the outset of this war it did look as if there were a division of domestic sentiment which might lead us to some errors of judgment and some errors of action; but I, for one, believe that that danger is passed. I never doubted that the danger was exaggerated, because I had learned long ago, and many of you will corroborate me by your experience, that it is not the men who are doing the talking always who represent the real sentiments of the Nation. I for my part always feel a serene confidence in waiting for the declaration of the principles and sentiments of the men who are not vociferous, do not go about seeking to make trouble, do their own thinking, attend to their own business, and love their own country.

I have at no time supposed that the men whose voices seemed to contain the threat of division amongst us were really uttering the sentiments even of those whom they pretended to represent. I for my part have no jealousy of family sentiment. I have no jealousy of that deep affection which runs back through long lineage. It would be a pity if we forget the fine things that our ancestors have done. But I also know the magic of America; I also know the great principles which thrill men in the singular body politic to which we belong in the United States. I know the impulses which have drawn men to our shores. They have not come idly; they have not come without conscious purpose to be free; they have not come without voluntary desire to unite themselves with the great nation on this side of the sea; and I know that whenever the test comes every man's heart will be first for America. It was principle and affection and ambition and hope that drew men to these shores, and they are not going to forget the errand upon which they came and allow America, the home of their refuge and hope, to suffer by any forgetfulness on their part. And so the trouble makers have shot their bolt, and it has been ineffectual. Some of them have been vociferous; all of them have been exceedingly irresponsible. Talk was cheap, and that was all it cost them. They did not have to do anything. But you will know without my telling you that the man whom for the time being you have charged with the duties of President of the United States must talk with a deep sense of responsibility, and he must remember, above all things else, the fine traditions of his office which some men seem to have forgotten. There is no precedent in American history for any action of aggression on the part of the United States or for any action which might mean that America is seeking to connect herself with the controversies on the other side of the water. Men who seek to provoke us to such action have forgotten the traditions of the United States, but it behooves those with whom you have entrusted office to remember the traditions of the United States and to see to it that the actions of the Government are made to square with those traditions.

But there are other dangers, my fellow-citizens, which are not past and which have not been overcome, and they are dangers which we cannot control. We can control irresponsible talkers amidst ourselves. All we have got to do is to encourage them to hire a hall and their folly will be abundantly advertised by themselves. But we cannot in this simple fashion control the dangers that surround us now and have surrounded us since this titanic struggle on the other side of the water began. I say on the other side of the water; you will ask me, "On the other side of which water," for this great struggle has extended to all quarters of the globe. There is no continent outside, I was about to say, of this Western Hemisphere which is not touched with it, but I recollected as I began the sentence that a part of our own continent was touched with it, because it involves our neighbors to the north in Canada. There is no part of the world, except South America, to which the direct influences of this struggle have not extended, so that now we are completely surrounded by this tremendous disturbance and you must realize what that involves.

Our thoughts are concentrated upon our own affairs and our own relations to the rest of the world, but the thoughts of the men who are engaged in this struggle are concentrated upon the struggle itself, and there is daily and hourly danger that they will feel themselves constrained to do things which are absolutely inconsistent with the rights of the United States. They are not thinking of us. I am not criticising them for not thinking of us. I dare say if I were in their place neither would I think of us. They believe that they are struggling for the lives and honor of their nations, and that if the United States puts its interests in the path of this great struggle, she ought to know beforehand that there is danger of very serious misunderstanding and difficulty. So that the very uncalculating, unpremeditated, one might almost say accidental, course of affairs may touch us to the quick at any moment, and I want you to realize that, standing in the midst of these difficulties, I feel that I am charged with a double duty of the utmost difficulty. In the first place, I know that you are depending upon me to keep this Nation out of the war. So far I have done so, and I pledge you my word that, God helping me, I will if it is possible. But you have laid another duty upon me. You have bidden me to see it that nothing stains or impairs the honor of the United States, and that is a matter not within my control; that depends upon what others do, not upon what the Government of the United States does. Therefore there may at any moment come a time when I cannot preserve both the honor and the peace of the United States. Do not exact of me an impossible and contradictory thing, but stand ready and insistent that everybody who represents you should stand ready to provide the necessary means for maintaining the honor of the United States.

I sometimes think that it is true that no people ever went to war with another people. Governments have gone to war with one another. Peoples, so far as I remember, have not, and this is a government of the people, and this people is not going to choose war. But we are not dealing with people; we are dealing with Governments. We are dealing with Governments now engaged in a great struggle, and therefore we do not know what a day or an hour will bring forth. All that we know is the character of our own duty. We do not want the question of peace and war, or the conduct of war, entrusted too entirely to our Government. We want war, if it must come, to be something that springs out of the sentiments and principles and actions of the people themselves; and it is on that account that I am counseling the Congress of the United States not to take the advice of those who recommend that we should have, and have very soon, a great standing Army, but, on the contrary, to see to it that the citizens of this country are so trained and that the military equipment is so sufficiently provided for them that when they choose they can take up arms and defend themselves.

The Constitution of the United States makes the President the Commander in Chief of the Army and Navy of the Nation, but I do not want a big Army subject to my personal command. If danger comes, I want to turn to you and the rest of my fellow-countrymen and say, "Men, are you ready?" and I know what the response will be. I know that there will spring up out of the body of the Nation a great host of free men, and I want those men not to be mere targets for shot and shell. I want them to know something of the arms they have in their hands. I want them to know something about how to guard against the diseases that creep into camps, where men are unaccustomed to live. I want them to know something of what the orders mean that they will be under when they enlist under arms for the Government of the United States. I want them to be men who can comprehend and easily and intelligently step into the duty of national defense. That is the reason that I am urging upon the Congress of the United States at any rate the beginnings of a system by which we may give a very considerable body of our fellow-citizens the necessary training.

I have not forgotten the great National Guard of this country, but in this country of 100,000,000 people there are only 129,000 men in the National Guard; and the National Guard, fine as it is, is not subject to the orders of the President of the United States. It is subject to the orders of the Governors of the several States, and the Constitution itself says that the President has no right to withdraw them from their States even, except in the case of actual invasion of the soil of the United States. I want the Congress of the United States to do a great deal for the National Guard, but I do not see how the Congress of the United States can put the National Guard at the disposal of the national authorities. Therefore it seems to me absolutely necessary that in addition to the National Guard there should be a considerable body of men with some training in the military art who will have pledged themselves to come at the call of the Nation.

I have been told by those who have a greater knack at guessing statistics than I have that there are probably several million men in the United States who, either in this country or in other countries from which they have come to the United States, have received training in arms. It may be; I do not know, and I suspect that they do not either, but even if it be true, these men are not subject to the call of the Federal Government. They would have to be found; they would have to be induced to enlist; they would have to be organized; their numbers are indefinite; and they would have to be equipped. Such are not the materials which we need. We want to know who these men are and where they are and to have everything ready for them if they should come to our assistance. For we have now got down, not to the sentiment of national defense, but to the business of national defense. It is a business proposition and it must be treated as such. And there are abundant precedents for the proposals which have been made to the Congress. Even that arch-Democrat, Thomas Jefferson, believed that there ought to be compulsory military training for the adult men of the Nation, because he believed, as every true believer in democracy believes, that it is upon the voluntary action of the men of a great Nation like this that it must depend for its military force.

There is another misapprehension that I want to remove from your minds: Do not think that I have come to talk to you about these things because I doubt whether they are going to be done or not. I do not doubt it for a moment, but I believe that when great things of this sort are going to be done the people of this country are entitled to know just what is being proposed. As a friend of mine says, I am not arguing with you; I am telling you. I am not trying to convert you to anything, because I know that in your hearts you are converted already, but I want you to know the motives of what is proposed and the character of what is proposed, in order that we should have only one attitude and counsel with regard to this great matter.

It is being very sedulously spread abroad in this country that the impulse back of all this is the desire of men who make the materials of warfare to get money out of the Treasury of the United States. I wish the people that say that could see meetings like this. Did you come here for that purpose? Did you come here because you are interested to see some of your fellow-citizens make money out of the present situation? Of course you did not. I am ready to admit that probably the equipment of those men whom we are training will have to be bought from somebody, and I know that if the equipment is bought, it will have to be paid for; and I dare say somebody will make some money out of it. It is also true, ladies and gentlemen, that there are men now, a great many men, in the belligerent countries who are growing rich out of the sale of the materials needed by the armies of those countries. If the Government itself does not manufacture everything that an army needs, somebody has got to make money out of it, and I for my part have been urging the Congress of the United States to make the necessary preparations by which the Government can manufacture armor plate and munitions, so that, being in the business itself and having the ability to manufacture all it needs, if it is put upon a business basis, it can at any rate keep the price that it pays within moderate and reasonable limits. The Government of the United States is not going to be imposed upon by anybody, and you may rest assured, therefore, that while I believe you prefer that private capital and private initiative should bestir themselves in these matters, it is also possible, and I assure you that it is most likely, that the Government of the United States will have adequate means of controlling this matter very thoroughly indeed. There need be no fear on that side. Let nobody suppose that this is a money-making agitation. I would for one be ashamed to be such a dupe as to be engaged in it if it had any suspicion of that about it, but I am not as innocent as I look; and I believe that I can say for my colleagues in Washington that they are just as watchful in such matters as you would desire them to be.

And there is another misapprehension that I do not wish you to entertain. Do not suppose that there is any new or sudden or recent inadequacy on the part of this Government in respect of preparation for national defense. I have heard some gentlemen say that we had no coast defenses worth talking about. Coast defenses are not nowadays advertised, you understand, and they are not visible to the naked eye, so that if you passed them and nothing exploded, you would not know they were there. The coast defenses of the United States, while not numerous enough, are equipped in the most modern and efficient fashion. You are told that there has been some sort of neglect about the Navy. There has not been any sort of neglect about the Navy. We have been slowly building up a Navy which in quality is second to no navy in the world. The only thing it lacks is quantity. In size it is the fourth navy in the world, though I have heard it said by some gentlemen in this very region that it was the second. In fighting force, though not in quality, it is reckoned by experts to be the fourth in rank in the world; and yet when I go on board those ships and see their equipment and talk with their officers I suspect that they could give an account of themselves which would raise them above the fourth class. It reminds me of that very quaint saying of the old darky preacher, "The Lord says unto Moses, come fourth, and he came fifth and lost the race." But I think this Navy would not come fourth in the race, but higher.

What we are proposing now is not the sudden creation of a Navy, for we have a splendid Navy, but the definite working out of a program by which within five years we shall bring the Navy to a fighting strength which otherwise might have taken eight or ten years; along exactly the same lines of development that have been followed and followed diligently and intelligently for at least a decade past. There is no sudden panic, there is no sudden change of plan; all that has happened is that we now see that we ought more rapidly and more thoroughly than ever before to do the things which have always been characteristic of America. For she has always been proud of her Navy and has always been addicted to the principle that her citizenship must do the fighting on land. We are working out American principle a little faster, because American pulses are beating a little faster, because the world is in a whirl, because there are incalculable elements of trouble abroad which we cannot control or alter. I would be derelict to the duty which you have laid upon me if I did not tell you that it was absolutely necessary to carry out our principles in this matter now and at once.

And yet all the time, my fellow-citizens, I believe that in these things we are merely interpreting the spirit of America. Who shall say what the spirit of America is? I have many times heard orators apostrophize this beautiful flag which is the emblem of the Nation. I have many times heard orators and philosophers speak of the spirit which was resident in America. I have always for my own part felt that it was an act of audacity to attempt to characterize anything of that kind, and when I have been outside of the country in foreign lands and have been asked if this, that, or the other was true of America I have habitually said, "Nothing stated in general terms is true of America, because it is the most variegated and varied and multiform land under the sun." Yet I know that if you turn away from the physical aspects of the country, if you turn away from the variety of the strains of blood that make up our great population, if you turn away from the great variations of occupation and of interest among our fellow-citizens, there is a spiritual unity in America. I know that there are some things which stir every heart in America, no matter what the racial derivation or the local environment, and one of the things that stirs every American is the love of individual liberty. We do not stand for occupations. We do not stand for material interests. We do not stand for any narrow conception even of political institutions; but we do stand for this, that we are banded together in America to see to it that no man shall serve any master who is not of his own choosing. And we have been very liberal and generous about this idea. We have seen great peoples, for the most part not of the same blood with ourselves, to the south of us build up politics in which this same idea pulsed and was regnant, this idea of free institutions and individual liberty, and when we have seen hands reached across the water from older political polities to interfere with the development of free institutions on the Western Hemisphere we have said: "No; we are the champions of the freedom of popular sovereignty wherever it displays or exercises itself throughout both Americas." We are the champions of a particular sort of freedom, the sort of freedom which is the only foundation and guarantee of peace.

Peace lies in the hearts of great industrial and agricultural populations, and we have arranged a government on this side of the water by which their preferences and their predilections and their interests are the mainsprings of government itself. And so when we prepare for national defense we prepare for national political integrity; we prepare to take care of the great ideals which gave birth to this Government; we are going back in spirit and in energy to those great first generations in America, when men banded themselves together, though they were but a handful upon a single coast of the Atlantic, to set up in the world the standards which have ever since floated everywhere that Americans asserted the power of their Government. As I came along the line of the railway to-day, I was touched to observe that everywhere, upon every railway station, upon every house, where a flag could be procured, some temporary standard had been raised from which there floated the stars and stripes. They seemed to have divined the errand upon which I had come, to remind you that we must subordinate every individual interest and every local interest to assert once more, if it should be necessary to assert them, the great principles for which that flag stands.

Do not deceive yourselves, ladies and gentlemen, as to where the colors of that flag came from. Those lines of red are lines of blood, nobly and unselfishly shed by men who loved the liberty of their fellow-men more than they loved their own lives and fortunes. God forbid that we should have to use the blood of America to freshen the color of that flag; but if it should ever be necessary again to assert the majesty and integrity of those ancient and honorable principles, that flag will be colored once more, and in being colored will be glorified and purified.

The Submarine Question

[Address delivered at a joint session of the two Houses of Congress, April 19, 1916.]

Gentlemen of the Congress:

A situation has arisen in the foreign relations of the country of which it is my plain duty to inform you very frankly.

It will be recalled that in February, 1915, the Imperial German Government announced its intention to treat the waters surrounding Great Britain and Ireland as embraced within the seat of war and to destroy all merchant ships owned by its enemies that might be found within any part of that portion of the high seas, and that it warned all vessels, of neutral as well as of belligerent ownership, to keep out of the waters it had thus proscribed or else enter them at their peril. The Government of the United States earnestly protested. It took the position that such a policy could not be pursued without the practical certainty of gross and palpable violations of the law of nations, particularly if submarine craft were to be employed as its instruments, inasmuch as the rules prescribed by that law, rules founded upon principles of humanity and established for the protection of the lives of non-combatants at sea, could not in the nature of the case be observed by such vessels. It based its protest on the ground that persons of neutral nationality and vessels of neutral ownership would be exposed to extreme and intolerable risks, and that no right to close any part of the high seas against their use or to expose them to such risks could lawfully be asserted by any belligerent government. The law of nations in these matters, upon which the Government of the United States based its protest, is not of recent origin or founded upon merely arbitrary principles set up by convention. It is based, on the contrary, upon manifest and imperative principles of humanity and has long been established with the approval and by the express assent of all civilized nations.

Notwithstanding the earnest protest of our Government, the Imperial German Government at once proceeded to carry out the policy it had announced. It expressed the hope that the dangers involved, at any rate the dangers to neutral vessels, would be reduced to a minimum by the instructions which it had issued to its submarine commanders, and assured the Government of the United States that it would take every possible precaution both to respect the rights of neutrals and to safeguard the lives of non-combatants.

What has actually happened in the year which has since elapsed has shown that those hopes were not justified, those assurances insusceptible of being fulfilled. In pursuance of the policy of submarine warfare against the commerce of its adversaries, thus announced and entered upon by the Imperial German Government in despite of the solemn protest of this Government, the commanders of German undersea vessels have attacked merchant ships with greater and greater activity, not only upon the high seas surrounding Great Britain and Ireland but wherever they could encounter them, in a way that has grown more and more ruthless, more and more indiscriminate as the months have gone by, less and less observant of restraints of any kind; and have delivered their attacks without compunction against vessels of every nationality and bound upon every sort of errand. Vessels of neutral ownership, even vessels of neutral ownership bound from neutral port to neutral port, have been destroyed along with vessels of belligerent ownership in constantly increasing numbers. Sometimes the merchantman attacked has been warned and summoned to surrender before being fired on or torpedoed; sometimes passengers or crews have been vouchsafed the poor security of being allowed to take to the ship's boats before she was sent to the bottom. But again and again no warning has been given, no escape even to the ship's boats allowed to those on board. What this Government foresaw must happen has happened. Tragedy has followed tragedy on the seas in such fashion, with such attendant circumstances, as to make it grossly evident that warfare of such a sort, if warfare it be, cannot be carried on without the most palpable violation of the dictates alike of right and of humanity. Whatever the disposition and intention of the Imperial German Government, it has manifestly proved impossible for it to keep such methods of attack upon the commerce of its enemies within the bounds set by either the reason or the heart of mankind.

In February of the present year the Imperial German Government informed this Government and the other neutral governments of the world that it had reason to believe that the Government of Great Britain had armed all merchant vessels of British ownership and had given them secret orders to attack any submarine of the enemy they might encounter upon the seas, and that the Imperial German Government felt justified in the circumstances in treating all armed merchantmen of belligerent ownership as auxiliary vessels of war, which it would have the right to destroy without warning. The law of nations has long recognized the right of merchantmen to carry arms for protection and to use them to repel attack, though to use them, in such circumstances, at their own risk; but the Imperial German Government claimed the right to set these understandings aside in circumstances which it deemed extraordinary. Even the terms in which it announced its purpose thus still further to relax the restraints it had previously professed its willingness and desire to put upon the operations of its submarines carried the plain implication that at least vessels which were not armed would still be exempt from destruction without warning and that personal safety would be accorded their passengers and crews; but even that limitation, if it was ever practicable to observe it, has in fact constituted no check at all upon the destruction of ships of every sort.

Again and again the Imperial German Government has given this Government its solemn assurances that at least passenger ships would not be thus dealt with, and yet it has again and again permitted its undersea commanders to disregard those assurances with entire impunity. Great liners like the *Lusitania* and the *Arabic* and mere ferryboats like the *Sussex* have been attacked without a moment's warning, sometimes before they had even become aware that they were in the presence of an armed vessel of the enemy, and the lives of non-combatants, passengers and crew, have been sacrificed wholesale, in a manner which the Government of the United States cannot but regard as wanton and without the slightest color of justification. No limit of any kind has in fact been set to the indiscriminate pursuit and destruction of merchantmen of all kinds and nationalities within the waters, constantly extending in area, where these operations have been carried on; and the roll of Americans who have lost their lives on ships thus attacked and destroyed has grown month by month until the ominous toll has mounted into the hundreds.

One of the latest and most shocking instances of this method of warfare was that of the destruction of the French cross-Channel steamer *Sussex*. It must stand forth, as the sinking of the steamer *Lusitania* did, as so singularly tragical and unjustifiable as to constitute a truly terrible example of the inhumanity of submarine warfare as the commanders of German vessels have for the past twelvemonth been conducting it. If this instance stood alone, some explanation, some disavowal by the German Government, some evidence of criminal mistake or wilful disobedience on the part of the commander of the vessel that fired the torpedo might be sought or entertained; but unhappily it does not stand alone. Recent events make the conclusion inevitable that it is only one instance, even though it be one of the most extreme and distressing instances, of the spirit and method of warfare which the Imperial German Government has mistakenly adopted, and which from the first exposed that Government to the reproach of thrusting all neutral rights aside in pursuit of its immediate objects.

The Government of the United States has been very patient. At every stage of this distressing experience of tragedy after tragedy in which its own citizens were involved it has sought to be restrained from any extreme course of action or of protest by a thoughtful consideration of the extraordinary circumstances of this unprecedented war, and actuated in all that it said or did by the sentiments of genuine friendship which the people of the United States have always entertained and continue to entertain towards the German nation. It has of course accepted the successive explanations and assurances of the Imperial German Government as given in entire sincerity and good faith, and has hoped, even against hope, that it would prove to be possible for the German Government so to order and control the acts of its naval commanders as to square its policy with the principles of humanity as embodied in the law of nations. It has been willing to wait until the significance of the facts became absolutely unmistakable and susceptible of but one interpretation.

That point has now unhappily been reached. The facts are susceptible of but one interpretation. The Imperial German Government has been unable to put any limits or restraints upon its warfare against either freight or passenger ships. It has therefore become painfully evident that the position which this Government took at the very outset is inevitable, namely, that the use of submarines for the destruction of an enemy's commerce is of necessity, because of the very character of the vessels employed and the very methods of attack which their employment of course involves, incompatible with the principles of humanity, the long established and incontrovertible rights of neutrals, and the sacred immunities of non-combatants.

I have deemed it my duty, therefore, to say to the Imperial German Government that if it is still its purpose to prosecute relentless and indiscriminate warfare against vessels of commerce by the use of submarines, notwithstanding the now demonstrated impossibility of conducting that warfare in accordance with what the Government of the United States must consider the sacred and indisputable rules of international law and the universally recognized dictates of humanity, the Government of the United States is at last forced to the conclusion that there is but one course it can pursue; and that unless the Imperial German Government should now immediately declare and effect an abandonment of its present methods of warfare against passenger and freight carrying vessels this Government can have no choice but to sever diplomatic relations with the Government of the German Empire altogether.

This decision I have arrived at with the keenest regret; the possibility of the action contemplated I am sure all thoughtful Americans will look forward to with unaffected reluctance. But we cannot forget that we are in some sort and by the force of circumstances the responsible spokesmen of the rights of humanity, and that we cannot remain silent while those rights seem in process of being swept utterly away in the maelstrom of this terrible war. We owe it to a due regard for our own rights as a nation, to our sense of duty as a representative of the rights of neutrals the world over, and to a just conception of the rights of mankind to take this stand now with the utmost solemnity and firmness.

I have taken it, and taken it in the confidence that it will meet with your approval and support. All sober-minded men must unite in hoping that the Imperial German Government, which has in other circumstances stood as the champion of all that we are now contending for in the interest of humanity, may recognize the justice of our demands and meet them in the spirit in which they are made.

American Principles

[Address delivered at the First Annual Assemblage of the League to Enforce Peace, May 27, 1916.]

When the invitation to be here to-night came to me, I was glad to accept it, —not because it offered me an opportunity to discuss the program of the League, —that you will, I am sure, not expect of me, —but because the desire of the whole world now turns eagerly, more and more eagerly, towards the hope of peace, and there is just reason why we should take our part in counsel upon this great theme. It is right that I, as spokesman of our Government, should attempt to give expression to what I believe to be the thought and purpose of the people of the United States in this vital matter.

This great war that broke so suddenly upon the world two years ago, and which has swept within its flame so great a part of the civilized world, has affected us very profoundly, and we are not only at liberty, it is perhaps our duty, to speak very frankly of it and of the great interests of civilization which it affects.

With its causes and its objects we are not concerned. The obscure fountains from which its stupendous flood has burst forth we are not interested to search for or explore. But so great a flood, spread far and wide to every quarter of the globe, has of necessity engulfed many a fair province of right that lies very near to us. Our own rights as a Nation, the liberties, the privileges, and the property of our people have been profoundly affected. We are not mere disconnected lookers-on. The longer the war lasts, the more deeply do we become concerned that it should be brought to an end and the world be permitted to resume its normal life and course again. And when it does come to an end we shall be as much concerned as the nations at war to see peace assume an aspect of permanence, give promise of days from which the anxiety of uncertainty shall be lifted, bring some assurance that peace and war shall always hereafter be reckoned part of the common interest of mankind. We are participants, whether we would or not, in the life of the world. The interests of all nations are our own also. We are partners with the rest. What affects mankind is inevitably our affair as well as the affair of the nations of Europe and of Asia.

One observation on the causes of the present war we are at liberty to make, and to make it may throw some light forward upon the future, as well as backward upon the past. It is plain that this war could have come only as it did, suddenly and out of secret counsels, without warning to the world, without discussion, without any of the deliberate movements of counsel with which it would seem natural to approach so stupendous a contest. It is probable that if it had been foreseen just what would happen, just what alliances would be formed, just what forces arrayed against one another, those who brought the great contest on would have been glad to substitute conference for force. If we ourselves had been afforded some opportunity to apprise the belligerents of the attitude which it would be our duty to take, of the policies and practices against which we would feel bound to use all our moral and economic strength, and in certain circumstances even our physical strength also, our own contribution to the counsel which might have averted the struggle would have been considered worth weighing and regarding.

And the lesson which the shock of being taken by surprise in a matter so deeply vital to all the nations of the world has made poignantly clear is, that the peace of the world must henceforth depend upon a new and more wholesome diplomacy. Only when the great nations of the world have reached some sort of agreement as to what they hold to be fundamental to their common interest, and as to some feasible method of acting in concert when any nation or group of nations seeks to disturb those fundamental things, can we feel that civilization is at last in a way of justifying its existence and claiming to be finally established. It is clear that nations must in the future be governed by the same high code of honor that we demand of individuals.

We must, indeed, in the very same breath with which we avow this conviction admit that we have ourselves upon occasion in the past been offenders against the law of diplomacy which we thus forecast; but our conviction is not the less clear, but rather the more clear, on that account. If this war has accomplished nothing else for the benefit of the world, it has at least disclosed a great moral necessity and set forward the thinking of the statesmen of the world by a whole age. Repeated utterances of the leading statesmen of most of the great nations now engaged in war have made it plain that their thought has come to this, that the principle of public right must henceforth take precedence over the individual interests of particular nations, and that the nations of the world must in some way band themselves together to see that that right prevails as against any sort of selfish aggression; that henceforth alliance must not be set up against alliance, understanding against understanding, but that there must be a common agreement for a common object, and that at the heart of that common object must lie the inviolable rights of peoples and of mankind. The nations of the world have become each other's neighbors. It is to their interest that they should understand each other. In order that they may understand each other, it is imperative that they should agree to coöperate in a common cause, and that they should so act that the guiding principle of that common cause shall be even-handed and impartial justice.

This is undoubtedly the thought of America. This is what we ourselves will say when there comes proper occasion to say it. In the dealings of nations with one another arbitrary force must be rejected and we must move forward to the thought of the modern world, the thought of which peace is the very atmosphere. That thought constitutes a chief part of the passionate conviction of America.

We believe these fundamental things: First, that every people has a right to choose the sovereignty under which they shall live. Like other nations, we have ourselves no doubt once and again offended against that principle when for a little while controlled by selfish passion, as our franker historians have been honorable enough to admit; but it has become more and more our rule of life and action. Second, that the small states of the world have a right to enjoy the same respect for their sovereignty and for their territorial integrity that great and powerful nations expect and insist upon. And, third, that the world has a right to be free from every disturbance of its peace that has its origin in aggression and disregard of the rights of peoples and nations.

So sincerely do we believe in these things that I am sure that I speak the mind and wish of the people of America when I say that the United States is willing to become a partner in any feasible association of nations formed in order to realize these objects and make them secure against violation.

There is nothing that the United States wants for itself that any other nation has. We are willing, on the contrary, to limit ourselves along with them to a prescribed course of duty and respect for the rights of others which will check any selfish passion of our own, as it will check any aggressive impulse of theirs.

If it should ever be our privilege to suggest or initiate a movement for peace among the nations now at war, I am sure that the people of the United States would wish their Government to move along these lines: First, such a settlement with regard to their own immediate interests as the belligerents may agree upon. We have nothing material of any kind to ask for ourselves, and are quite aware that we are in no sense or degree parties to the present quarrel. Our interest is only in peace and its future guarantees. Second, an universal association of the nations to maintain the inviolate security of the highway of the seas for the common and unhindered use of all the nations of the world, and to prevent any war begun either contrary to treaty covenants or without warning and full submission of the causes to the opinion of the world, —a virtual guarantee of territorial integrity and political independence.

But I did not come here, let me repeat, to discuss a program. I came only to avow a creed and give expression to the confidence I feel that the world is even now upon the eve of a great consummation, when some common force will be brought into existence which shall safeguard right as the first and most fundamental interest of all peoples and all governments, when coercion shall be summoned not to the service of political ambition or selfish hostility, but to the service of a common order, a common justice, and a common peace. God grant that the dawn of that day of frank dealing and of settled peace, concord, and coöperation may be near at hand!

The Demands of Railway Employees

[Address delivered at a joint session of the two Houses of Congress, August 29, 1916.]

Gentlemen of the Congress:

I have come to you to seek your assistance in dealing with a very grave situation which has arisen out of the demand of the employees of the railroads engaged in freight train service that they be granted an eight-hour working day, safeguarded by payment for an hour and a half of service for every hour of work beyond the eight.

The matter has been agitated for more than a year. The public has been made familiar with the demands of the men and the arguments urged in favor of them, and even more familiar with the objections of the railroads and their counter demand that certain privileges now enjoyed by their men and certain bases of payment worked out through many years of contest be reconsidered, especially in their relation to the adoption of an eight-hour day. The matter came some three weeks ago to a final issue and resulted in a complete deadlock between the parties. The means provided by law for the mediation of the controversy failed and the means of arbitration for which the law provides were rejected. The representatives of the railway executives proposed that the demands of the men be submitted in their entirety to arbitration, along with certain questions of readjustment as to pay and conditions of employment which seemed to them to be either closely associated with the demands or to call for reconsideration on their own merits; the men absolutely declined arbitration, especially if any of their established privileges were by that means to be drawn again in question. The law in the matter put no compulsion upon them. The four hundred thousand men from whom the demands proceeded had voted to strike if their demands were refused; the strike was imminent; it has since been set for the fourth of September next. It affects the men who man the freight trains on practically every railway in the country. The freight service throughout the United States must stand still until their places are filled, if, indeed, it should prove possible to fill them at all. Cities will be cut off from their food supplies, the whole commerce of the nation will be paralyzed, men of every sort and occupation will be thrown out of employment, countless thousands will in all likelihood be brought, it may be, to the very point of starvation, and a tragical national calamity brought on, to be added to the other distresses of the time, because no basis of accommodation or settlement has been found.

Just so soon as it became evident that mediation under the existing law had failed and that arbitration had been rendered impossible by the attitude of the men, I considered it my duty to confer with the representatives of both the railways and the brotherhoods, and myself offer mediation, not as an arbitrator, but merely as spokesman of the nation, in the interest of justice, indeed, and as a friend of both parties, but not as judge, only as the representative of one hundred millions of men, women, and children who would pay the price, the incalculable price, of loss and suffering should these few men insist upon approaching and concluding the matters in controversy between them merely as employers and employees, rather than as patriotic citizens of the United States looking before and after and accepting the larger responsibility which the public would put upon them.

It seemed to me, in considering the subject-matter of the controversy, that the whole spirit of the time and the preponderant evidence of recent economic experience spoke for the eight-hour day. It has been adjudged by the thought and experience of recent years a thing upon which society is justified in insisting as in the interest of health, efficiency, contentment, and a general increase of economic vigor. The whole presumption of modern experience would, it seemed to me, be in its favor, whether there was arbitration or not, and the debatable points to settle were those which arose out of the acceptance of the eight-hour day rather than those which affected its establishment. I, therefore, proposed that the eight-hour day be adopted by the railway managements and put into practice for the present as a substitute for the existing ten-hour basis of pay and service; that I should appoint, with the permission of the Congress, a small commission to observe the results of the change, carefully studying the figures of the altered operating costs, not only, but also the conditions of labor under which the men worked and the operation of their existing agreements with the railroads, with instructions to report the facts as they found them to the Congress at the earliest possible day, but without recommendation; and that, after the facts had been thus disclosed, an adjustment should in some orderly manner be sought of all the matters now left unadjusted between the railroad managers and the men.

These proposals were exactly in line, it is interesting to note, with the position taken by the Supreme Court of the United States when appealed to to protect certain litigants from the financial losses which they confidently expected if they should submit to the regulation of their charges and of their methods of service by public legislation. The Court has held that it would not undertake to form a judgment upon forecasts, but could base its action only upon actual experience; that it must be supplied with facts, not with calculations and opinions, however scientifically attempted. To undertake to arbitrate the question of the adoption of an eight-hour day in the light of results merely estimated and predicted would be to undertake an enterprise of conjecture. No wise man could undertake it, or, if he did undertake it, could feel assured of his conclusions.

I unhesitatingly offered the friendly services of the administration to the railway managers to see to it that justice was done the railroads in the outcome. I felt warranted in assuring them that no obstacle of law would be suffered to stand in the way of their increasing their revenues to meet the expenses resulting from the change so far as the development of their business and of their administrative efficiency did not prove adequate to meet them. The public and the representatives of the public, I felt justified in assuring them, were disposed to nothing but justice in such cases and were willing to serve those who served them.

The representatives of the brotherhoods accepted the plan; but the representatives of the railroads declined to accept it. In the face of what I cannot but regard as the practical certainty that they will be ultimately obliged to accept the eight-hour day by the concerted action of organized labor, backed by the favorable judgment of society, the representatives of the railway management have felt justified in declining a peaceful settlement which would engage all the forces of justice, public and private, on their side to take care of the event. They fear the hostile influence of shippers, who would be opposed to an increase of freight rates (for which, however, of course, the public itself would pay); they apparently feel no confidence that the Interstate Commerce Commission could withstand the objections that would be made. They do not care to rely upon the friendly assurances of the Congress or the President. They have thought it best that they should be forced to yield, if they must yield, not by counsel, but by the suffering of the country. While my conferences with them were in progress, and when to all outward appearance those conferences had come to a standstill, the representatives of the brotherhoods suddenly acted and set the strike for the fourth of September.

The railway managers based their decision to reject my counsel in this matter upon their conviction that they must at any cost to themselves or to the country stand firm for the principle of arbitration which the men had rejected. I based my counsel upon the indisputable fact that there was no means of obtaining arbitration. The law supplied none; earnest efforts at mediation had failed to influence the men in the least. To stand firm for the principle of arbitration and yet not get arbitration seemed to me futile, and something more than futile, because it involved incalculable distress to the country and consequences in some respects worse than those of war, and that in the midst of peace.

I yield to no man in firm adherence, alike of conviction and of purpose, to the principle of arbitration in industrial disputes; but matters have come to a sudden crisis in this particular dispute and the country had been caught unprovided with any practicable means of enforcing that conviction in practice (by whose fault we will not now stop to inquire). A situation had to be met whose elements and fixed conditions were indisputable. The practical and patriotic course to pursue, as it seemed to me, was to secure immediate peace by conceding the one thing in the demands of the men which society itself and any arbitrators who represented public sentiment were most likely to approve, and immediately lay the foundations for securing arbitration with regard to everything else involved. The event has confirmed that judgment.

I was seeking to compose the present in order to safeguard the future; for I wished an atmosphere of peace and friendly coöperation in which to take counsel with the representatives of the nation with regard to the best means for providing, so far as it might prove possible to provide, against the recurrence of such unhappy situations in the future,—the best and most practicable means of securing calm and fair arbitration of all industrial disputes in the days to come. This is assuredly the best way of vindicating a principle, namely, having failed to make certain of its observance in the present, to make certain of its observance in the future.

But I could only propose. I could not govern the will of others who took an entirely different view of the circumstances of the case, who even refused to admit the circumstances to be what they have turned out to be.

Having failed to bring the parties to this critical controversy to an accommodation, therefore, I turn to you, deeming it clearly our duty as public servants to leave nothing undone that we can do to safeguard the life and interests of the nation. In the spirit of such a purpose, I earnestly recommend the following legislation:

First, immediate provision for the enlargement and administrative reorganization of the Interstate Commerce Commission along the lines embodied in the bill recently passed by the House of Representatives and now awaiting action by the Senate; in order that the Commission may be enabled to deal with the many great and various duties now devolving upon it with a promptness and thoroughness which are with its present constitution and means of action practically impossible.

Second, the establishment of an eight-hour day as the legal basis alike of work and of wages in the employment of all railway employees who are actually engaged in the work of operating trains in interstate transportation.

Third, the authorization of the appointment by the President of a small body of men to observe the actual results in experience of the adoption of the eight-hour day in railway transportation alike for the men and for the railroads; its effects in the matter of operating costs, in the application of the existing practices and agreements to the new conditions, and in all other practical aspects, with the provision that the investigators shall report their conclusions to the Congress at the earliest possible date, but without recommendation as to legislative action; in order that the public may learn from an unprejudiced source just what actual developments have ensued.

Fourth, explicit approval by the Congress of the consideration by the Interstate Commerce Commission of an increase of freight rates to meet such additional expenditures by the railroads as may have been rendered necessary by the adoption of the eight-hour day and which have not been offset by administrative readjustments and economies, should the facts disclosed justify the increase.

Fifth, an amendment of the existing federal statute which provides for the mediation, conciliation, and arbitration of such controversies as the present by adding to it a provision that in case the methods of accommodation now provided for should fail, a full public investigation of the merits of every such dispute shall be instituted and completed before a strike or lockout may lawfully be attempted.

And, sixth, the lodgment in the hands of the Executive of the power, in case of military necessity, to take control of such portions and such rolling stock of the railways of the country as may be required for military use and to operate them for military purposes, with authority to draft into the military service of the United States such train crews and administrative officials as the circumstances require for their safe and efficient use.

This last suggestion I make because we cannot in any circumstances suffer the nation to be hampered in the essential matter of national defense. At the present moment circumstances render this duty particularly obvious. Almost the entire military force of the nation is stationed upon the Mexican border to guard our territory against hostile raids. It must be supplied, and steadily supplied, with whatever it needs for its maintenance and efficiency. If it should be necessary for purposes of national defense to transfer any portion of it upon short notice to some other part of the country, for reasons now unforeseen, ample means of transportation must be available, and available without delay. The power conferred in this matter should be carefully and explicitly limited to cases of military necessity, but in all such cases it should be clear and ample.

There is one other thing we should do if we are true champions of arbitration. We should make all arbitral awards judgments by record of a court of law in order that their interpretation and enforcement may lie, not with one of the parties to the arbitration, but with an impartial and authoritative tribunal.

These things I urge upon you, not in haste or merely as a means of meeting a present emergency, but as permanent and necessary additions to the law of the land, suggested, indeed, by circumstances we had hoped never to see, but imperative as well as just, if such emergencies are to be prevented in the future. I feel that no extended argument is needed to commend them to your favorable consideration. They demonstrate themselves. The time and the occasion only give emphasis to their importance. We need them now and we shall continue to need them.

Speech of Acceptance

[On being offered the nomination for President by the Democratic Party. Delivered at Shadow Lawn, Sea Girt, N.J., Saturday, September 2, 1916.]

Senator James, Gentlemen of the Notification Committee, Fellow-Citizens:

I cannot accept the leadership and responsibility which the National Democratic Convention has again, in such generous fashion, asked me to accept without first expressing my profound gratitude to the party for the trust it reposes in me after four years of fiery trial in the midst of affairs of unprecedented difficulty, and the keen sense of added responsibility with which this honor fills (I had almost said burdens) me as I think of the great issues of national life and policy involved in the present and immediate future conduct of our Government. I shall seek, as I have always sought, to justify the extraordinary confidence thus reposed in me by striving to purge my heart and purpose of every personal and of every misleading party motive and devoting every energy I have to the service of the nation as a whole, praying that I may continue to have the counsel and support of all forward-looking men at every turn of the difficult business.

For I do not doubt that the people of the United States will wish the Democratic Party to continue in control of the Government. They are not in the habit of rejecting those who have actually served them for those who are making doubtful and conjectural promises of service. Least of all are they likely to substitute those who promised to render them particular services and proved false to that promise for those who have actually rendered those very services.

Boasting is always an empty business, which pleases nobody but the boaster, and I have no disposition to boast of what the Democratic Party has accomplished. It has merely done its duty. It has merely fulfilled its explicit promises. But there can be no violation of good taste in calling attention to the manner in which those promises have been carried out or in adverting to the interesting fact that many of the things accomplished were what the opposition party had again and again promised to do but had left undone. Indeed that is manifestly part of the business of this year of reckoning and assessment. There is no means of judging the future except by assessing the past. Constructive action must be weighed against destructive comment and reaction. The Democrats either have or have not understood the varied interests of the country. The test is contained in the record.

What is that record? What were the Democrats called into power to do? What things had long waited to be done, and how did the Democrats do them? It is a record of extraordinary length and variety, rich in elements of many kinds, but consistent in principle throughout and susceptible of brief recital.

The Republican Party was put out of power because of failure, practical failure and moral failure; because it had served special interests and not the country at large; because, under the leadership of its preferred and established guides, of those who still make its choices, it had lost touch with the thoughts and the needs of the nation and was living in a past age and under a fixed illusion, the illusion of greatness. It had framed tariff laws based upon a fear of foreign trade, a fundamental doubt as to American skill, enterprise, and capacity, and a very tender regard for the profitable privileges of those who had gained control of domestic markets and domestic credits; and yet had enacted anti-trust laws which hampered the very things they meant to foster, which were stiff and inelastic, and in part unintelligible. It had permitted the country throughout the long period of its control to stagger from one financial crisis to another under the operation of a national banking law of its own framing which made stringency and panic certain and the control of the larger business operations of the country by the bankers of a few reserve centers inevitable; had made as if it meant to reform the law but had faint-heartedly failed in the attempt, because it could not bring itself to do the one thing necessary to make the reform genuine and effectual, namely, break up the control of small groups of bankers.

It had been oblivious, or indifferent, to the fact that the farmers, upon whom the country depends for its food and in the last analysis for its prosperity, were without standing in the matter of commercial credit, without the protection of standards in their market transactions, and without systematic knowledge of the markets themselves; that the laborers of the country, the great army of men who man the industries it was professing to father and promote, carried their labor as a mere commodity to market, were subject to restraint by novel and drastic process in the courts, were without assurance of compensation for industrial accidents, without federal assistance in accommodating labor disputes, and without national aid or advice in finding the places and the industries in which their labor was most needed. The country had no national system of road construction and development. Little intelligent attention was paid to the army, and not enough to the navy. The other republics of America distrusted us, because they found that we thought first of the profits of American investors and only as an afterthought of impartial justice and helpful friendship. Its policy was provincial in all things; its purposes were out of harmony with the temper and purpose of the people and the timely development of the nation's interests.

So things stood when the Democratic Party came into power. How do they stand now? Alike in the domestic field and in the wide field of the commerce of the world, American business and life and industry have been set free to move as they never moved before.

The tariff has been revised, not on the principle of repelling foreign trade, but upon the principle of encouraging it, upon something like a footing of equality with our own in respect of the terms of competition, and a Tariff Board has been created whose function it will be to keep the relations of American with foreign business and industry under constant observation, for the guidance alike of our business men and of our Congress. American energies are now directed towards the markets of the world.

The laws against trusts have been clarified by definition, with a view to making it plain that they were not directed against big business but only against unfair business and the pretense of competition where there was none; and a Trade Commission has been created with powers of guidance and accommodation which have relieved business men of unfounded fears and set them upon the road of hopeful and confident enterprise.

By the Federal Reserve Act the supply of currency at the disposal of active business has been rendered elastic, taking its volume, not from a fixed body of investment securities, but from the liquid assets of daily trade; and these assets are assessed and accepted, not by distant groups of bankers in control of unavailable reserves, but by bankers at the many centers of local exchange who are in touch with local conditions everywhere.

Effective measures have been taken for the re-creation of an American merchant marine and the revival of the American carrying trade indispensable to our emancipation from the control which foreigners have so long exercised over the opportunities, the routes, and the methods of our commerce with other countries.

The Interstate Commerce Commission is about to be reorganized to enable it to perform its great and important functions more promptly and more efficiently. We have created, extended and improved the service of the parcels post.

So much we have done for business. What other party has understood the task so well or executed it so intelligently and energetically? What other party has attempted it at all? The Republican leaders, apparently, know of no means of assisting business but "protection." How to stimulate it and put it upon a new footing of energy and enterprise they have not suggested.

For the farmers of the country we have virtually created commercial credit, by means of the Federal Reserve Act and the Rural Credits Act. They now have the standing of other business men in the money market. We have successfully regulated speculation in "futures" and established standards in the marketing of grains. By an intelligent Warehouse Act we have assisted to make the standard crops available as never before both for systematic marketing and as a security for loans from the banks. We have greatly added to the work of neighborhood demonstration on the farm itself of improved methods of cultivation, and, through the intelligent extension of the functions of the Department of Agriculture, have made it possible for the farmer to learn systematically where his best markets are and how to get at them.

The workingmen of America have been given a veritable emancipation, by the legal recognition of a man's labor as part of his life, and not a mere marketable commodity; by exempting labor organizations from processes of the courts which treated their members like fractional parts of mobs and not like accessible and responsible individuals; by releasing our seamen from involuntary servitude; by making adequate provision for compensation for industrial accidents; by providing suitable machinery for mediation and conciliation in industrial disputes; and by putting the Federal Department of Labor at the disposal of the workingman when in search of work.

We have effected the emancipation of the children of the country by releasing them from hurtful labor. We have instituted a system of national aid in the building of highroads such as the country has been feeling after for a century. We have sought to equalize taxation by means of an equitable income tax. We have taken the steps that ought to have been taken at the outset to open up the resources of Alaska. We have provided for national defense upon a scale never before seriously proposed upon the responsibility of an entire political party. We have driven the tariff lobby from cover and obliged it to substitute solid argument for private influence.

This extraordinary recital must sound like a platform, a list of sanguine promises; but it is not. It is a record of promises made four years ago and now actually redeemed in constructive legislation.

These things must profoundly disturb the thoughts and confound the plans of those who have made themselves believe that the Democratic Party neither understood nor was ready to assist the business of the country in the great enterprises which it is its evident and inevitable destiny to undertake and carry through. The breaking up of the lobby must especially disconcert them: for it was through the lobby that they sought and were sure they had found the heart of things. The game of privilege can be played successfully by no other means.

This record must equally astonish those who feared that the Democratic Party had not opened its heart to comprehend the demands of social justice. We have in four years come very near to carrying out the platform of the Progressive Party as well as our own; for we also are progressives.

There is one circumstance connected with this program which ought to be very plainly stated. It was resisted at every step by the interests which the Republican Party had catered to and fostered at the expense of the country, and these same interests are now earnestly praying for a reaction which will save their privileges, —for the restoration of their sworn friends to power before it is too late to recover what they have lost. They fought with particular desperation and infinite resourcefulness the reform of the banking and currency system, knowing that to be the citadel of their control; and most anxiously are they hoping and planning for the amendment of the Federal Reserve Act by the concentration of control in a single bank which the old familiar group of bankers can keep under their eye and direction. But while the "big men" who used to write the tariffs and command the assistance of the Treasury have been hostile, —all but a few with vision, —the average business man knows that he has been delivered, and that the fear that was once every day in his heart, that the men who controlled credit and directed enterprise from the committee rooms of Congress would crush him, is there no more, and will not return, —unless the party that consulted only the "big men" should return to power, —the party of masterly inactivity and cunning resourcefulness in standing pat to resist change.

The Republican Party is just the party that *cannot* meet the new conditions of a new age. It does not know the way and it does not wish new conditions. It tried to break away from the old leaders and could not. They still select its candidates and dictate its policy, still resist change, still hanker after the old conditions, still know no methods of encouraging business but the old methods. When it changes its leaders and its purposes and brings its ideas up to date it will have the right to ask the American people to give it power again; but not until then. A new age, an age of revolutionary change, needs new purposes and new ideas.

In foreign affairs we have been guided by principles clearly conceived and consistently lived up to. Perhaps they have not been fully comprehended because they have hitherto governed international affairs only in theory, not in practice. They are simple, obvious, easily stated, and fundamental to American ideals.

We have been neutral not only because it was the fixed and traditional policy of the United States to stand aloof from the politics of Europe and because we had had no part either of action or of policy in the influences which brought on the present war, but also because it was manifestly our duty to prevent, if it were possible, the indefinite extension of the fires of hate and desolation kindled by that terrible conflict and seek to serve mankind by reserving our strength and our resources for the anxious and difficult days of restoration and healing which must follow, when peace will have to build its house anew.

The rights of our own citizens of course became involved: that was inevitable. Where they did this was our guiding principle: that property rights can be vindicated by claims for damages and no modern nation can decline to arbitrate such claims; but the fundamental rights of humanity cannot be. The loss of life is irreparable. Neither can direct violations of a nation's sovereignty await vindication in suits for damages. The nation that violates these essential rights must expect to be checked and called to account by direct challenge and resistance. It at once makes the quarrel in part our own. These are plain principles and we have never lost sight of them or departed from them, whatever the stress or the perplexity of circumstance or the provocation to hasty resentment. The record is clear and consistent throughout and stands distinct and definite for anyone to judge who wishes to know the truth about it.

The seas were not broad enough to keep the infection of the conflict out of our own politics. The passions and intrigues of certain active groups and combinations of men amongst us who were born under foreign flags injected the poison of disloyalty into our own most critical affairs, laid violent hands upon many of our industries, and subjected us to the shame of divisions of sentiment and purpose in which America was contemned and forgotten. It is part of the business of this year of reckoning and settlement to speak plainly and act with unmistakable purpose in rebuke of these things, in order that they may be forever hereafter impossible. I am the candidate of a party, but I am above all things else an American citizen. I neither seek the favor nor fear the displeasure of that small alien element amongst us which puts loyalty to any foreign power before loyalty to the United States.

While Europe was at war our own continent, one of our own neighbors, was shaken by revolution. In that matter, too, principle was plain and it was imperative that we should live up to it if we were to deserve the trust of any real partisan of the right as free men see it. We have professed to believe, and we do believe, that the people of small and weak states have the right to expect to be dealt with exactly as the people of big and powerful states would be. We have acted upon that principle in dealing with the people of Mexico.

Our recent pursuit of bandits into Mexican territory was no violation of that principle. We ventured to enter Mexican territory only because there were no military forces in Mexico that could protect our border from hostile attack and our own people from violence, and we have committed there no single act of hostility or interference even with the sovereign authority of the Republic of Mexico herself. It was a plain case of the violation of our own sovereignty which could not wait to be vindicated by damages and for which there was no other remedy. The authorities of Mexico were powerless to prevent it.

Many serious wrongs against the property, many irreparable wrongs against the persons of Americans have been committed within the territory of Mexico herself during this confused revolution, wrongs which could not be effectually checked so long as there was no constituted power in Mexico which was in a position to check them. We could not act directly in that matter ourselves without denying Mexicans the right to any revolution at all which disturbed us and making the emancipation of her own people await our own interest and convenience.

For it is their emancipation that they are seeking, —blindly, it may be, and as yet ineffec-tually, but with profound and passionate purpose and within their unquestionable right, apply what true American principle you will, —any principle that an American would publicly avow. The people of Mexico have not been suffered to own their own country or direct their own institutions. Outsiders, men out of other nations and with interests too often alien to their own, have dictated what their privileges and opportunities should be and who should control their land, their lives, and their resources, —some of them Americans, pressing for things they could never have got in their own country. The Mexican people are entitled to attempt their liberty from such influences; and so long as I have anything to do with the action of our great Government I shall do everything in my power to prevent anyone standing in their way. I know that this is hard for some persons to understand; but it is not hard for the plain people of the United States to understand. It is hard doctrine only for those who wish to get something for themselves out of Mexico. There are men, and noble women, too, not a few, of our own people, thank God! whose fortunes are invested in great properties in Mexico who yet see the case with true vision and assess its issues with true American feeling. The rest can be left for the present out of the reckoning until this enslaved people has had its day of struggle towards the light. I have heard no one who was free from such influences propose interference by the United States with the internal affairs of Mexico. Certainly no friend of the Mexican people has proposed it.

The people of the United States are capable of great sympathies and a noble pity in dealing with problems of this kind. As their spokesman and representative, I have tried to act in the spirit they would wish me show. The people of Mexico are striving for the rights that are fundamental to life and happiness, —15,000,000 oppressed men, overburdened women, and pitiful children in virtual bondage in their own home of fertile lands and inexhaustible treasure! Some of the leaders of the revolution may often have been mistaken and violent and selfish, but the revolution itself was inevitable and is right. The unspeakable Huerta betrayed the very comrades he served, traitorously overthrew the government of which he was a trusted part, impudently spoke for the very forces that had driven his people to the rebellion with which he had pretended to sympathize. The men who overcame him and drove him out represent at least the fierce passion of reconstruction which lies at the very heart of liberty; and so long as they represent, however imperfectly, such a struggle for deliverance, I am ready to serve their ends when I can. So long as the power of recognition rests with me the Government of the United States will refuse to extend the hand of welcome to any one who obtains power in a sister republic by treachery and violence. No permanency can be given the affairs of any republic by a title based upon intrigue and assassination. I declared that to be the policy of this Administration within three weeks after I assumed the presidency. I here again vow it. I am more interested in the fortunes of oppressed men and pitiful women and children than in any property rights whatever. Mistakes I have no doubt made in this perplexing business, but not in purpose or object.

More is involved than the immediate destinies of Mexico and the relations of the United States with a distressed and distracted people. All America looks on. Test is now being made of us whether we be sincere lovers of popular liberty or not and are indeed to be trusted to respect national sovereignty among our weaker neighbors. We have undertaken these many years to play big brother to the republics of this hemisphere. This is the day of our test whether we mean, or have ever meant, to play that part for our own benefit wholly or also for theirs. Upon the outcome of that test (its outcome in their minds, not in ours) depends every relationship of the United States with Latin America, whether in politics or in commerce and enterprise. These are great issues and lie at the heart of the gravest tasks of the future, tasks both economic and political and very intimately inwrought with many of the most vital of the new issues of the politics of the world. The republics of America have in the last three years been drawing together in a new spirit of accommodation, mutual understanding, and cordial coöperation. Much of the politics of the world in the years to come will depend upon their relationships with one another. It is a barren and provincial statesmanship that loses sight of such things!

The future, the immediate future, will bring us squarely face to face with many great and exacting problems which will search us through and through whether we be able and ready to play the part in the world that we mean to play. It will not bring us into their presence slowly, gently, with ceremonious introduction, but suddenly and at once, the moment the war in Europe is over. They will be new problems, most of them; many will be old problems in a new setting and with new elements which we have never dealt with or reckoned the force and meaning of before. They will require for their solution new thinking, fresh courage and resourcefulness, and in some matters radical reconsiderations of policy. We must be ready to mobilize our resources alike of brains and of materials.

It is not a future to be afraid of. It is, rather, a future to stimulate and excite us to the display of the best powers that are in us. We may enter it with confidence when we are sure that we understand it, —and we have provided ourselves already with the means of understanding it.

Look first at what it will be necessary that the nations of the world should do to make the days to come tolerable and fit to live and work in; and then look at our part in what is to follow and our own duty of preparation. For we must be prepared both in resources and in policy.

There must be a just and settled peace, and we here in America must contribute the full force of our enthusiasm and of our authority as a nation to the organization of that peace upon world-wide foundations that cannot easily be shaken. No nation should be forced to take sides in any quarrel in which its own honor and integrity and the fortunes of its own people are not involved; but no nation can any longer remain neutral as against any wilful disturbance of the peace of the world. The effects of war can no longer be confined to the areas of battle. No nation stands wholly apart in interest when the life and interests of all nations are thrown into confusion and peril. If hopeful and generous enterprise is to be renewed, if the healing and helpful arts of life are indeed to be revived when peace comes again, a new atmosphere of justice and friendship must be generated by means the world has never tried before. The nations of the world must unite in joint guarantees that whatever is done to disturb the whole world's life must first be tested in the court of the whole world's opinion before it is attempted.

These are the new foundations the world must build for itself, and we must play our part in the reconstruction, generously and without too much thought of our separate interests. We must make ourselves ready to play it intelligently, vigorously, and well.

One of the contributions we must make to the world's peace is this: We must see to it that the people in our insular possessions are treated in their own lands as we would treat them here, and make the rule of the United States mean the same thing everywhere, —the same justice, the same consideration for the essential rights of men.

Besides contributing our ungrudging moral and practical support to the establishment of peace throughout the world we must actively and intelligently prepare ourselves to do our full service in the trade and industry which are to sustain and develop the life of the nations in the days to come.

We have already been provident in this great matter and supplied ourselves with the instrumentalities of prompt adjustment. We have created, in the Federal Trade Commission, a means of inquiry and of accommodation in the field of commerce which ought both to coördinate the enterprises of our traders and manufacturers and to remove the barriers of misunderstanding and of a too technical interpretation of the law. In the new Tariff Commission we have added another instrumentality of observation and adjustment which promises to be immediately serviceable. The Trade Commission substitutes counsel and accommodation for the harsher processes of legal restraint, and the Tariff Commission ought to substitute facts for prejudices and theories. Our exporters have for some time had the advantage of working in the new light thrown upon foreign markets and opportunities of trade by the intelligent inquiries and activities of the Bureau of Foreign and Domestic Commerce which the Democratic Congress so wisely created in 1912. The Tariff Commission completes the machinery by which we shall be enabled to open up our legislative policy to the facts as they develop.

We can no longer indulge our traditional provincialism. We are to play a leading part in the world drama whether we wish it or not. We shall lend, not borrow; act for ourselves, not imitate or follow; organize and initiate, not peep about merely to see where we may get in.

We have already formulated and agreed upon a policy of law which will explicitly remove the ban now supposed to rest upon coöperation amongst our exporters in seeking and securing their proper place in the markets of the world. The field will be free, the instrumentalities at hand. It will only remain for the masters of enterprise amongst us to act in energetic concert, and for the Government of the United States to insist upon the maintenance throughout the world of those conditions of fairness and of even-handed justice in the commercial dealings of the nations with one another upon which, after all, in the last analysis, the peace and ordered life of the world must ultimately depend.

At home also we must see to it that the men who plan and develop and direct our business enterprises shall enjoy definite and settled conditions of law, a policy accommodated to the freest progress. We have set the just and necessary limits. We have put all kinds of unfair competition under the ban and penalty of the law. We have barred monopoly. These fatal and ugly things being excluded, we must now quicken action and facilitate enterprise by every just means within our choice. There will be peace in the business world, and, with peace, revived confidence and life.

We ought both to husband and to develop our natural resources, our mines, our forests, our water power. I wish we could have made more progress than we have made in this vital matter; and I call once more, with the deepest earnestness and solicitude, upon the advocates of a careful and provident conservation, on the one hand, and the advocates of a free and inviting field for private capital, on the other, to get together in a spirit of genuine accommodation and agreement and set this great policy forward at once.

We must hearten and quicken the spirit and efficiency of labor throughout our whole industrial system by everywhere and in all occupations doing justice to the laborer, not only by paying a living wage but also by making all the conditions that surround labor what they ought to be. And we must do more than justice. We must safeguard life and promote health and safety in every occupation in which they are threatened or imperilled. That is more than justice, and better, because it is humanity and economy.

We must coördinate the railway systems of the country for national use, and must facilitate and promote their development with a view to that coördination and to their better adaptation as a whole to the life and trade and defense of the nation. The life and industry of the country can be free and unhampered only if these arteries are open, efficient, and complete.

Thus shall we stand ready to meet the future as circumstance and international policy effect their unfolding, whether the changes come slowly or come fast and without preface.

I have not spoken explicitly, Gentlemen, of the platform adopted at St. Louis; but it has been implicit in all that I have said. I have sought to interpret its spirit and meaning. The people of the United States do not need to be assured now that that platform is a definite pledge, a practical program. We have proved to them that our promises are made to be kept.

We hold very definite ideals. We believe that the energy and initiative of our people have been too narrowly coached and superintended; that they should be set free, as we have set them free, to disperse themselves throughout the nation; that they should not be concentrated in the hands of a few powerful guides and guardians, as our opponents have again and again, in effect if not in purpose, sought to concentrate them. We believe, moreover, —who that looks about him now with comprehending eye can fail to believe? —that the day of Little Americanism, with its narrow horizons, when methods of "protection" and industrial nursing were the chief study of our provincial statesmen, are past and gone and that a day of enterprise has at last dawned for the United States whose field is the wide world.

We hope to see the stimulus of that new day draw all America, the republics of both continents, on to a new life and energy and initiative in the great affairs of peace. We are Americans for Big America, and rejoice to look forward to the days in which America shall strive to stir the world without irritating it or drawing it on to new antagonisms, when the nations with which we deal shall at last come to see upon what deep foundations of humanity and justice our passion for peace rests, and when all mankind shall look upon our great people with a new sentiment of admiration, friendly rivalry and real affection, as upon a people who, though keen to succeed, seeks always to be at once generous and just and to whom humanity is dearer than profit or selfish power.

Upon this record and in the faith of this purpose we go to the country.

Lincoln's Beginnings

[Address delivered September 4, 1916, on the acceptance of a deed of gift to the Nation, by the Lincoln Farm Association, of the Lincoln Birthplace Farm, at Hodgenville, Kentucky.]

No more significant memorial could have been presented to the nation than this. It expresses so much of what is singular and noteworthy in the history of the country; it suggests so many of the things that we prize most highly in our life and in our system of government. How eloquent this little house within this shrine is of the vigor of democracy! There is nowhere in the land any home so remote, so humble, that it may not contain the power of mind and heart and conscience to which nations yield and history submits its processes. Nature pays no tribute to aristocracy, subscribes to no creed of caste, renders fealty to no monarch or master of any name or kind. Genius is no snob. It does not run after titles or seek by preference the high circles of society. It affects humble company as well as great. It pays no special tribute to universities or learned societies or conventional standards of greatness, but serenely chooses its own comrades, its own haunts, its own cradle even, and its own life of adventure and of training. Here is proof of it. This little hut was the cradle of one of the great sons of men, a man of singular, delightful, vital genius who presently emerged upon the great stage of the nation's history, gaunt, shy, ungainly, but dominant and majestic, a natural ruler of men, himself inevitably the central figure of the great plot. No man can explain this, but every man can see how it demonstrates the vigor of democracy, where every door is open, in every hamlet and countryside, in city and wilderness alike, for the ruler to emerge when he will and claim his leadership in the free life. Such are the authentic proofs of the validity and vitality of democracy.

Here, no less, hides the mystery of democracy. Who shall guess this secret of nature and providence and a free polity? Whatever the vigor and vitality of the stock from which he sprang, its mere vigor and soundness do not explain where this man got his great heart that seemed to comprehend all mankind in its catholic and benignant sympathy, the mind that sat enthroned behind those brooding, melancholy eyes, whose vision swept many an horizon which those about him dreamed not of, —that mind that comprehended what it had never seen, and understood the language of affairs with the ready ease of one to the manner born, —or that nature which seemed in its varied richness to be the familiar of men of every way of life. This is the sacred mystery of democracy, that its richest fruits spring up out of soils which no man has prepared and in circumstances amidst which they are the least expected. This is a place alike of mystery and of reassurance.

It is likely that in a society ordered otherwise than our own Lincoln could not have found himself or the path of fame and power upon which he walked serenely to his death. In this place it is right that we should remind ourselves of the solid and striking facts upon which our faith in democracy is founded. Many another man besides Lincoln has served the nation in its highest places of counsel and of action whose origins were as humble as his. Though the greatest example of the universal energy, richness, stimulation, and force of democracy, he is only one example among many. The permeating and all-pervasive virtue of the freedom which challenges us in America to make the most of every gift and power we possess every page of our history serves to emphasize and illustrate. Standing here in this place, it seems almost the whole of the stirring story.

Here Lincoln had his beginnings. Here the end and consummation of that great life seem remote and a bit incredible. And yet there was no break anywhere between beginning and end, no lack of natural sequence anywhere. Nothing really incredible happened. Lincoln was unaffectedly as much at home in the White House as he was here. Do you share with me the feeling, I wonder, that he was permanently at home nowhere? It seems to me that in the case of a man, —I would rather say of a spirit, —like Lincoln the question *where* he was is of little significance, that it is always *what* he was that really arrests our thought and takes hold of our imagination. It is the spirit always that is sovereign. Lincoln, like the rest of us, was put through the discipline of the world, —a very rough and exacting discipline for him, an indispensable discipline for every man who would know what he is about in the midst of the world's affairs; but his spirit got only its schooling there. It did not derive its character or its vision from the experiences which brought it to its full revelation. The test of every American must always be, not where he is, but what he is. That, also, is of the essence of democracy, and is the moral of which this place is most gravely expressive.

We would like to think of men like Lincoln and Washington as typical Americans, but no man can be typical who is so unusual as these great men were. It was typical of American life that it should produce such men with supreme indifference as to the manner in which it produced them, and as readily here in this hut as amidst the little circle of cultivated gentlemen to whom Virginia owed so much in leadership and example. And Lincoln and Washington were typical Americans in the use they made of their genius. But there will be few such men at best, and we will not look into the mystery of how and why they come. We will only keep the door open for them always, and a hearty welcome, —after we have recognized them.

I have read many biographies of Lincoln; I have sought out with the greatest interest the many intimate stories that are told of him, the narratives of nearby friends, the sketches at close quarters, in which those who had the privilege of being associated with him have tried to depict for us the very man himself "in his habit as he lived;" but I have nowhere found a real intimate of Lincoln's. I nowhere get the impression in any narrative or reminiscence that the writer had in fact penetrated to the heart of his mystery, or that any man could penetrate to the heart of it. That brooding spirit had no real familiars. I get the impression that it never spoke out in complete self-revelation, and that it could not reveal itself completely to anyone. It was a very lonely spirit that looked out from underneath those shaggy brows and comprehended men without fully communing with them, as if, in spite of all its genial efforts at comradeship, it dwelt apart, saw its visions of duty where no man looked on. There is a very holy and very terrible isolation for the conscience of every man who seeks to read the destiny in affairs for others as well as for himself, for a nation as well as for individuals. That privacy no man can intrude upon. That lonely search of the spirit for the right perhaps no man can assist. This strange child of the cabin kept company with invisible things, was born into no intimacy but that of its own silently assembling and deploying thoughts.

I have come here to-day, not to utter a eulogy on Lincoln; he stands in need of none, but to endeavor to interpret the meaning of this gift to the nation of the place of his birth and origin. Is not this an altar upon which we may forever keep alive the vestal fire of democracy as upon a shrine at which some of the deepest and most sacred hopes of mankind may from age to age be rekindled? For these hopes must constantly be rekindled, and only those who live can rekindle them. The only stuff that can retain the life-giving heat is the stuff of living hearts. And the hopes of mankind cannot be kept alive by words merely, by constitutions and doctrines of right and codes of liberty. The object of democracy is to transmute these into the life and action of society, the self-denial and self-sacrifice of heroic men and women willing to make their lives an embodiment of right and service and enlightened purpose. The commands of democracy are as imperative as its privileges and opportunities are wide and generous. Its compulsion is upon us. It will be great and lift a great light for the guidance of the nations only if we are great and carry that light high for the guidance of our own feet. We are not worthy to stand here unless we ourselves be in deed and in truth real democrats and servants of mankind, ready to give our very lives for the freedom and justice and spiritual exaltation of the great nation which shelters and nurtures us.

The Triumph of Women's Suffrage

[Address at the Suffrage Convention, Atlantic City, New Jersey, September 8, 1916.]

Madam President, Ladies of the Association:

I have found it a real privilege to be here to-night and to listen to the addresses which you have heard. Though you may not all of you believe it, I would a great deal rather hear somebody else speak than speak myself; but I should feel that I was omitting a duty if I did not address you to-night and say some of the things that have been in my thought as I realized the approach of this evening and the duty that would fall upon me.

The astonishing thing about the movement which you represent is, not that it has grown so slowly, but that it has grown so rapidly. No doubt for those who have been a long time in the struggle, like your honored president, it seems a long and arduous path that has been trodden, but when you think of the cumulating force of this movement in recent decades, you must agree with me that it is one of the most astonishing tides in modern history. Two generations ago, no doubt Madam President will agree with me in saying, it was a handful of women who were fighting this cause. Now it is a great multitude of women who are fighting it.

And there are some interesting historical connections which I would like to attempt to point out to you. One of the most striking facts about the history of the United States is that at the outset it was a lawyers' history. Almost all of the questions to which America addressed itself, say a hundred years ago, were legal questions, were questions of method, not questions of what you were going to do with your Government, but questions of how you were going to constitute your Government, —how you were going to balance the powers of the States and the Federal Government, how you were going to balance the claims of property against the processes of liberty, how you were going to make your governments up so as to balance the parts against each other so that the legislature would check the executive, and the executive the legislature, and the courts both of them put together. The whole conception of government when the United States became a Nation was a mechanical conception of government, and the mechanical conception of government which underlay it was the Newtonian theory of the universe. If you pick up the Federalist, some parts of it read like a treatise on astronomy instead of a treatise on government. They speak of the centrifugal and the centripetal forces, and locate the President somewhere in a rotating system. The whole thing is a calculation of power and an adjustment of parts. There was a time when nobody but a lawyer could know enough to run the Government of the United States, and a distinguished English publicist once remarked, speaking of the complexity of the American Government, that it was no proof of the excellence of the American Constitution that it had been successfully operated, because the Americans could run any constitution. But there have been a great many technical difficulties in running it.

And then something happened. A great question arose in this country which, though complicated with legal elements, was at bottom a human question, and nothing but a question of humanity. That was the slavery question. And is it not significant that it was then, and then for the first time, that women became prominent in politics in America? Not many women; those prominent in that day were so few that you can name them over in a brief catalogue, but, nevertheless, they then began to play a part in writing, not only, but in public speech, which was a very novel part for women to play in America. After the Civil War had settled some of what seemed to be the most difficult legal questions of our system, the life of the Nation began not only to unfold, but to accumulate. Life in the United States was a comparatively simple matter at the time of the Civil War. There was none of that underground struggle which is now so manifest to those who look only a little way beneath the surface. Stories such as Dr. Davis has told to-night were uncommon in those simpler days. The pressure of low wages, the agony of obscure and unremunerated toil, did not exist in America in anything like the same proportions that they exist now. And as our life has unfolded and accumulated, as the contacts of it have become hot, as the populations have assembled in the cities, and the cool spaces of the country have been supplanted by the feverish urban areas, the whole nature of our political questions has been altered. They have ceased to be legal questions. They have more and more become social questions, questions with regard to the relations of human beings to one another, —not merely their legal relations, but their moral and spiritual relations to one another. This has been most characteristic of American life in the last few decades, and as these questions have assumed greater and greater prominence, the movement which this association represents has gathered cumulative force. So that, if anybody asks himself, "What does this gathering force mean," if he knows anything about the history of the country, he knows that it means something that has not only come to stay, but has come with conquering power.

I get a little impatient sometimes about the discussion of the channels and methods by which it is to prevail. It is going to prevail, and that is a very superficial and ignorant view of it which attributes it to mere social unrest. It is not merely because the women are discontented. It is because the women have seen visions of duty, and that is something which we not only cannot resist, but, if we be true Americans, we do not wish to resist. America took its origin in visions of the human spirit, in aspirations for the deepest sort of liberty of the mind and of the heart, and as visions of that sort come up to the sight of those who are spiritually minded in America, America comes more and more into her birthright and into the perfection of her development.

So that what we have to realize in dealing with forces of this sort is that we are dealing with the substance of life itself. I have felt as I sat here to-night the wholesome contagion of the occasion. Almost every other time that I ever visited Atlantic City, I came to fight somebody. I hardly know how to conduct myself when I have not come to fight against anybody, but with somebody. I have come to suggest, among other things, that when the forces of nature are steadily working and the tide is rising to meet the moon, you need not be afraid that it will not come to its flood. We feel the tide; we rejoice in the strength of it; and we shall not quarrel in the long run as to the method of it. Because, when you are working with masses of men and organized bodies of opinion, you have got to carry the organized body along. The whole art and practice of government consists not in moving individuals, but in moving masses. It is all very well to run ahead and beckon, but, after all, you have got to wait for the body to follow. I have not come to ask you to be patient, because you have been, but I have come to congratulate you that there was a force behind you that will beyond any peradventure be triumphant, and for which you can afford a little while to wait.

The Terms of Peace

[Address to the Senate of the United States, delivered January 22, 1917.]

Gentlemen of the Senate:

On the eighteenth of December last I addressed an identic note to the governments of the nations now at war requesting them to state, more definitely than they had yet been stated by either group of belligerents, the terms upon which they would deem it possible to make peace. I spoke on behalf of humanity and of the rights of all neutral nations like our own, many of whose most vital interests the war puts in constant jeopardy. The Central Powers united in a reply which stated merely that they were ready to meet their antagonists in conference to discuss terms of peace. The Entente Powers have replied much more definitely and have stated, in general terms, indeed, but with sufficient definiteness to imply details, the arrangements, guarantees, and acts of reparation which they deem to be the indispensable conditions of a satisfactory settlement. We are that much nearer a definite discussion of the peace which shall end the present war. We are that much nearer the discussion of the international concert which must thereafter hold the world at peace. In every discussion of the peace that must end this war it is taken for granted that that peace must be followed by some definite concert of power which will make it virtually impossible that any such catastrophe should ever overwhelm us again. Every lover of mankind, every sane and thoughtful man must take that for granted.

I have sought this opportunity to address you because I thought that I owed it to you, as the council associated with me in the final determination of our international obligations, to disclose to you without reserve the thought and purpose that have been taking form in my mind in regard to the duty of our Government in the days to come when it will be necessary to lay afresh and upon a new plan the foundations of peace among the nations.

It is inconceivable that the people of the United States should play no part in that great enterprise. To take part in such a service will be the opportunity for which they have sought to prepare themselves by the very principles and purposes of their polity and the approved practices of their Government ever since the days when they set up a new nation in the high and honorable hope that it might in all that it was and did show mankind the way to liberty. They cannot in honor withhold the service to which they are now about to be challenged. They do not wish to withhold it. But they owe it to themselves and to the other nations of the world to state the conditions under which they will feel free to render it.

That service is nothing less than this, to add their authority and their power to the authority and force of other nations to guarantee peace and justice throughout the world. Such a settlement cannot now be long postponed. It is right that before it comes this Government should frankly formulate the conditions upon which it would feel justified in asking our people to approve its formal and solemn adherence to a League for Peace. I am here to attempt to state those conditions.

The present war must first be ended; but we owe it to candor and to a just regard for the opinion of mankind to say that, so far as our participation in guarantees of future peace is concerned, it makes a great deal of difference in what way and upon what terms it is ended. The treaties and agreements which bring it to an end must embody terms which will create a peace that is worth guaranteeing and preserving, a peace that will win the approval of mankind, not merely a peace that will serve the several interests and immediate aims of the nations engaged. We shall have no voice in determining what those terms shall be, but we shall, I feel sure, have a voice in determining whether they shall be made lasting or not by the guarantees of a universal covenant; and our judgment upon what is fundamental and essential as a condition precedent to permanency should be spoken now, not afterwards when it may be too late.

No covenant of coöperative peace that does not include the peoples of the New World can suffice to keep the future safe against war; and yet there is only one sort of peace that the peoples of America could join in guaranteeing. The elements of that peace must be elements that engage the confidence and satisfy the principles of the American governments, elements consistent with their political faith and with the practical convictions which the peoples of America have once for all embraced and undertaken to defend.

I do not mean to say that any American government would throw any obstacle in the way of any terms of peace the governments now at war might agree upon, or seek to upset them when made, whatever they might be. I only take it for granted that mere terms of peace between the belligerents will not satisfy even the belligerents themselves. Mere agreements may not make peace secure. It will be absolutely necessary that a force be created as a guarantor of the permanency of the settlement so much greater than the force of any nation now engaged or any alliance hitherto formed or projected that no nation, no probable combination of nations could face or withstand it. If the peace presently to be made is to endure, it must be a peace made secure by the organized major force of mankind.

The terms of the immediate peace agreed upon will determine whether it is a peace for which such a guarantee can be secured. The question upon which the whole future peace and policy of the world depends is this: Is the present war a struggle for a just and secure peace, or only for a new balance of power? If it be only a struggle for a new balance of power, who will guarantee, who can guarantee, the stable equilibrium of the new arrangement? Only a tranquil Europe can be a stable Europe. There must be, not a balance of power, but a community of power; not organized rivalries, but an organized common peace.

Fortunately we have received very explicit assurances on this point. The statesmen of both of the groups of nations now arrayed against one another have said, in terms that could not be misinterpreted, that it was no part of the purpose they had in mind to crush their antagonists. But the implications of these assurances may not be equally clear to all, —may not be the same on both sides of the water. I think it will be serviceable if I attempt to set forth what we understand them to be.

They imply, first of all, that it must be a peace without victory. It is not pleasant to say this. I beg that I may be permitted to put my own interpretation upon it and that it may be understood that no other interpretation was in my thought. I am seeking only to face realities and to face them without soft concealments. Victory would mean peace forced upon the loser, a victor's terms imposed upon the vanquished. It would be accepted in humiliation, under duress, at an intolerable sacrifice, and would leave a sting, a resentment, a bitter memory upon which terms of peace would rest, not permanently, but only as upon quicksand. Only a peace between equals can last. Only a peace the very principle of which is equality and a common participation in a common benefit. The right state of mind, the right feeling between nations, is as necessary for a lasting peace as is the just settlement of vexed questions of territory or of racial and national allegiance.

The equality of nations upon which peace must be founded if it is to last must be an equality of rights; the guarantees exchanged must neither recognize nor imply a difference between big nations and small, between those that are powerful and those that are weak. Right must be based upon the common strength, not upon the individual strength, of the nations upon whose concert peace will depend. Equality of territory or of resources there of course cannot be; nor any other sort of equality not gained in the ordinary peaceful and legitimate development of the peoples themselves. But no one asks or expects anything more than an equality of rights. Mankind is looking now for freedom of life, not for equipoises of power.

And there is a deeper thing involved than even equality of right among organized nations. No peace can last, or ought to last, which does not recognize and accept the principle that governments derive all their just powers from the consent of the governed, and that no right anywhere exists to hand peoples about from sovereignty to sovereignty as if they were property.

I take it for granted, for instance, if I may venture upon a single example, that statesmen everywhere are agreed that there should be a united, independent, and autonomous Poland, and that henceforth inviolable security of life, of worship, and of industrial and social development should be guaranteed to all peoples who have lived hitherto under the power of governments devoted to a faith and purpose hostile to their own.

I speak of this, not because of any desire to exalt an abstract political principle which has always been held very dear by those who have sought to build up liberty in America, but for the same reason that I have spoken of the other conditions of peace which seem to me clearly indispensable, —because I wish frankly to uncover realities. Any peace which does not recognize and accept this principle will inevitably be upset. It will not rest upon the affections or the convictions of mankind. The ferment of spirit of whole populations will fight subtly and constantly against it, and all the world will sympathize. The world can be at peace only if its life is stable, and there can be no stability where the will is in rebellion, where there is not tranquillity of spirit and a sense of justice, of freedom, and of right.

So far as practicable, moreover, every great people now struggling towards a full development of its resources and of its powers should be assured a direct outlet to the great highways of the sea. Where this cannot be done by the cession of territory, it can no doubt be done by the neutralization of direct rights of way under the general guarantee which will assure the peace itself. With a right comity of arrangement no nation need be shut away from free access to the open paths of the world's commerce.

And the paths of the sea must alike in law and in fact be free. The freedom of the seas is the *sine qua non* of peace, equality, and coöperation. No doubt a somewhat radical reconsideration of many of the rules of international practice hitherto thought to be established may be necessary in order to make the seas indeed free and common in practically all circumstances for the use of mankind, but the motive for such changes is convincing and compelling. There can be no trust or intimacy between the peoples of the world without them. The free, constant, unthreatened intercourse of nations is an essential part of the process of peace and of development. It need not be difficult either to define or to secure the freedom of the seas if the governments of the world sincerely desire to come to an agreement concerning it.

It is a problem closely connected with the limitation of naval armaments and the coöperation of the navies of the world in keeping the seas at once free and safe. And the question of limiting naval armaments opens the wider and perhaps more difficult question of the limitation of armies and of all programs of military preparation. Difficult and delicate as these questions are, they must be faced with the utmost candor and decided in a spirit of real accommodation if peace is to come with healing in its wings, and come to stay. Peace cannot be had without concession and sacrifice. There can be no sense of safety and equality among the nations if great preponderating armaments are henceforth to continue here and there to be built up and maintained. The statesmen of the world must plan for peace and nations must adjust and accommodate their policy to it as they have planned for war and made ready for pitiless contest and rivalry. The question of armaments, whether on land or sea, is the most immediately and intensely practical question connected with the future fortunes of nations and of mankind.

I have spoken upon these great matters without reserve and with the utmost explicitness because it has seemed to me to be necessary if the world's yearning desire for peace was anywhere to find free voice and utterance. Perhaps I am the only person in high authority amongst all the peoples of the world who is at liberty to speak and hold nothing back. I am speaking as an individual, and yet I am speaking also, of course, as the responsible head of a great government, and I feel confident that I have said what the people of the United States would wish me to say. May I not add that I hope and believe that I am in effect speaking for liberals and friends of humanity in every nation and of every program of liberty? I would fain believe that I am speaking for the silent mass of mankind everywhere who have as yet had no place or opportunity to speak their real hearts out concerning the death and ruin they see to have come already upon the persons and the homes they hold most dear.

And in holding out the expectation that the people and Government of the United States will join the other civilized nations of the world in guaranteeing the permanence of peace upon such terms as I have named I speak with the greater boldness and confidence because it is clear to every man who can think that there is in this promise no breach in either our traditions or our policy as a nation, but a fulfilment, rather, of all that we have professed or striven for.

I am proposing, as it were, that the nations should with one accord adopt the doctrine of President Monroe as the doctrine of the world: that no nation should seek to extend its polity over any other nation or people, but that every people should be left free to determine its own polity, its own way of development, unhindered, unthreatened, unafraid, the little along with the great and powerful.

I am proposing that all nations henceforth avoid entangling alliances which would draw them into competitions of power, catch them in a net of intrigue and selfish rivalry, and disturb their own affairs with influences intruded from without. There is no entangling alliance in a concert of power. When all unite to act in the same sense and with the same purpose all act in the common interest and are free to live their own lives under a common protection.

I am proposing government by the consent of the governed; that freedom of the seas which in international conference after conference representatives of the United States have urged with the eloquence of those who are the convinced disciples of liberty; and that moderation of armaments which makes of armies and navies a power for order merely, not an instrument of aggression or of selfish violence.

These are American principles, American policies. We could stand for no others. And they are also the principles and policies of forward looking men and women everywhere, of every modern nation, of every enlightened community. They are the principles of mankind and must prevail.

Meeting Germany's Challenge

[Address delivered at a joint session of the two Houses of Congress, February 3, 1917.]

Gentlemen of the Congress:

The Imperial German Government on the thirty-first of January announced to this Government and to the governments of the other neutral nations that on and after the first day of February, the present month, it would adopt a policy with regard to the use of submarines against all shipping seeking to pass through certain designated areas of the high seas to which it is clearly my duty to call your attention.

Let me remind the Congress that on the eighteenth of April last, in view of the sinking on the twenty-fourth of March of the cross-Channel passenger steamer *Sussex* by a German submarine, without summons or warning, and the consequent loss of the lives of several citizens of the United States who were passengers aboard her, this Government addressed a note to the Imperial German Government in which it made the following declaration:

"If it is still the purpose of the Imperial Government to prosecute relentless and indiscriminate warfare against vessels of commerce by the use of submarines without regard to what the Government of the United States must consider the sacred and indisputable rules of international law and the universally recognized dictates of humanity, the Government of the United States is at last forced to the conclusion that there is but one course it can pursue. Unless the Imperial Government should now immediately declare and effect an abandonment of its present methods of submarine warfare against passenger and freight-carrying vessels, the Government of the United States can have no choice but to sever diplomatic relations with the German Empire altogether."

In reply to this declaration the Imperial German Government gave this Government the following assurance:

"The German Government is prepared to do its utmost to confine the operations of war for the rest of its duration to the fighting forces of the belligerents, thereby also insuring the freedom of the seas, a principle upon which the German Government believes, now as before, to be in agreement with the Government of the United States.

"The German Government, guided by this idea, notifies the Government of the United States that the German naval forces have received the following orders: In accordance with the general principles of visit and search and destruction of merchant vessels recognized by international law, such vessels, both within and without the area declared as naval war zone, shall not be sunk without warning and without saving human lives, unless these ships attempt to escape or offer resistance.

"But," it added, "neutrals cannot expect that Germany, forced to fight for her existence, shall, for the sake of neutral interest, restrict the use of an effective weapon if her enemy is permitted to continue to apply at will methods of warfare violating the rules of international law. Such a demand would be incompatible with the character of neutrality, and the German Government is convinced that the Government of the United States does not think of making such a demand, knowing that the Government of the United States has repeatedly declared that it is determined to restore the principle of the freedom of the seas, from whatever quarter it has been violated."

To this the Government of the United States replied on the eighth of May, accepting, of course, the assurances given, but adding,

"The Government of the United States feels it necessary to state that it takes it for granted that the Imperial German Government does not intend to imply that the maintenance of its newly announced policy is in any way contingent upon the course or result of diplomatic negotiations between the Government of the United States and any other belligerent Government, notwithstanding the fact that certain passages in the Imperial Government's note of the fourth instant might appear to be susceptible of that construction. In order, however, to avoid any possible misunderstanding, the Government of the United States notifies the Imperial Government that it cannot for a moment entertain, much less discuss, a suggestion that respect by German naval authorities for the rights of citizens of the United States upon the high seas should in any way or in the slightest degree be made contingent upon the conduct of any other Government affecting the rights of neutrals and non-combatants. Responsibility in such matters is single, not joint; absolute, not relative."

To this note of the eighth of May the Imperial German Government made no reply.

On the thirty-first of January, the Wednesday of the present week, the German Ambassador handed to the Secretary of State, along with a formal note, a memorandum which contains the following statement:

"The Imperial Government, therefore, does not doubt that the Government of the United States will understand the situation thus forced upon Germany by the Entente-Allies' brutal methods of war and by their determination to destroy the Central Powers, and that the Government of the United States will further realize that the now openly disclosed intentions of the Entente-Allies give back to Germany the freedom of action which she reserved in her note addressed to the Government of the United States on May 4, 1916.

"Under these circumstances Germany will meet the illegal measures of her enemies by forcibly preventing after February 1, 1917, in a zone around Great Britain, France, Italy, and in the Eastern Mediterranean all navigation, that of neutrals included, from and to England and from and to France, etc., etc. All ships met within the zone will be sunk."

I think that you will agree with me that, in view of this declaration, which suddenly and without prior intimation of any kind deliberately withdraws the solemn assurance given in the Imperial Government's note of the fourth of May, 1916, this Government has no alternative consistent with the dignity and honor of the United States but to take the course which, in its note of the eighteenth of April, 1916, it announced that it would take in the event that the German Government did not declare and effect an abandonment of the methods of submarine warfare which it was then employing and to which it now purposes again to resort.

I have, therefore, directed the Secretary of State to announce to His Excellency the German Ambassador that all diplomatic relations between the United States and the German Empire are severed, and that the American Ambassador at Berlin will immediately be withdrawn; and, in accordance with this decision, to hand to His Excellency his passports.

Notwithstanding this unexpected action of the German Government, this sudden and deeply deplorable renunciation of its assurances, given this Government at one of the most critical moments of tension in the relations of the two governments, I refuse to believe that it is the intention of the German authorities to do in fact what they have warned us they will feel at liberty to do. I cannot bring myself to believe that they will indeed pay no regard to the ancient friendship between their people and our own or to the solemn obligations which have been exchanged between them and destroy American ships and take the lives of American citizens in the willful prosecution of the ruthless naval program they have announced their intention to adopt. Only actual overt acts on their part can make me believe it even now.

If this inveterate confidence on my part in the sobriety and prudent foresight of their purpose should unhappily prove unfounded; if American ships and American lives should in fact be sacrificed by their naval commanders in heedless contravention of the just and reasonable understandings of international law and the obvious dictates of humanity, I shall take the liberty of coming again before the Congress, to ask that authority be given me to use any means that may be necessary for the protection of our seamen and our people in the prosecution of their peaceful and legitimate errands on the high seas. I can do nothing less. I take it for granted that all neutral governments will take the same course.

We do not desire any hostile conflict with the Imperial German Government. We are the sincere friends of the German people and earnestly desire to remain at peace with the Government which speaks for them. We shall not believe that they are hostile to us unless and until we are obliged to believe it; and we purpose nothing more than the reasonable defense of the undoubted rights of our people. We wish to serve no selfish ends. We seek merely to stand true alike in thought and in action to the immemorial principles of our people which I sought to express in my address to the Senate only two weeks ago, —seek merely to vindicate our right to liberty and justice and an unmolested life. These are the bases of peace, not war. God grant we may not be challenged to defend them by acts of wilful injustice on the part of the Government of Germany!

Request for Authority

[Address delivered at a joint session of the two Houses of Congress, February 26, 1917.]

Gentlemen of the Congress:

I have again asked the privilege of addressing you because we are moving through critical times during which it seems to me to be my duty to keep in close touch with the Houses of Congress, so that neither counsel nor action shall run at cross purposes between us.

On the third of February I officially informed you of the sudden and unexpected action of the Imperial German Government in declaring its intention to disregard the promises it had made to this Government in April last and undertake immediate submarine operations against all commerce, whether of belligerents or of neutrals, that should seek to approach Great Britain and Ireland, the Atlantic coasts of Europe, or the harbors of the eastern Mediterranean, and to conduct those operations without regard to the established restrictions of international practice, without regard to any considerations of humanity even which might interfere with their object. That policy was forthwith put into practice. It has now been in active execution for nearly four weeks.

Its practical results are not yet fully disclosed. The commerce of other neutral nations is suffering severely, but not, perhaps, very much more severely than it was already suffering before the first of February, when the new policy of the Imperial Government was put into operation. We have asked the coöperation of the other neutral governments to prevent these depredations, but so far none of them has thought it wise to join us in any common course of action. Our own commerce has suffered, is suffering, rather in apprehension than in fact, rather because so many of our ships are timidly keeping to their home ports than because American ships have been sunk.

Two American vessels have been sunk, the *Housatonic* and the *Lyman M. Law*. The case of the *Housatonic,* which was carrying food-stuffs consigned to a London firm, was essentially like the case of the *Fry,* in which, it will be recalled, the German Government admitted its liability for damages, and the lives of the crew, as in the case of the *Fry,* were safeguarded with reasonable care. The case of the *Law,* which was carrying lemon-box staves to Palermo, disclosed a ruthlessness of method which deserves grave condemnation, but was accompanied by no circumstances which might not have been expected at any time in connection with the use of the submarine against merchantmen as the German Government has used it.

In sum, therefore, the situation we find ourselves in with regard to the actual conduct of the German submarine warfare against commerce and its effects upon our own ships and people is substantially the same that it was when I addressed you on the third of February, except for the tying up of our shipping in our own ports because of the unwillingness of our shipowners to risk their vessels at sea without insurance or adequate protection, and the very serious congestion of our commerce which has resulted, a congestion which is growing rapidly more and more serious every day. This in itself might presently accomplish, in effect, what the new German submarine orders were meant to accomplish, so far as we are concerned. We can only say, therefore, that the overt act which I have ventured to hope the German commanders would in fact avoid has not occurred.

But, while this is happily true, it must be admitted that there have been certain additional indications and expressions of purpose on the part of the German press and the German authorities which have increased rather than lessened the impression that, if our ships and our people are spared, it will be because of fortunate circumstances or because the commanders of the German submarines which they may happen to encounter exercise an unexpected discretion and restraint rather than because of the instructions under which those commanders are acting.

It would be foolish to deny that the situation is fraught with the gravest possibilities and dangers. No thoughtful man can fail to see that the necessity for definite action may come at any time, if we are in fact, and not in word merely, to defend our elementary rights as a neutral nation. It would be most imprudent to be unprepared.

I cannot in such circumstances be unmindful of the fact that the expiration of the term of the present Congress is immediately at hand, by constitutional limitation; and that it would in all likelihood require an unusual length of time to assemble and organize the Congress which is to succeed it. I feel that I ought, in view of that fact, to obtain from you full and immediate assurance of the authority which I may need at any moment to exercise. No doubt I already possess that authority without special warrant of law, by the plain implication of my constitutional duties and powers; but I prefer, in the present circumstances, not to act upon general implication. I wish to feel that the authority and the power of the Congress are behind me in whatever it may become necessary for me to do. We are jointly the servants of the people and must act together and in their spirit, so far as we can divine and interpret it.

No one doubts what it is our duty to do. We must defend our commerce and the lives of our people in the midst of the present trying circumstances, with discretion but with clear and steadfast purpose. Only the method and the extent remain to be chosen, upon the occasion, if occasion should indeed arise. Since it has unhappily proved impossible to safeguard our neutral rights by diplomatic means against the unwarranted infringements they are suffering at the hands of Germany, there may be no recourse but to *armed* neutrality, which we shall know how to maintain and for which there is abundant American precedent.

It is devoutly to be hoped that it will not be necessary to put armed force anywhere into action. The American people do not desire it, and our desire is not different from theirs. I am sure that they will understand the spirit in which I am now acting, the purpose I hold nearest my heart and would wish to exhibit in everything I do. I am anxious that the people of the nations at war also should understand and not mistrust us. I hope that I need give no further proofs and assurances than I have already given throughout nearly three years of anxious patience that I am the friend of peace and mean to preserve it for America so long as I am able. I am not now proposing or contemplating war or any steps that need lead to it. I merely request that you will accord me by your own vote and definite bestowal the means and the authority to safeguard in practice the right of a great people who are at peace and who are desirous of exercising none but the rights of peace to follow the pursuits of peace in quietness and good will, —rights recognized time out of mind by all the civilized nations of the world. No course of my choosing or of theirs will lead to war. War can come only by the wilful acts and aggressions of others.

You will understand why I can make no definite proposals or forecasts of action now and must ask for your supporting authority in the most general terms. The form in which action may become necessary cannot yet be foreseen. I believe that the people will be willing to trust me to act with restraint, with prudence, and in the true spirit of amity and good faith that they have themselves displayed throughout these trying months; and it is in that belief that I request that you will authorize me to supply our merchant ships with defensive arms, should that become necessary, and with the means of using them, and to employ any other instrumentalities or methods that may be necessary and adequate to protect our ships and our people in their legitimate and peaceful pursuits on the seas. I request also that you will grant me at the same time, along with the powers I ask, a sufficient credit to enable me to provide adequate means of protection where they are lacking, including adequate insurance against the present war risks.

I have spoken of our commerce and of the legitimate errands of our people on the seas, but you will not be misled as to my main thought, the thought that lies beneath these phrases and gives them dignity and weight. It is not of material interests merely that we are thinking. It is, rather, of fundamental human rights, chief of all the right of life itself. I am thinking, not only of the rights of Americans to go and come about their proper business by way of the sea, but also of something much deeper, much more fundamental than that. I am thinking of those rights of humanity without which there is no civilization. My theme is of those great principles of compassion and of protection which mankind has sought to throw about human lives, the lives of non-combatants, the lives of men who are peacefully at work keeping the industrial processes of the world quick and vital, the lives of women and children and of those who supply the labor which ministers to their sustenance. We are speaking of no selfish material rights but of rights which our hearts support and whose foundation is that righteous passion for justice upon which all law, all structures alike of family, of state, and of mankind must rest, as upon the ultimate base of our existence and our liberty. I cannot imagine any man with American principles at his heart hesitating to defend these things.

The Call to War

[Address delivered at a joint session of the two Houses of Congress, April 2, 1917.]

Gentlemen of the Congress:

I have called the Congress into extraordinary session because there are serious, very serious, choices of policy to be made, and made immediately, which it was neither right nor constitutionally permissible that I should assume the responsibility of making.

On the third of February last I officially laid before you the extraordinary announcement of the Imperial German Government that on and after the first day of February it was its purpose to put aside all restraints of law or of humanity and use its submarines to sink every vessel that sought to approach either the ports of Great Britain and Ireland or the western coasts of Europe or any of the ports controlled by the enemies of Germany within the Mediterranean. That had seemed to be the object of the German submarine warfare earlier in the war, but since April of last year the Imperial Government had somewhat restrained the commanders of its undersea craft in conformity with its promise then given to us that passenger boats should not be sunk and that due warning would be given to all other vessels which its submarines might seek to destroy, when no resistance was offered or escape attempted, and care taken that their crews were given at least a fair chance to save their lives in their open boats. The precautions taken were meager and haphazard enough, as was proved in distressing instance after instance in the progress of the cruel and unmanly business, but a certain degree of restraint was observed. The new policy has swept every restriction aside. Vessels of every kind, whatever their flag, their character, their cargo, their destination, their errand, have been ruthlessly sent to the bottom without warning and without thought of help or mercy for those on board, the vessels of friendly neutrals along with those of belligerents. Even hospital ships and ships carrying relief to the sorely bereaved and stricken people of Belgium, though the latter were provided with safe conduct through the proscribed areas by the German Government itself and were distinguished by unmistakable marks of identity, have been sunk with the same reckless lack of compassion or of principle.

I was for a little while unable to believe that such things would in fact be done by any government that had hitherto subscribed to the humane practices of civilized nations. International law had its origin in the attempt to set up some law which would be respected and observed upon the seas, where no nation had right of dominion and where lay the free highways of the world. By painful stage after stage has that law been built up, with meager enough results, indeed, after all was accomplished that could be accomplished, but always with a clear view, at least, of what the heart and conscience of mankind demanded. This minimum of right the German Government has swept aside under the plea of retaliation and necessity and because it had no weapons which it could use at sea except these which it is impossible to employ as it is employing them without throwing to the winds all scruples of humanity or of respect for the understandings that were supposed to underlie the intercourse of the world. I am not now thinking of the loss of property involved, immense and serious as that is, but only of the wanton and wholesale destruction of the lives of non-combatants, men, women, and children, engaged in pursuits which have always, even in the darkest periods of modern history, been deemed innocent and legitimate. Property can be paid for; the lives of peaceful and innocent people cannot be. The present German submarine warfare against commerce is a warfare against mankind.

It is a war against all nations. American ships have been sunk, American lives taken, in ways which it has stirred us very deeply to learn of, but the ships and people of other neutral and friendly nations have been sunk and overwhelmed in the waters in the same way. There has been no discrimination. The challenge is to all mankind. Each nation must decide for itself how it will meet it. The choice we make for ourselves must be made with a moderation of counsel and a temperateness of judgment befitting our character and our motives as a nation. We must put excited feeling away. Our motive will not be revenge or the victorious assertion of the physical might of the nation, but only the vindication of right, of human right, of which we are only a single champion.

When I addressed the Congress on the twenty-sixth of February last I thought that it would suffice to assert our neutral rights with arms, our right to use the seas against unlawful interference, our right to keep our people safe against unlawful violence. But armed neutrality, it now appears, is impracticable. Because submarines are in effect outlaws when used as the German submarines have been used against merchant shipping, it is impossible to defend ships against their attacks as the law of nations has assumed that merchantmen would defend themselves against privateers or cruisers, visible craft giving chase upon the open sea. It is common prudence in such circumstances, grim, necessity indeed, to endeavor to destroy them before they have shown their own intention. They must be dealt with upon sight, if dealt with at all. The German Government denies the right of neutrals to use arms at all within the areas of the sea which it has proscribed, even in the defense of rights which no modern publicist has ever before questioned their right to defend. The intimation is conveyed that the armed guards which we have placed on our merchant ships will be treated as beyond the pale of law and subject to be dealt with as pirates would be. Armed neutrality is ineffectual enough at best; in such circumstances and in the face of such pretensions it is worse than ineffectual: it is likely only to produce what it was meant to prevent; it is practically certain to draw us into the war without either the rights or the effectiveness of belligerents. There is one choice we cannot make, we are incapable of making: we will not choose the path of submission and suffer the most sacred rights of our nation and our people to be ignored or violated. The wrongs against which we now array ourselves are no common wrongs; they cut to the very roots of human life.

With a profound sense of the solemn and even tragical character of the step I am taking and of the grave responsibilities which it involves, but in unhesitating obedience to what I deem my constitutional duty, I advise that the Congress declare the recent course of the Imperial German Government to be in fact nothing less than war against the government and people of the United States; that it formally accept the status of belligerent which has thus been thrust upon it; and that it take immediate steps not only to put the country in a more thorough state of defense but also to exert all its power and employ all its resources to bring the Government of the German Empire to terms and end the war.

What this will involve is clear. It will involve the utmost practicable coöperation in counsel and action with the governments now at war with Germany, and, as incident to that, the extension to those governments of the most liberal financial credits, in order that our resources may so far as possible be added to theirs. It will involve the organization and mobilization of all the material resources of the country to supply the materials of war and serve the incidental needs of the nation in the most abundant and yet the most economical and efficient way possible. It will involve the immediate full equipment of the navy in all respects but particularly in supplying it with the best means of dealing with the enemy's submarines. It will involve the immediate addition to the armed forces of the United States already provided for by law in case of war at least 500,000 men, who should, in my opinion, be chosen upon the principle of universal liability to service, and also the authorization of subsequent additional increments of equal force so soon as they may be needed and can be handled in training. It will involve also, of course, the granting of adequate credits to the Government, sustained, I hope, so far as they can equitably be sustained by the present generation, by well conceived taxation.

I say sustained so far as may be equitable by taxation because it seems to me that it would be most unwise to base the credits which will now be necessary entirely on money borrowed. It is our duty, I most respectfully urge, to protect our people so far as we may against the very serious hardships and evils which would be likely to arise out of the inflation which would be produced by vast loans.

In carrying out the measures by which these things are to be accomplished we should keep constantly in mind the wisdom of interfering as little as possible in our own preparation and in the equipment of our own military forces with the duty, —for it will be a very practical duty, —of supplying the nations already at war with Germany with the materials which they can obtain only from us or by our assistance. They are in the field and we should help them in every way to be effective there.

I shall take the liberty of suggesting, through the several executive departments of the Government, for the consideration of your committees, measures for the accomplishment of the several objects I have mentioned. I hope that it will be your pleasure to deal with them as having been framed after very careful thought by the branch of the Government upon which the responsibility of conducting the war and safeguarding the nation will most directly fall.

While we do these things, these deeply momentous things, let us be very clear, and make very clear to all the world what our motives and our objects are. My own thought has not been driven from its habitual and normal course by the unhappy events of the last two months, and I do not believe that the thought of the nation has been altered or clouded by them. I have exactly the same things in mind now that I had in mind when I addressed the Senate on the twenty-second of January last; the same that I had in mind when I addressed the Congress on the third of February and on the twenty-sixth of February. Our object now, as then, is to vindicate the principles of peace and justice in the life of the world as against selfish, and autocratic power and to set up amongst the really free and self-governed peoples of the world such a concert of purpose and of action as will henceforth ensure the observance of those principles. Neutrality is no longer feasible or desirable where the peace of the world is involved and the freedom of its peoples, and the menace to that peace and freedom lies in the existence of autocratic governments backed by organized force which is controlled wholly by their will, not by the will of their people. We have seen the last of neutrality in such circumstances. We are at the beginning of an age in which it will be insisted that the same standards of conduct and of responsibility for wrong done shall be observed among nations and their governments that are observed among the individual citizens of civilized states.

We have no quarrel with the German people. We have no feeling towards them but one of sympathy and friendship. It was not upon their impulse that their government acted in entering this war. It was not with their previous knowledge or approval. It was a war determined upon as wars used to be determined upon in the old, unhappy days when peoples were nowhere consulted by their rulers and wars were provoked and waged in the interest of dynasties or of little groups of ambitious men who were accustomed to use their fellow-men as pawns and tools. Self-governed nations do not fill their neighbor states with spies or set the course of intrigue to bring about some critical posture of affairs which will give them an opportunity to strike and make conquest. Such designs can be successfully worked out only under cover and where no one has the right to ask questions. Cunningly contrived plans of deception or aggression, carried, it may be, from generation to generation, can be worked out and kept from the light only within the privacy of courts or behind the carefully guarded confidences of a narrow and privileged class. They are happily impossible where public opinion commands and insists upon full information concerning all the nation's affairs.

A steadfast concert for peace can never be maintained except by a partnership of democratic nations. No autocratic government could be trusted to keep faith within it or observe its covenants. It must be a league of honor, a partnership of opinion. Intrigue would eat its vitals away; the plottings of inner circles who could plan what they would and render account to no one would be a corruption seated at its very heart. Only free peoples can hold their purpose and their honor steady to a common end and prefer the interests of mankind to any narrow interest of their own.

Does not every American feel that assurance has been added to our hope for the future peace of the world by the wonderful and heartening things that have been happening within the last few weeks in Russia? Russia was known by those who knew it best to have been always in fact democratic at heart, in all the vital habits of her thought, in all the intimate relationships of her people that spoke their natural instinct, their habitual attitude towards life. The autocracy that crowned the summit of her political structure, long as it had stood and terrible as was the reality of its power, was not in fact Russian in origin, character, or purpose; and now it has been shaken off and the great, generous Russian people have been added in all their naïve majesty and might to the forces that are fighting for freedom in the world, for justice, and for peace. Here is a fit partner for a League of Honor.

One of the things that has served to convince us that the Prussian autocracy was not and could never be our friend is that from the very outset of the present war it has filled our unsuspecting communities and even our offices of government with spies and set criminal intrigues everywhere afoot against our national unity of counsel, our peace within and without, our industries and our commerce. Indeed it is now evident that its spies were here even before the war began; and it is unhappily not a matter of conjecture but a fact proved in our courts of justice that the intrigues which have more than once come perilously near to disturbing the peace and dislocating the industries of the country have been carried on at the instigation, with the support, and even under the personal direction of official agents of the Imperial Government accredited to the Government of the United States. Even in checking these things and trying to extirpate them we have sought to put the most generous interpretation possible upon them because we knew that their source lay, not in any hostile feeling or purpose of the German people towards us (who were, no doubt as ignorant of them as we ourselves were), but only in the selfish designs of a Government that did what it pleased and told its people nothing. But they have played their part in serving to convince us at last that that Government entertains no real friendship for us and means to act against our peace and security at its convenience. That it means to stir up enemies against us at our very doors the intercepted note to the German Minister at Mexico City is eloquent evidence.

We are accepting this challenge of hostile purpose because we know that in such a government, following such methods, we can never have a friend; and that in the presence of its organized power, always lying in wait to accomplish we know not what purpose, there can be no assured security for the democratic governments of the world. We are now about to accept gauge of battle with this natural foe to liberty and shall, if necessary, spend the whole force of the nation to check and nullify its pretensions and its power. We are glad, now that we see the facts with no veil of false pretense about them, to fight thus for the ultimate peace of the world and for the liberation of its peoples, the German peoples included: for the rights of nations great and small and the privilege of men everywhere to choose their way of life and of obedience. The world must be made safe for democracy. Its peace must be planted upon the tested foundations of political liberty. We have no selfish ends to serve. We desire no conquest, no dominion. We seek no indemnities for ourselves, no material compensation for the sacrifices we shall freely make. We are but one of the champions of the rights of mankind. We shall be satisfied when those rights have been made as secure as the faith and the freedom of nations can make them.

Just because we fight without rancor and without selfish object, seeking nothing for ourselves but what we shall wish to share with all free peoples, we shall, I feel confident, conduct our operations as belligerents without passion and ourselves observe with proud punctilio the principles of right and of fair play we profess to be fighting for.

I have said nothing of the governments allied with the Imperial Government of Germany because they have not made war upon us or challenged us to defend our right and our honor. The Austro-Hungarian Government has, indeed, avowed its unqualified endorsement and acceptance of the reckless and lawless submarine warfare adopted now without disguise by the Imperial German Government, and it has therefore not been possible for this Government to receive Count Tarnowski, the Ambassador recently accredited to this Government by the Imperial and Royal Government of Austria-Hungary; but that Government has not actually engaged in warfare against citizens of the United States on the seas, and I take the liberty, for the present at least, of postponing a discussion of our relations with the authorities at Vienna. We enter this war only where we are clearly forced into it because there are no other means of defending our rights.

It will be all the easier for us to conduct ourselves as belligerents in a high spirit of right and fairness because we act without animus, not in enmity towards a people or with the desire to bring any injury or disadvantage upon them, but only in armed opposition to an irresponsible government which has thrown aside all considerations of humanity and of right and is running amuck. We are, let me say again, the sincere friends of the German people, and shall desire nothing so much as the early reëstablishment of intimate relations of mutual advantage between us, —however hard it may be for them, for the time being, to believe that this is spoken from our hearts. We have borne with their present government through all these bitter months because of that friendship, —exercising a patience and forbearance which would otherwise have been impossible. We shall, happily, still have an opportunity to prove that friendship in our daily attitude and actions towards the millions of men and women of German birth and native sympathy who live amongst us and share our life, and we shall be proud to prove it towards all who are in fact loyal to their neighbors and to the Government in the hour of test. They are, most of them, as true and loyal Americans as if they had never known any other fealty or allegiance. They will be prompt to stand with us in rebuking and restraining the few who may be of a different mind and purpose. If there should be disloyalty, it will be dealt with with a firm hand of stern repression; but, if it lifts its head at all, it will lift it only here and there and without countenance except from a lawless and malignant few.

It is a distressing and oppressive duty, Gentlemen of the Congress, which I have performed in thus addressing you. There are, it may be, many months of fiery trial and sacrifice ahead of us. It is a fearful thing to lead this great peaceful people into war, into the most terrible and disastrous of all wars, civilization itself seeming to be in the balance. But the right is more precious than peace, and we shall fight for the things which we have always carried nearest our hearts, —for democracy, for the right of those who submit to authority to have a voice in their own governments, for the rights and liberties of small nations, for a universal dominion of right by such a concert of free peoples as shall bring peace and safety to all nations and make the world itself at last free. To such a task we can dedicate our lives and our fortunes, everything that we are and everything that we have, with the pride of those who know that the day has come when America is privileged to spend her blood and her might for the principles that gave her birth and happiness and the peace which she has treasured. God helping her, she can do no other.

To the Country

[President Wilson's Address to his Fellow-Countrymen, April 16, 1917.]

My Fellow-Countrymen:

The entrance of our own beloved country into the grim and terrible war for democracy and human rights which has shaken the world creates so many problems of national life and action which call for immediate consideration and settlement that I hope you will permit me to address to you a few words of earnest counsel and appeal with regard to them.

We are rapidly putting our navy upon an effective war footing and are about to create and equip a great army, but these are the simplest parts of the great task to which we have addressed ourselves. There is not a single selfish element, so far as I can see, in the cause we are fighting for. We are fighting for what we believe and wish to be the rights of mankind and for the future peace and security of the world. To do this great thing worthily and successfully we must devote ourselves to the service without regard to profit or material advantage and with an energy and intelligence that will rise to the level of the enterprise itself. We must realize to the full how great the task is and how many things, how many kinds and elements of capacity and service and self-sacrifice, it involves.

These, then, are the things we must do, and do well, besides fighting, —the things without which mere fighting would be fruitless:

We must supply abundant food for ourselves and for our armies and our seamen not only, but also for a large part of the nations with whom we have now made common cause, in whose support and by whose sides we shall be fighting.

We must supply ships by the hundreds out of our shipyards to carry to the other side of the sea, submarines or no submarines, what will every day be needed there, and abundant materials out of our fields and our mines and our factories with which not only to clothe and equip our own forces on land and sea but also to clothe and support our people for whom the gallant fellows under arms can no longer work, to help clothe and equip the armies with which we are coöperating in Europe, and to keep the looms and manufactories there in raw material; coal to keep the fires going in ships at sea and in the furnaces of hundreds of factories across the sea; steel out of which to make arms and ammunition both here and there; rails for worn-out railways back of the fighting fronts; locomotives and rolling stock to take the place of those every day going to pieces; mules, horses, cattle for labor and for military service; everything with which the people of England and France and Italy and Russia have usually supplied themselves but cannot now afford the men, the materials, or the machinery to make.

It is evident to every thinking man that our industries, on the farms, in the shipyards, in the mines, in the factories, must be made more prolific and more efficient than ever and that they must be more economically managed and better adapted to the particular requirements of our task than they have been; and what I want to say is that the men and the women who devote their thought and their energy to these things will be serving the country and conducting the fight for peace and freedom just as truly and just as effectively as the men on the battlefield or in the trenches. The industrial forces of the country, men and women alike, will be a great national, a great international, Service Army, —a notable and honored host engaged in the service of the nation and the world, the efficient friends and saviors of free men everywhere. Thousands, nay, hundreds of thousands, of men otherwise liable to military service will of right and of necessity be excused from that service and assigned to the fundamental, sustaining work of the fields and factories and mines, and they will be as much part of the great patriotic forces of the nation as the men under fire.

I take the liberty, therefore, of addressing this word to the farmers of the country and to all who work on the farms: The supreme need of our own nation and of the nations with which we are coöperating is an abundance of supplies, and especially of food-stuffs. The importance of an adequate food supply, especially for the present year, is superlative. Without abundant food, alike for the armies and the peoples now at war, the whole great enterprise upon which we have embarked will break down and fail. The world's food reserves are low. Not only during the present emergency but for some time after peace shall have come both our own people and a large proportion of the people of Europe must rely upon the harvests in America. Upon the farmers of this country, therefore, in large measure, rests the fate of the war and the fate of the nations. May the nation not count upon them to omit no step that will increase the production of their land or that will bring about the most effectual coöperation in the sale and distribution of their products? The time is short. It is of the most imperative importance that everything possible be done and done immediately to make sure of large harvests. I call upon young men and old alike and upon the able-bodied boys of the land to accept and act upon this duty-to turn in hosts to the farms and make certain that no pains and no labor is lacking in this great matter.

I particularly appeal to the farmers of the South to plant abundant food-stuffs as well as cotton. They can show their patriotism in no better or more convincing way than by resisting the great temptation of the present price of cotton and helping, helping upon a great scale, to feed the nation and the peoples everywhere who are fighting for their liberties and for our own. The variety of their crops will be the visible measure of their comprehension of their national duty.

The Government of the United States and the governments of the several States stand ready to coöperate. They will do everything possible to assist farmers in securing an adequate supply of seed, an adequate force of laborers when they are most needed, at harvest time, and the means of expediting shipments of fertilizers and farm machinery, as well as of the crops themselves when harvested. The course of trade shall be as unhampered as it is possible to make it and there shall be no unwarranted manipulation of the nation's food supply by those who handle it on its way to the consumer. This is our opportunity to demonstrate the efficiency of a great Democracy and we shall not fall short of it!

This let me say to the middlemen of every sort, whether they are handling our food-stuffs or our raw materials of manufacture or the products of our mills and factories: The eyes of the country will be especially upon you. This is your opportunity for signal service, efficient and disinterested. The country expects you, as it expects all others, to forego unusual profits, to organize and expedite shipments of supplies of every kind, but especially of food, with an eye to the service you are rendering and in the spirit of those who enlist in the ranks, for their people, not for themselves. I shall confidently expect you to deserve and win the confidence of people of every sort and station.

To the men who run the railways of the country, whether they be managers or operative employees, let me say that the railways are the arteries of the nation's life and that upon them rests the immense responsibility of seeing to it that those arteries suffer no obstruction of any kind, no inefficiency or slackened power. To the merchant let me suggest the motto, "Small profits and quick service"; and to the shipbuilder the thought that the life of the war depends upon him. The food and the war supplies must be carried across the seas no matter how many ships are sent to the bottom. The places of those that go down must be supplied and supplied at once. To the miner let me say that he stands where the farmer does: the work of the world waits on him. If he slackens or fails, armies and statesmen are helpless. He also is enlisted in the great Service Army. The manufacturer does not need to be told, I hope, that the nation looks to him to speed and perfect every process; and I want only to remind his employees that their service is absolutely indispensable and is counted on by every man who loves the country and its liberties.

Let me suggest, also, that everyone who creates or cultivates a garden helps, and helps greatly, to solve the problem of the feeding of the nations; and that every housewife who practices strict economy puts herself in the ranks of those who serve the nation. This is the time for America to correct her unpardonable fault of wastefulness and extravagance. Let every man and every woman assume the duty of careful, provident use and expenditure as a public duty, as a dictate of patriotism which no one can now expect ever to be excused or forgiven for ignoring.

In the hope that this statement of the needs of the nation and of the world in this hour of supreme crisis may stimulate those to whom it comes and remind all who need reminder of the solemn duties of a time such as the world has never seen before, I beg that all editors and publishers everywhere will give as prominent publication and as wide circulation as possible to this appeal. I venture to suggest, also, to all advertising agencies that they would perhaps render a very substantial and timely service to the country if they would give it widespread repetition. And I hope that clergymen will not think the theme of it an unworthy or inappropriate subject of comment and homily from their pulpits.

The supreme test of the nation has come. We must all speak, act, and serve together!

WOODROW WILSON.

The German Plot

[Speech in Washington Monument Grounds, June 14, 1917.]

We know now clearly, as we knew before we ourselves were engaged in the War, that we are not enemies of the German people, and they are not our enemies. They did not originate, or desire, this hideous war, or wish that we should be drawn into it, and we are vaguely conscious that we are fighting their cause, as they will some day see it themselves, as well as our own. They themselves are in the grip of the same sinister power that has stretched its ugly talons out and drawn blood from us.

The War was begun by the military masters of Germany, who have proved themselves to be also the masters of Austria-Hungary. These men never regarded nations as peoples of men, women, and children of like blood and frame as themselves, for whom Governments existed and in whom Governments had their life. They regarded them merely as serviceable organizations, which they could, either by force or intrigue, bend or corrupt to their own purpose. They regarded the smaller States, particularly, and those peoples, who could be overwhelmed by force, as their natural tools and instruments of domination.

Their purpose had long been avowed. The statesmen of other nations, to whom that purpose was incredible, paid little attention, and regarded what the German professors expounded in their class-rooms and the German writers set forth to the world as the goal of German policy as rather the dream of minds detached from practical affairs and the preposterous private conceptions of Germany's destiny than the actual plans of responsible rulers. But the rulers of Germany knew all the while what concrete plans, what well-advanced intrigue, lay at the back of what professors and writers were saying, and were glad to go forward unmolested, filling the thrones of the Balkan States with German princes, putting German officers at the service of Turkey, developing plans of sedition and rebellion in India and Egypt, and setting their fires in Persia.

The demands made by Austria upon Serbia were a mere single step in the plan which compassed Europe and Asia from Berlin to Bagdad. They hoped that these demands might not arouse Europe, but they meant to press them, whether they did or not. For they thought themselves ready for the final issue of arms. Their plan was to throw a belt of German military power and political control across the very center of Europe and beyond the Mediterranean into the heart of Asia, and Austria-Hungary was to be as much their tool and pawn as Serbia, Bulgaria, Turkey, or the ponderous States of the East. Austria-Hungary, indeed, was to become a part of the Central German Empire, absorbed and dominated by the same forces and influences that originally cemented the German States themselves.

The dream had its heart at Berlin. It could have had its heart nowhere else. It rejected entirely the idea of the solidarity of race. The choice of peoples played no part at all in the contemplated binding together of the racial and political units, which could keep together only by force. And they actually carried the greater part of that amazing plan into execution.

Look how things stand. Austria, at their mercy, has acted, not upon its own initiative or upon the choice of its own people, but at Berlin's dictation ever since the War began. Its people now desire peace, but they cannot have it until leave is granted from Berlin. The so-called Central Powers are, in fact, but a single Power. Serbia is at its mercy should its hand be but for a moment freed; Bulgaria consented to its will; Rumania is overrun by the Turkish armies, which the Germans trained into serving Germany, and the guns of the German warships lying in the harbor at Constantinople remind the Turkish statesmen every day that they have no choice but to take their orders from Berlin.

From Hamburg to the Persian Gulf the net is spread. Is it not easy to understand the eagerness for peace that has been manifested by Berlin ever since the snare was set and sprung?

"Peace, peace, peace" has been the talk of her Foreign Office for a year or more, not peace upon her own initiative, but upon the initiative of the nations over which she now deems herself to hold the advantage. A little of the talk has been public, but most of it has been private, through all sorts of channels. It has come to me in all sorts of guises, but never with the terms disclosed which the German Government would be willing to accept.

That Government has other valuable pawns in its hands besides those I have mentioned. It still holds a valuable part of France, though with a slowly relaxing grasp, and practically the whole of Belgium. Its armies press close on Russia and overrun Poland. It cannot go farther-it dare not go back. It wishes to close its bargain before it is too late and it has little left to offer for the pound of flesh it will demand. The military masters under whom Germany is bleeding see very clearly to what point fate has brought them: if they fall back or are forced back an inch, their power abroad and at home will fall to pieces. It is their power at home of which they are thinking now more than of their power abroad. It is that power which is trembling under their very feet.

Deep fear has entered their hearts. They have but one chance to perpetuate their military power, or even their controlling political influence. If they can secure peace now, with the immense advantage still in their hands, they will have justified themselves before the German people. They will have gained by force what they promised to gain by it-an immense expansion of German power and an immense enlargement of German industrial and commercial opportunities. Their prestige will be secure, and with their prestige their political power.

If they fail, their people will thrust them aside. A Government accountable to the people themselves will be set up in Germany, as has been the case in England, the United States, and France-in all great countries of modern times except Germany. If they succeed they are safe, and Germany and the world are undone. If they fail, Germany is saved and the world will be at peace. If they succeed, America will fall within the menace, and we, and all the rest of the world, must remain armed, as they will remain, and must make ready for the next step in their aggression. If they fail, the world may unite for peace and Germany may be of the union.

Do you not now understand the new intrigue for peace, and why the masters of Germany do not hesitate to use any agency that promises to effect their purpose, the deceit of nations? Their present particular aim is to deceive all those who, throughout the world, stand for the rights of peoples and the self-government of nations, for they see what immense strength the forces of justice and liberalism are gathering out of this war. They are employing Liberals in their enterprises. Let them once succeed, and these men, now their tools, will be ground to powder beneath the weight of the great military Empire; the Revolutionists of Russia will be cut off from all succour and the coöperation of Western Europe, and a counter-revolution will be fostered and supported; Germany herself will lose her chance of freedom, and all Europe will arm for the next final struggle.

The sinister intrigue is being no less actively conducted in this country than in Russia and in every country of Europe into which the agents and dupes of the Imperial German Government can get access. That Government has many spokesmen here, in places both high and low. They have learned discretion; they keep within the law. It is opinion they utter now, not sedition. They proclaim the liberal purposes of their masters, and they declare that this is a foreign war, which can touch America with no danger either to her lands or institutions. They set England at the center of the stage, and talk of her ambition to assert her economic dominion throughout the world. They appeal to our ancient tradition of isolation, and seek to undermine the Government with false professions of loyalty to its principles.

But they will make no headway. Falsehood betrays them in every accent. These facts are patent to all the world, and nowhere more plainly than in the United States, where we are accustomed to deal with facts, not sophistries; and the great fact that stands out above all the rest is that this is a peoples' war for freedom, justice and self-government among all the nations of the world, a war to make the world safe for the peoples who live upon it, the German people included, and that with us rests the choice to break through all these hypocrisies, the patent cheats and masks of brute force, and help set the world free, or else stand aside and let it be dominated through sheer weight of arms and the arbitrary choices of the self-constituted masters by the nation which can maintain the biggest armies, the most irresistible armaments, a power to which the world has afforded no parallel, in the face of which political freedom must wither and perish.

For us there was but one choice. We have made it, and woe be to that man, or that group of men, that seeks to stand in our way in this day of high resolution, when every principle we hold dearest is to be vindicated and made secure for the salvation of the nation. We are ready to plead at the bar of history, and our flag shall wear a new luster. Once more we shall make good with our lives and fortunes the great faith to which we are born, and a new glory shall shine in the face of our people.

Reply to the Pope

[This important and eloquent document, though signed by the Secretary of State, was of course authorized by the President, and indeed bears internal marks of being his own composition. The Pope had made a plea for peace, which was by our government deemed premature.]

AUGUST 27, 1917.

To His Holiness Benedictus XV, Pope:

In acknowledgment of the communication of Your Holiness to the belligerent peoples, dated August 1, 1917, the President of the United States requests me to transmit the following reply:

Every heart that has not been blinded and hardened by this terrible war must be touched by this moving appeal of His Holiness the Pope, must feel the dignity and force of the humane and generous motives which prompted it, and must fervently wish that we might take the path of peace he so persuasively points out. But it would be folly to take it if it does not in fact lead to the goal he proposes. Our response must be based upon the stern facts and upon nothing else. It is not a mere cessation of arms he desires; it is a stable and enduring peace. This agony must not be gone through with again, and it must be a matter of very sober judgment that will insure us against it.

His Holiness in substance proposes that we return to the status quo ante bellum, and that then there be a general condonation, disarmament, and a concert of nations based upon an acceptance of the principle of arbitration; that by a similar concert freedom of the seas be established; and that the territorial claims of France and Italy, the perplexing problems of the Balkan States, and the restitution of Poland be left to such conciliatory adjustments as may be possible in the new temper of such a peace, due regard being paid to the aspirations of the peoples whose political fortunes and affiliations will be involved.

It is manifest that no part of this program can be successfully carried out unless the restitution of the status quo ante furnishes a firm and satisfactory basis for it. The object of this war is to deliver the free peoples of the world from the menace and the actual power of a vast military establishment controlled by an irresponsible government which, having secretly planned to dominate the world, proceeded to carry the plan out without regard either to the sacred obligations of treaty or the long-established practices and long-cherished principles of international action and honor; which chose its own time for the war; delivered its blow fiercely and suddenly; stopped at no barrier either of law or of mercy; swept a whole continent within the tide of blood-not the blood of soldiers only, but the blood of innocent women and children also and of the helpless poor; and now stands balked but not defeated, the enemy of four-fifths of the world. This power is not the German people. It is the ruthless master of the German people. It is no business of ours how that great people came under its control or submitted with temporary zest to the domination of its purpose; but it is our business to see to it that the history of the rest of the world is no longer left to its handling.

To deal with such a power by way of peace upon the plan proposed by His Holiness the Pope would, so far as we can see, involve a recuperation of its strength and a renewal of its policy; would make it necessary to create a permanent hostile combination of nations against the German people who are its instruments; and would result in abandoning the newborn Russia to the intrigue, the manifold subtle interference, and the certain counter-revolution which would be attempted by all the malign influences to which the German Government has of late accustomed the world. Can peace be based upon a restitution of its power or upon any word of honor it could pledge in a treaty of settlement and accommodation?

Responsible statesmen must now everywhere see, if they never saw before, that no peace can rest securely upon political or economic restrictions meant to benefit some nations and cripple or embarrass others, upon vindictive action of any sort, or any kind of revenge or deliberate injury. The American people have suffered intolerable wrongs at the hands of the Imperial German Government, but they desire no reprisal upon the German people who have themselves suffered all things in this war which they did not choose. They believe that peace should rest upon the rights of peoples, not the rights of Governments-the rights of peoples great or small, weak or powerful-their equal right to freedom and security and self-government and to a participation upon fair terms in the economic opportunities of the world, the German people of course included if they will accept equality and not seek domination.

The test, therefore, of every plan of peace is this: Is it based upon the faith of all the peoples involved or merely upon the word of an ambitious and intriguing government on the one hand and of a group of free peoples on the other? This is a test which goes to the root of the matter; and it is the test which must be applied.

The purposes of the United States in this war are known to the whole world, to every people to whom the truth has been permitted to come. They do not need to be stated again. We seek no material advantage of any kind. We believe that the intolerable wrongs done in this war by the furious and brutal power of the Imperial German Government ought to be repaired, but not at the expense of the sovereignty of any people-rather a vindication of the sovereignty both of those that are weak and of those that are strong. Punitive damages, the dismemberment of empires, the establishment of selfish and exclusive economic leagues, we deem inexpedient and in the end worse than futile, no proper basis for a peace of any kind, least of all for an enduring peace. That must be based upon justice and fairness and the common rights of mankind.

We cannot take the word of the present rulers of Germany as a guaranty of anything that is to endure, unless explicitly supported by such conclusive evidence of the will and purpose of the German people themselves as the other peoples of the world would be justified in accepting. Without such guaranties treaties of settlement, agreements for disarmament, covenants to set up arbitration in the place of force, territorial adjustments, reconstitutions of small nations, if made with the German Government, no man, no nation could now depend on. We must await some new evidence of the purposes of the great peoples of the central powers. God grant it may be given soon and in a way to restore the confidence of all peoples everywhere in the faith of nations and the possibility of a covenanted peace.

Robert Lansing,
Secretary of State of the United States of America.

Labor Must be Free

[Address to the American Federation of Labor Convention, Buffalo, New York, November 12, 1917.]

Mr. President, Delegates of the American Federation of Labor, Ladies and Gentlemen:

I esteem it a great privilege and a real honor to be thus admitted to your public counsels. When your executive committee paid me the compliment of inviting me here I gladly accepted the invitation because it seems to me that this, above all other times in our history, is the time for common counsel, for the drawing together not only of the energies but of the minds of the Nation. I thought that it was a welcome opportunity for disclosing to you some of the thoughts that have been gathering in my mind during these last momentous months.

CRITICAL TIME IN HISTORY

I am introduced to you as the President of the United States, and yet I would be pleased if you would put the thought of the office into the background and regard me as one of your fellow-citizens who has come here to speak, not the words of authority, but the words of counsel; the words which men should speak to one another who wish to be frank in a moment more critical perhaps than the history of the world has ever yet known; a moment when it is every man's duty to forget himself, to forget his own interests, to fill himself with the nobility of a great national and world conception, and act upon a new platform elevated above the ordinary affairs of life and lifted to where men have views of the long destiny of mankind.

I think that in order to realize just what this moment of counsel is it is very desirable that we should remind ourselves just how this war came about and just what it is for. You can explain most wars very simply, but the explanation of this is not so simple. Its roots run deep into all the obscure soils of history, and in my view this is the last decisive issue between the old principle of power and the new principle of freedom.

WAR STARTED BY GERMANY

The war was started by Germany. Her authorities deny that they started it, but I am willing to let the statement I have just made await the verdict of history. And the thing that needs to be explained is why Germany started the war. Remember what the position of Germany in the world was-as enviable a position as any nation has ever occupied. The whole world stood at admiration of her wonderful intellectual and material achievements. All the intellectual men of the world went to school to her. As a university man I have been surrounded by men trained in Germany, men who had resorted to Germany because nowhere else could they get such thorough and searching training, particularly in the principles of science and the principles that underlie modern material achievement. Her men of science had made her industries perhaps the most competent industries of the world, and the label "Made in Germany" was a guarantee of good workmanship and of sound material. She had access to all the markets of the world, and every other nation who traded in those markets feared Germany because of her effective and almost irresistible competition. She had a "place in the sun."

GERMANY'S INDUSTRIAL GROWTH

Why was she not satisfied? What more did she want? There was nothing in the world of peace that she did not already have and have in abundance. We boast of the extraordinary pace of American advancement. We show with pride the statistics of the increase of our industries and of the population of our cities. Well, those statistics did not match the recent statistics of Germany. Her old cities took on youth and grew faster than any American cities ever grew. Her old industries opened their eyes and saw a new world and went out for its conquest. And yet the authorities of Germany were not satisfied.

You have one part of the answer to the question why she was not satisfied in her methods of competition. There is no important industry in Germany upon which the Government has not laid its hands, to direct it and, when necessity arose, control it; and you have only to ask any man whom you meet who is familiar with the conditions that prevailed before the war in the matter of national competition to find out the methods of competition which the German manufacturers and exporters used under the patronage and support of the Government of Germany. You will find that they were the same sorts of competition that we have tried to prevent by law within our own borders. If they could not sell their goods cheaper than we could sell ours at a profit to themselves they could get a subsidy from the Government which made it possible to sell them cheaper anyhow, and the conditions of competition were thus controlled in large measure by the German Government itself.

BERLIN-BAGDAD RAILWAY

But that did not satisfy the German Government. All the while there was lying behind its thought and in its dreams of the future a political control which would enable it in the long run to dominate the labor and the industry of the world. They were not content with success by superior achievement; they wanted success by authority. I suppose very few of you have thought much about the Berlin-to-Bagdad Railway. The Berlin-Bagdad Railway was constructed in order to run the threat of force down the flank of the industrial undertakings of half a dozen other countries; so that when German competition came in it would not be resisted too far, because there was always the possibility of getting German armies into the heart of that country quicker than any other armies could be got there.

Look at the map of Europe now! Germany is thrusting upon us again and again the discussion of peace talks, —about what? Talks about Belgium; talks about northern France; talks about Alsace-Lorraine. Well, those are deeply interesting subjects to us and to them, but they are not the heart of the matter. Take the map and look at it. Germany has absolute control of Austria-Hungary, practical control of the Balkan States, control of Turkey, control of Asia Minor. I saw a map in which the whole thing was printed in appropriate black the other day, and the black stretched all the way from Hamburg to Bagdad-the bulk of German power inserted into the heart of the world. If she can keep that, she has kept all that her dreams contemplated when the war began. If she can keep that, her power can disturb the world as long as she keeps it, always provided, for I feel bound to put this proviso in-always provided the present influences that control the German Government continue to control it. I believe that the spirit of freedom can get into the hearts of Germans and find as fine a welcome there as it can find in any other hearts, but the spirit of freedom does not suit the plans of the Pan-Germans. Power cannot be used with concentrated force against free peoples if it is used by free people.

PEACE RUMORS

You know how many intimations come to us from one of the central powers that it is more anxious for peace than the chief central power, and you know that it means that the people in that central power know that if the war ends as it stands they will in effect themselves be vassals of Germany, notwithstanding that their populations are compounded of all the peoples of that part of the world, and notwithstanding the fact that they do not wish in their pride and proper spirit of nationality to be so absorbed and dominated. Germany is determined that the political power of the world shall belong to her. There have been such ambitions before. They have been in part realized, but never before have those ambitions been based upon so exact and precise and scientific a plan of domination.

May I not say that it is amazing to me that any group of persons should be so ill-informed as to suppose, as some groups in Russia apparently suppose, that any reforms planned in the interest of the people can live in the presence of a Germany powerful enough to undermine or overthrow them by intrigue or force? Any body of free men that compounds with the present German Government is compounding for its own destruction. But that is not the whole of the story. Any man in America or anywhere else that supposes that the free industry and enterprise of the world can continue if the Pan-German plan is achieved and German power fastened upon the world is as fatuous as the dreamers in Russia. What I am opposed to is not the feeling of the pacifists, but their stupidity. My heart is with them, but my mind has a contempt for them. I want peace, but I know how to get it, and they do not.

COLONEL HOUSE'S MISSION

You will notice that I sent a friend of mine, Colonel House, to Europe, who is as great a lover of peace as any man in the world; but I didn't send him on a peace mission yet. I sent him to take part in a conference as to how the war was to be won, and he knows, as I know, that that is the way to get peace, if you want it for more than a few minutes.

All of this is a preface to the conference that I have referred to with regard to what we are going to do. If we are true friends of freedom, our own or anybody else's, we will see that the power of this country and the productivity of this country is raised to its absolute maximum, and that absolutely nobody is allowed to stand in the way of it. When I say that nobody is allowed to stand in the way I do not mean that they shall be prevented by the power of the Government but by the power of the American spirit. Our duty, if we are to do this great thing and show America to be what we believe her to be-the greatest hope and energy of the world-is to stand together night and day until the job is finished.

LABOR MUST BE FREE

While we are fighting for freedom we must see, among other things, that labor is free; and that means a number of interesting things. It means not only that we must do what we have declared our purpose to do, see that the conditions of labor are not rendered more onerous by the war, but also that we shall see to it that the instrumentalities by which the conditions of labor are improved are not blocked or checked. That we must do. That has been the matter about which I have taken pleasure in conferring from time to time with your president, Mr. Gompers; and if I may be permitted to do so, I want to express my admiration of his patriotic courage, his large vision, and his statesmanlike sense of what has to be done. I like to lay my mind alongside of a mind that knows how to pull in harness. The horses that kick over the traces will have to be put in corral.

Now, to stand together means that nobody must interrupt the processes of our energy if the interruption can possibly be avoided without the absolute invasion of freedom. To put it concretely, that means this: Nobody has a right to stop the processes of labor until all the methods of conciliation and settlement have been exhausted. And I might as well say right here that I am not talking to you alone. You sometimes stop the courses of labor, but there are others who do the same, and I believe I am speaking from my own experience not only, but from the experience of others when I say that you are reasonable in a larger number of cases than the capitalists. I am not saying these things to them personally yet, because I have not had a chance, but they have to be said, not in any spirit of criticism, but in order to clear the atmosphere and come down to business. Everybody on both sides has now got to transact business, and a settlement is never impossible when both sides want to do the square and right thing.

SETTLEMENT HARD TO AVOID

Moreover, a settlement is always hard to avoid when the parties can be brought face to face. I can differ from a man much more radically when he is not in the room than I can when he is in the room, because then the awkward thing is he can come back at me and answer what I say. It is always dangerous for a man to have the floor entirely to himself. Therefore, we must insist in every instance that the parties come into each other's presence and there discuss the issues between them, and not separately in places which have no communication with each other. I always like to remind myself of a delightful saying of an Englishman of the past generation, Charles Lamb. He stuttered a little bit, and once when he was with a group of friends he spoke very harshly of some man who was not present. One of his friends said: "Why, Charles, I didn't know that you knew so and so." "O-o-oh," he said, "I-I d-d-don't; I-I can't h-h-h hate a m-m-man I-I know." There is a great deal of human nature, of very pleasant human nature, in the saying. It is hard to hate a man you know. I may admit, parenthetically, that there are some politicians whose methods I do not at all believe in, but they are jolly good fellows, and if they only would not talk the wrong kind of politics to me, I would love to be with them.

NO SYMPATHY WITH MOB SPIRIT

So it is all along the line, in serious matters and things less serious. We are all of the same clay and spirit, and we can get together if we desire to get together. Therefore, my counsel to you is this: Let us show ourselves Americans by showing that we do not want to go off in separate camps or groups by ourselves, but that we want to coöperate with all other classes and all other groups in the common enterprise which is to release the spirits of the world from bondage. I would be willing to set that up as the final test of an American. That is the meaning of democracy. I have been very much distressed, my fellow-citizens, by some of the things that have happened recently. The mob spirit is displaying itself here and there in this country. I have no sympathy with what some men are saying, but I have no sympathy with the men who take their punishment into their own hands; and I want to say to every man who does join such a mob that I do not recognize him as worthy of the free institutions of the United States. There are some organizations in this country whose object is anarchy and the destruction of law, but I would not meet their efforts by making myself partner in destroying the law. I despise and hate their purposes as much as any man, but I respect the ancient processes of justice; and I would be too proud not to see them done justice, however wrong they are.

MUST OBEY COMMON COUNSEL

So I want to utter my earnest protest against any manifestation of the spirit of lawlessness anywhere or in any cause. Why, gentlemen, look what it means. We claim to be the greatest democratic people in the world, and democracy means first of all that we can govern ourselves. If our men have not self-control, then they are not capable of that great thing which we call democratic government. A man who takes the law into his own hands is not the right man to coöperate in any formation or development of law and institutions, and some of the processes by which the struggle between capital and labor is carried on are processes that come very near to taking the law into your own hands. I do not mean for a moment to compare them with what I have just been speaking of, but I want you to see that they are mere gradations in this manifestation of the unwillingness to coöperate, and that the fundamental lesson of the whole situation is that we must not only take common counsel, but that we must yield to and obey common counsel. Not all of the instrumentalities for this are at hand. I am hopeful that in the very near future new instrumentalities may be organized by which we can see to it that various things that are now going on ought not to go on. There are various processes of the dilution of labor and the unnecessary substitution of labor and the bidding in distant markets and unfairly upsetting the whole competition of labor which ought not to go on. I mean now on the part of employers, and we must interject some instrumentality of coöperation by which the fair thing will be done all around. I am hopeful that some such instrumentalities may be devised, but whether they are or not, we must use those that we have and upon every occasion where it is necessary have such an instrumentality originated upon that occasion.

So, my fellow-citizens, the reason I came away from Washington is that I sometimes get lonely down there. So many people come to Washington who know things that are not so, and so few people who know anything about what the people of the United States are thinking about. I have to come away and get reminded of the rest of the country. I have to come away and talk to men who are up against the real thing, and say to them, "I am with you if you are with me." And the only test of being with me is not to think about me personally at all, but merely to think of me as the expression for the time being of the power and dignity and hope of the United States.

The Call for War with Austria-Hungary

[Address delivered at a joint session of the two Houses of Congress, December 4, 1917.]

Gentlemen of the Congress:

Eight months have elapsed since I last had the honor of addressing you. They have been months crowded with events of immense and grave significance for us. I shall not undertake to retail or even to summarize those events. The practical particulars of the part we have played in them will be laid before you in the reports of the Executive Departments. I shall discuss only our present outlook upon these vast affairs, our present duties, and the immediate means of accomplishing the objects we shall hold always in view.

I shall not go back to debate the causes of the war. The intolerable wrongs done and planned against us by the sinister masters of Germany have long since become too grossly obvious and odious to every true American to need to be rehearsed. But I shall ask you to consider again and with a very grave scrutiny our objectives and the measures by which we mean to attain them; for the purpose of discussion here in this place is action, and our action must move straight towards definite ends. Our object is, of course, to win the war; and we shall not slacken or suffer ourselves to be diverted until it is won. But it is worth while asking and answering the question, When shall we consider the war won?

From one point of view it is not necessary to broach this fundamental matter. I do not doubt that the American people know what the war is about and what sort of an outcome they will regard as a realization of their purpose in it. As a nation we are united in spirit and intention. I pay little heed to those who tell me otherwise. I hear the voices of dissent, —who does not? I hear the criticism and the clamor of the noisily thoughtless and troublesome. I also see men here and there fling themselves in impotent disloyalty against the calm, indomitable power of the nation. I hear men debate peace who understand neither its nature not the way in which we may attain it with uplifted eyes and unbroken spirits. But I know that none of these speaks for the nation. They do not touch the heart of anything. They may safely be left to strut their uneasy hour and be forgotten.

But from another point of view I believe that it is necessary to say plainly what we here at the seat of action consider the war to be for and what part we mean to play in the settlement of its searching issues. We are the spokesmen of the American people and they have a right to know whether their purpose is ours. They desire peace by the overcoming of evil, by the defeat once for all of the sinister forces that interrupt peace and render it impossible, and they wish to know how closely our thought runs with theirs and what action we propose. They are impatient with those who desire peace by any sort of compromise, —deeply and indignantly impatient, —but they will be equally impatient with us if we do not make it plain to them what our objectives are and what we are planning for in seeking to make conquest of peace by arms.

I believe that I speak for them when I say two things: First, that this intolerable Thing of which the masters of Germany have shown us the ugly face, this menace of combined intrigue and force which we now see so clearly as the German power, a Thing without conscience or honor or capacity for covenanted peace, must be crushed and, if it be not utterly brought to an end, at least shut out from the friendly intercourse of the nations; and, second, that when this Thing and its power are indeed defeated and the time comes that we can discuss peace, —when the German people have spokesmen whose word we can believe and when those spokesmen are ready in the name of their people to accept the common judgment of the nations as to what shall henceforth be the bases of law and of covenant for the life of the world, —we shall be willing and glad to pay the full price for peace, and pay it ungrudgingly. We know what that price will be. It will be full, impartial justice, —justice done at every point and to every nation that the final settlement must affect, our enemies as well as our friends.

You catch, with me, the voices of humanity that are in the air. They grow daily more audible, more articulate, more persuasive, and they come from the hearts of men everywhere. They insist that the war shall not end in vindictive action of any kind; that no nation or people shall be robbed or punished because the irresponsible rulers of a single country have themselves done deep and abominable wrong. It is this thought that has been expressed in the formula "No annexations, no contributions, no punitive indemnities." Just because this crude formula expresses the instinctive judgment as to right of plain men everywhere it has been made diligent use of by the masters of German intrigue to lead the people of Russia astray-and the people of every other country their agents could reach, in order that a premature peace might be brought about before autocracy has been taught its final and convincing lesson, and the people of the world put in control of their own destinies.

But the fact that a wrong use has been made of a just idea is no reason why a right use should not be made of it. It ought to be brought under the patronage of its real friends. Let it be said again that autocracy must first be shown the utter futility of its claims to power or leadership in the modern world. It is impossible to apply any standard of justice so long as such forces are unchecked and undefeated as the present masters of Germany command. Not until that has been done can Right be set up as arbiter and peace-maker among the nations. But when that has been done, —as, God willing, it assuredly will be, —we shall at last be free to do an unprecedented thing, and this is the time to avow our purpose to do it. We shall be free to base peace on generosity and justice, to the exclusion of all selfish claims to advantage even on the part of the victors.

Let there be no misunderstanding. Our present and immediate task is to win the war, and nothing shall turn us aside from it until it is accomplished. Every power and resource we possess, whether of men, of money, or of materials, is being devoted and will continue to be devoted to that purpose until it is achieved. Those who desire to bring peace about before that purpose is achieved I counsel to carry their advice elsewhere. We will not entertain it. We shall regard the war as won only when the German people say to us, through properly accredited representatives, that they are ready to agree to a settlement based upon justice and the reparation of the wrongs their rulers have done. They have done a wrong to Belgium which must be repaired. They have established a power over other lands and peoples than their own, —over the great Empire of Austria-Hungary, over hitherto free Balkan states, over Turkey, and within Asia, —which must be relinquished.

Germany's success by skill, by industry, by knowledge, by enterprise we did not grudge or oppose, but admired, rather. She had built up for herself a real empire of trade and influence, secured by the peace of the world. We were content to abide the rivalries of manufacture, science, and commerce that were involved for us in her success and stand or fall as we had or did not have the brains and the initiative to surpass her. But at the moment when she had conspicuously won her triumphs of peace she threw them away, to establish in their stead what the world will no longer permit to be established, military and political domination by arms, by which to oust where she could not excel the rivals she most feared and hated. The peace we make must remedy that wrong. It must deliver the once fair lands and happy peoples of Belgium and northern France from the Prussian conquest and the Prussian menace, but it must also deliver the peoples of Austria-Hungary, the peoples of the Balkans, and the peoples of Turkey, alike in Europe and in Asia, from the impudent and alien dominion of the Prussian military and commercial autocracy.

We owe it, however, to ourselves to say that we do not wish in any way to impair or to rearrange the Austro-Hungarian Empire. It is no affair of ours what they do with their own life, either industrially or politically. We do not purpose or desire to dictate to them in any way. We only desire to see that their affairs are left in their own hands, in all matters, great or small. We shall hope to secure for the peoples of the Balkan peninsula and for the people of the Turkish Empire the right and opportunity to make their own lives safe, their own fortunes secure against oppression or injustice and from the dictation of foreign courts or parties.

And our attitude and purpose with regard to Germany herself are of a like kind. We intend no wrong against the German Empire, no interference with her internal affairs. We should deem either the one or the other absolutely unjustifiable, absolutely contrary to the principles we have professed to live by and to hold most sacred throughout our life as a nation.

The people of Germany are being told by the men whom they now permit to deceive them and to act as their masters that they are fighting for the very life and existence of their Empire, a war of desperate self-defense against deliberate aggression. Nothing could be more grossly or wantonly false, and we must seek by the utmost openness and candor as to our real aims to convince them of its falseness. We are in fact fighting for their emancipation from fear, along with our own, —from the fear as well as from the fact of unjust attack by neighbors or rivals or schemers after world empire. No one is threatening the existence or the independence or the peaceful enterprise of the German Empire.

The worst that can happen to the detriment of the German people is this, that if they should still, after the war is over, continue to be obliged to live under ambitious and intriguing masters interested to disturb the peace of the world, men or classes of men whom the other peoples of the world could not trust, it might be impossible to admit them to the partnership of nations which must henceforth guarantee the world's peace. That partnership must be a partnership of peoples, not a mere partnership of governments. It might be impossible, also, in such untoward circumstances, to admit Germany to the free economic intercourse which must inevitably spring out of the other partnerships of a real peace. But there would be no aggression in that; and such a situation, inevitable because of distrust, would in the very nature of things sooner or later cure itself, by processes which would assuredly set in.

The wrongs, the very deep wrongs, committed in this war will have to be righted. That of course. But they cannot and must not be righted by the commission of similar wrongs against Germany and her allies. The world will not permit the commission of similar wrongs as a means of reparation and settlement. Statesmen must by this time have learned that the opinion of the world is everywhere wide awake and fully comprehends the issues involved. No representative of any self-governed nation will dare disregard it by attempting any such covenants of selfishness and compromise as were entered into at the Congress of Vienna. The thought of the plain people here and everywhere throughout the world, the people who enjoy no privilege and have very simple and unsophisticated standards of right and wrong, is the air all governments must henceforth breathe if they would live. It is in the full disclosing light of that thought that all policies must be conceived and executed in this midday hour of the world's life. German rulers have been able to upset the peace of the world only because the German people were not suffered under their tutelage to share the comradeship of the other peoples of the world either in thought or in purpose. They were allowed to have no opinion of their own which might be set up as a rule of conduct for those who exercised authority over them. But the congress that concludes this war will feel the full strength of the tides that run now in the hearts and consciences of free men everywhere. Its conclusions will run with those tides.

All these things have been true from the very beginning of this stupendous war; and I cannot help thinking that if they had been made plain at the very outset the sympathy and enthusiasm of the Russian people might have been once for all enlisted on the side of the Allies, suspicion and distrust swept away, and a real and lasting union of purpose effected. Had they believed these things at the very moment of their revolution and had they been confirmed in that belief since, the sad reverses which have recently marked the progress of their affairs towards an ordered and stable government of free men might have been avoided. The Russian people have been poisoned by the very same falsehoods that have kept the German people in the dark, and the poison has been administered by the very same hands. The only possible antidote is the truth. It cannot be uttered too plainly or too often.

From every point of view, therefore, it has seemed to be my duty to speak these declarations of purpose, to add these specific interpretations to what I took the liberty of saying to the Senate in January. Our entrance into the war has not altered our attitude towards the settlement that must come when it is over. When I said in January that the nations of the world were entitled not only to free pathways upon the sea but also to assured and unmolested access to those pathways I was thinking, and I am thinking now, not of the smaller and weaker nations alone, which need our countenance and support, but also of the great and powerful nations, and of our present enemies as well as our present associates in the war. I was thinking, and am thinking now, of Austria herself, among the rest, as well as of Serbia and of Poland. Justice and equality of rights can be had only at a great price. We are seeking permanent, not temporary, foundations for the peace of the world and must seek them candidly and fearlessly. As always, the right will prove to be the expedient.

What shall we do, then, to push this great war of freedom and justice to its righteous conclusion? We must clear away with a thorough hand all impediments to success and we must make every adjustment of law that will facilitate the full and free use of our whole capacity and force as a fighting unit.

One very embarrassing obstacle that stands in our way is that we are at war with Germany but not with her allies. I therefore very earnestly recommend that the Congress immediately declare the United States in a state of war with Austria-Hungary. Does it seem strange to you that this should be the conclusion of the argument I have just addressed to you? It is not. It is in fact the inevitable logic of what I have said. Austria-Hungary is for the time being not her own mistress but simply the vassal of the German Government. We must face the facts as they are and act upon them without sentiment in this stern business. The government of Austria-Hungary is not acting upon its own initiative or in response to the wishes and feelings of its own peoples but as the instrument of another nation. We must meet its force with our own and regard the Central Powers as but one. The war can be successfully conducted in no other way. The same logic would lead also to a declaration of war against Turkey and Bulgaria. They also are the tools of Germany. But they are mere tools and do not yet stand in the direct path of our necessary action. We shall go wherever the necessities of this war carry us, but it seems to me that we should go only where immediate and practical considerations lead us and not heed any others.

The financial and military measures which must be adopted will suggest themselves as the war and its undertakings develop, but I will take the liberty of proposing to you certain other acts of legislation which seem to me to be needed for the support of the war and for the release of our whole force and energy.

It will be necessary to extend in certain particulars the legislation of the last session with regard to alien enemies; and also necessary, I believe, to create a very definite and particular control over the entrance and departure of all persons into and from the United States.

Legislation should be enacted defining as a criminal offense every wilful violation of the presidential proclamations relating to alien enemies promulgated under section 4067 of the Revised Statutes and providing appropriate punishments; and women as well as men should be included under the terms of the acts placing restraints upon alien enemies. It is likely that as time goes on many alien enemies will be willing to be fed and housed at the expense of the Government in the detention camps and it would be the purpose of the legislation I have suggested to confine offenders among them in penitentiaries and other similar institutions where they could be made to work as other criminals do.

Recent experience has convinced me that the Congress must go further in authorizing the Government to set limits to prices. The law of supply and demand, I am sorry to say, has been replaced by the law of unrestrained selfishness. While we have eliminated profiteering in several branches of industry it still runs impudently rampant in others. The farmers, for example, complain with a great deal of justice that, while the regulation of food prices restricts their incomes, no restraints are placed upon the prices of most of the things they must themselves purchase; and similar inequities obtain on all sides.

It is imperatively necessary that the consideration of the full use of the water power of the country and also the consideration of the systematic and yet economical development of such of the natural resources of the country as are still under the control of the federal government should be immediately resumed and affirmatively and constructively dealt with at the earliest possible moment. The pressing need of such legislation is daily becoming more obvious.

The legislation proposed at the last session with regard to regulated combinations among our exporters, in order to provide for our foreign trade a more effective organization and method of coöperation, ought by all means to be completed at this session.

And I beg that the members of the House of Representatives will permit me to express the opinion that it will be impossible to deal in any but a very wasteful and extravagant fashion with the enormous appropriations of the public moneys which must continue to be made, if the war is to be properly sustained, unless the House will consent to return to its former practice of initiating and preparing all appropriation bills through a single committee, in order that responsibility may be centered, expenditures standardized and made uniform, and waste and duplication as much as possible avoided.

Additional legislation may also become necessary before the present Congress again adjourns in order to effect the most efficient coördination and operation of the railway and other transportation systems of the country; but to that I shall, if circumstances should demand, call the attention of the Congress upon another occasion.

If I have overlooked anything that ought to be done for the more effective conduct of the war, your own counsels will supply the omission. What I am perfectly clear about is that in the present session of the Congress our whole attention and energy should be concentrated on the vigorous, rapid, and successful prosecution of the great task of winning the war.

We can do this with all the greater zeal and enthusiasm because we know that for us this is a war of high principle, debased by no selfish ambition of conquest or spoliation; because we know, and all the world knows, that we have been forced into it to save the very institutions we live under from corruption and destruction. The purposes of the Central Powers strike straight at the very heart of everything we believe in; their methods of warfare outrage every principle of humanity and of knightly honor; their intrigue has corrupted the very thought and spirit of many of our people; their sinister and secret diplomacy has sought to take our very territory away from us and disrupt the Union of the States. Our safety would be at an end, our honor forever sullied and brought into contempt were we to permit their triumph. They are striking at the very existence of democracy and liberty.

It is because it is for us a war of high, disinterested purpose, in which all the free peoples of the world are banded together for the vindication of right, a war for the preservation of our nation and of all that it has held dear of principle and of purpose, that we feel ourselves doubly constrained to propose for its outcome only that which is righteous and of irreproachable intention, for our foes as well as for our friends. The cause being just and holy, the settlement must be of like motive and quality. For this we can fight, but for nothing less noble or less worthy of our traditions. For this cause we entered the war and for this cause will we battle until the last gun is fired.

I have spoken plainly because this seems to me the time when it is most necessary to speak plainly, in order that all the world may know that even in the heat and ardor of the struggle and when our whole thought is of carrying the war through to its end we have not forgotten any ideal or principle for which the name of America has been held in honor among the nations and for which it has been our glory to contend in the great generations that went before us. A supreme moment of history has come. The eyes of the people have been opened and they see. The hand of God is laid upon the nations. He will show them favor, I devoutly believe, only if they rise to the clear heights of His own justice and mercy.

Government Administration of Railways

[Address delivered at a joint session of the two Houses of Congress, January 4, 1918.]

Gentlemen of the Congress:

I have asked the privilege of addressing you in order to report to you that on the twenty-eighth of December last, during the recess of the Congress, acting through the Secretary of War and under the authority conferred upon me by the Act of Congress approved August 29, 1916, I took possession and assumed control of the railway lines of the country and the systems of water transportation under their control. This step seemed to be imperatively necessary in the interest of the public welfare, in the presence of the great tasks of war with which we are now dealing. As our own experience develops difficulties and makes it clear what they are, I have deemed it my duty to remove those difficulties wherever I have the legal power to do so. To assume control of the vast railway systems of the country is, I realize, a very great responsibility, but to fail to do so in the existing circumstances would have been a much greater. I assumed the less responsibility rather than the weightier.

I am sure that I am speaking the mind of all thoughtful Americans when I say that it is our duty as the representatives of the nation to do everything that it is necessary to do to secure the complete mobilization of the whole resources of America by as rapid and effective means as can be found. Transportation supplies all the arteries of, mobilization. Unless it be under a single and unified direction, the whole process of the nation's action is embarrassed.

It was in the true spirit of America, and it was right, that we should first try to effect the necessary unification under the voluntary action of those who were in charge of the great railway properties; and we did try it. The directors of the railways responded to the need promptly and generously. The group of railway executives who were charged with the task of actual coördination and general direction performed their difficult duties with patriotic zeal and marked ability, as was to have been expected, and did, I believe, everything that it was possible for them to do in the circumstances. If I have taken the task out of their hands, it has not been because of any dereliction or failure on their part but only because there were some things which the Government can do and private management cannot. We shall continue to value most highly the advice and assistance of these gentlemen and I am sure we shall not find them withholding it.

It had become unmistakably plain that only under government administration can the entire equipment of the several systems of transportation be fully and unreservedly thrown into a common service without injurious discrimination against particular properties. Only under government administration can an absolutely unrestricted and unembarrassed common use be made of all tracks, terminals, terminal facilities and equipment of every kind. Only under that authority can new terminals be constructed and developed without regard to the requirements or limitations of particular roads. But under government administration all these things will be possible, —not instantly, but as fast as practical difficulties, which cannot be merely conjured away, give way before the new management.

The common administration will be carried out with as little disturbance of the present operating organizations and personnel of the railways as possible. Nothing will be altered or disturbed which it is not necessary to disturb. We are serving the public interest and safeguarding the public safety, but we are also regardful of the interest of those by whom these great properties are owned and glad to avail ourselves of the experience and trained ability of those who have been managing them. It is necessary that the transportation of troops and of war materials, of food and of fuel, and of everything that is necessary for the full mobilization of the energies and resources of the country, should be first considered, but it is clearly in the public interest also that the ordinary activities and the normal industrial and commercial life of the country should be interfered with and dislocated as little as possible, and the public may rest assured that the interest and convenience of the private shipper will be as carefully served and safeguarded as it is possible to serve and safeguard it in the present extraordinary circumstances.

While the present authority of the Executive suffices for all purposes of administration, and while of course all private interests must for the present give way to the public necessity, it is, I am sure you will agree with me, right and necessary that the owners and creditors of the railways, the holders of their stocks and bonds, should receive from the Government an unqualified guarantee that their properties will be maintained throughout the period of federal control in as good repair and as complete equipment as at present, and that the several roads will receive under federal management such compensation as is equitable and just alike to their owners and to the general public. I would suggest the average net railway operating income of the three years ending June 30, 1917. I earnestly recommend that these guarantees be given by appropriate legislation, and given as promptly as circumstances permit.

I need not point out the essential justice of such guarantees and their great influence and significance as elements in the present financial and industrial situation of the country. Indeed, one of the strong arguments for assuming control of the railroads at this time is the financial argument. It is necessary that the values of railway securities should be justly and fairly protected and that the large financial operations every year necessary in connection with the maintenance, operation and development of the roads should, during the period of the war, be wisely related to the financial operations of the Government. Our first duty is, of course, to conserve the common interest and the common safety and to make certain that nothing stands in the way of the successful prosecution of the great war for liberty and justice, but it is also an obligation of public conscience and of public honor that the private interests we disturb should be kept safe from unjust injury, and it is of the utmost consequence to the Government itself that all great financial operations should be stabilized and coördinated with the financial operations of the Government. No borrowing should run athwart the borrowings of the federal treasury, and no fundamental industrial values should anywhere be unnecessarily impaired. In the hands of many thousands of small investors in the country, as well as in national banks, in insurance companies, in savings banks, in trust companies, in financial agencies of every kind, railway securities, the sum total of which runs up to some ten or eleven thousand millions, constitute a vital part of the structure of credit, and the unquestioned solidity of that structure must be maintained.

The Secretary of War and I easily agreed that, in view of the many complex interests which must be safeguarded and harmonized, as well as because of his exceptional experience and ability in this new field of governmental action, the Honorable William G. McAdoo was the right man to assume direct administrative control of this new executive task. At our request, he consented to assume the authority and duties of organizer and Director General of the new Railway Administration. He has assumed those duties and his work is in active progress.

It is probably too much to expect that even under the unified railway administration which will now be possible sufficient economies can be effected in the operation of the railways to make it possible to add to their equipment and extend their operative facilities as much as the present extraordinary demands upon their use will render desirable without resorting to the national treasury for the funds. If it is not possible, it will, of course, be necessary to resort to the Congress for grants of money for that purpose. The Secretary of the Treasury will advise with your committees with regard to this very practical aspect of the matter. For the present, I suggest only the guarantees I have indicated and such appropriations as are necessary at the outset of this task. I take the liberty of expressing the hope that the Congress may grant these promptly and ungrudgingly. We are dealing with great matters and will, I am sure, deal with them greatly.

The Conditions of Peace

[Address delivered at a joint session of the two Houses of Congress, January 8, 1918.]

Gentlemen of the Congress:

Once more, as repeatedly before, the spokesmen of the Central Empires have indicated their desire to discuss the objects of the war and the possible bases of a general peace. Parleys have been in progress at Brest-Litovsk between Russian representatives and representatives of the Central Powers to which the attention of all the belligerents has been invited for the purpose of ascertaining whether it may be possible to extend these parleys into a general conference with regard to terms of peace and settlement. The Russian representatives presented not only a perfectly definite statement of the principles upon which they would be willing to conclude peace but also an equally definite program of the concrete application of those principles. The representatives of the Central Powers, on their part, presented an outline of settlement which, if much less definite, seemed susceptible of liberal interpretation until their specific program of practical terms was added. That program proposed no concessions at all either to the sovereignty of Russia or to the preferences of the populations with whose fortunes it dealt, but meant, in a word, that the Central Empires were to keep every foot of territory their armed forces had occupied, —every province, every city, every point of vantage, —as a permanent addition to their territories and their power. It is a reasonable conjecture that the general principles of settlement which they at first suggested originated with the more liberal statesmen of Germany and Austria, the men who have begun to feel the force of their own peoples' thought and purpose, while the concrete terms of actual settlement came from the military leaders who have no thought but to keep what they have got. The negotiations have been broken off. The Russian representatives were sincere and in earnest. They cannot entertain such proposals of conquest and domination.

The whole incident is full of significance. It is also full of perplexity. With whom are the Russian representatives dealing? For whom are the representatives of the Central Empires speaking? Are they speaking for the majorities of their respective parliaments or for the minority parties, that military and imperialistic minority which has so far dominated their whole policy and controlled the affairs of Turkey and of the Balkan states which have felt obliged to become their associates in this war? The Russian representatives have insisted, very justly, very wisely, and in the true spirit of modern democracy, that the conferences they have been holding with the Teutonic and Turkish statesmen should be held within open, not closed, doors, and all the world has been audience, as was desired. To whom have we been listening, then? To those who speak the spirit and intention of the Resolutions of the German Reichstag of the ninth of July last, the spirit and intention of the liberal leaders and parties of Germany, or to those who resist and defy that spirit and intention and insist upon conquest and subjugation? Or are we listening, in fact, to both, unreconciled and in open and hopeless contradiction? These are very serious and pregnant questions. Upon the answer to them depends the peace of the world.

But, whatever the results of the parleys at Brest-Litovsk, whatever the confusions of counsel and of purpose in the utterances of the spokesmen of the Central Empires, they have again attempted to acquaint the world with their objects in the war and have again challenged their adversaries to say what their objects are and what sort of settlement they would deem just and satisfactory. There is no good reason why that challenge should not be responded to, and responded to with the utmost candor. We did not wait for it. Not once, but again and again, we have laid our whole thought and purpose before the world, not in general terms only, but each time with sufficient definition to make it clear what sort of definitive terms of settlement must necessarily spring out of them. Within the last week Mr. Lloyd George has spoken with admirable candor and in admirable spirit for the people and Government of Great Britain. There is no confusion of counsel among the adversaries of the Central Powers, no uncertainty of principle, no vagueness of detail. The only secrecy of counsel, the only lack of fearless frankness, the only failure to make definite statement of the objects of the war, lies with Germany and her Allies. The issues of life and death hang upon these definitions. No statesman who has the least conception of his responsibility ought for a moment to permit himself to continue this tragical and appalling outpouring of blood and treasure unless he is sure beyond a peradventure that the objects of the vital sacrifice are part and parcel of the very life of society and that the people for whom he speaks think them right and imperative as he does.

There is, moreover, a voice calling for these definitions of principle and of purpose which is, it seems to me, more thrilling and more compelling than any of the many moving voices with which the troubled air of the world is filled. It is the voice of the Russian people. They are prostrate and all but helpless, it would seem, before the grim power of Germany, which has hitherto known no relenting and no pity. Their power, apparently, is shattered. And yet their soul is not subservient. They will not yield either in principle or in action. Their conception of what is right, of what it is humane and honorable for them to accept, has been stated with a frankness, a largeness of view, a generosity of spirit, and a universal human sympathy which must challenge the admiration of every friend of mankind; and they have refused to compound their ideals or desert others that they themselves may be safe. They call to us to say what it is that we desire, in what, if in anything, our purpose and our spirit differ from theirs; and I believe that the people of the United States would wish me to respond, with utter simplicity and frankness. Whether their present leaders believe it or not, it is our heartfelt desire and hope that some way may be opened whereby we may be privileged to assist the people of Russia to attain their utmost hope of liberty and ordered peace.

It will be our wish and purpose that the processes of peace, when they are begun, shall be absolutely open and that they shall involve and permit henceforth no secret understandings of any kind. The day of conquest and aggrandizement is gone by; so is also the day of secret covenants entered into in the interest of particular governments and likely at some unlooked-for moment to upset the peace of the world. It is this happy fact, now clear to the view of every public man whose thoughts do not still linger in an age that is dead and gone, which makes it possible for every nation whose purposes are consistent with justice and the peace of the world to avow now or at any other time the objects it has in view.

We entered this war because violations of right had occurred which touched us to the quick and made the life of our own people impossible unless they were corrected and the world secured once for all against their recurrence. What we demand in this war, therefore, is nothing peculiar to ourselves. It is that the world be made fit and safe to live in; and particularly that it be made safe for every peace-loving nation which, like our own, wishes to live its own life, determine its own institutions, be assured of justice and fair dealing by the other peoples of the world as against force and selfish aggression. All the peoples of the world are in effect partners in this interest, and for our own part we see very clearly that unless justice be done to others it will not be done to us. The program of the world's peace, therefore, is our program; and that program, the only possible program, as we see it, is this:

I. Open covenants of peace, openly arrived at, after which there shall be no private international understandings of any kind, but diplomacy shall proceed always frankly and in the public view.

II. Absolute freedom of navigation upon the seas, outside territorial waters, alike in peace and in war, except as the seas may be closed in whole or in part by international action for the enforcement of international covenants.

III. The removal, so far as possible, of all economic barriers and the establishment of an equality of trade conditions among all the nations consenting to the peace and associating themselves for its maintenance.

IV. Adequate guarantees given and taken that national armaments will be reduced to the lowest point consistent with domestic safety.

V. A free, open-minded, and absolutely impartial adjustment of all colonial claims, based upon a strict observance of the principle that in determining all such questions of sovereignty the interests of the populations concerned must have equal weight with the equitable claims of the government whose title is to be determined.

VI. The evacuation of all Russian territory and such a settlement of all questions affecting Russia as will secure the best and freest coöperation of the other nations of the world in obtaining for her an unhampered and unembarrassed opportunity for the independent determination of her own political development and national policy and assure her of a sincere welcome into the society of free nations under institutions of her own choosing; and, more than a welcome, assistance also of every kind that she may need and may herself desire. The treatment accorded Russia by her sister nations in the months to come will be the acid test of their good will, of their comprehension of her needs as distinguished from their own interests, and of their intelligent and unselfish sympathy.

VII. Belgium, the whole world will agree, must be evacuated and restored, without any attempt to limit the sovereignty which she enjoys in common with all other free nations. No other single act will serve as this will serve to restore confidence among the nations in the laws which they have themselves set and determined for the government of their relations with one another. Without this healing act the whole structure and validity of international law is forever impaired.

VIII. All French territory should be freed and the invaded portions restored, and the wrong done to France by Prussia in 1871 in the matter of Alsace-Lorraine, which has unsettled the peace of the world for nearly fifty years, should be righted, in order that peace may once more be made secure in the interest of all.

IX. A readjustment of the frontiers of Italy should be effected along clearly recognizable lines of nationality.

X. The peoples of Austria-Hungary, whose place among the nations we wish to see safeguarded and assured, should be accorded the freest opportunity of autonomous development.

XI. Rumania, Serbia, and Montenegro should be evacuated; occupied territories restored; Serbia accorded free and secure access to the sea; and the relations of the several Balkan states to one another determined by friendly counsel along historically established lines of allegiance and nationality; and international guarantees of the political and economic independence and territorial integrity of the several Balkan states should be entered into.

XII. The Turkish portions of the present Ottoman Empire should be assured a secure sovereignty, but the other nationalities which are now under Turkish rule should be assured an undoubted security of life and an absolutely unmolested opportunity of autonomous development and the Dardanelles should be permanently opened as a free passage to the ships and commerce of all nations under international guarantees.

XIII. An independent Polish state should be erected which should include the territories inhabited by indisputably Polish populations, which should be assured a free and secure access to the sea, and whose political and economic independence and territorial integrity should be guaranteed by international covenant.

XIV. A general association of nations must be formed under specific covenants for the purpose of affording mutual guarantees of political independence and territorial integrity to great and small states alike.

In regard to these essential rectifications of wrong and assertions of right we feel ourselves to be intimate partners of all the governments and peoples associated together against the Imperialists. We cannot be separated in interest or divided in purpose. We stand together until the end.

For such arrangements and covenants we are willing to fight and to continue to fight until they are achieved; but only because we wish the right to prevail and desire a just and stable peace such as can be secured only by removing the chief provocations to war, which this program does remove. We have no jealousy of German greatness, and there is nothing in this program that impairs it. We grudge her no achievement or distinction of learning or of pacific enterprise such as have made her record very bright and very enviable. We do not wish to injure her or to block in any way her legitimate influence or power. We do not wish to fight her either with arms or with hostile arrangements of trade if she is willing to associate herself with us and the other peace-loving nations of the world in covenants of justice and law and fair dealing. We wish her only to accept a place of equality among the peoples of the world, —the new world in which we now live, —instead of a place of mastery.

Neither do we presume to suggest to her any alteration or modification of her institutions. But it is necessary, we must frankly say, and necessary as a preliminary to any intelligent dealings with her on our part, that we should know whom her spokesmen speak for when they speak to us, whether for the Reichstag majority or for the military party and the men whose creed is imperial domination.

We have spoken now, surely, in terms too concrete to admit of any further doubt or question. An evident principle runs through the whole program I have outlined. It is the principle of justice to all peoples and nationalities, and their right to live on equal terms of liberty and safety with one another, whether they be strong or weak. Unless this principle be made its foundation no part of the structure of international justice can stand. The people of the United States could act upon no other principle; and to the vindication of this principle they are ready to devote their lives, their honor, and everything that they possess. The moral climax of this the culminating and final war for human liberty has come, and they are ready to put their own strength, their own highest purpose, their own integrity and devotion to the test.

Force to the Utmost

[Speech at the Opening of the Third Liberty Loan Campaign, delivered in the Fifth Regiment Armory, Baltimore, April 6, 1918.]

Fellow-Citizens:

This is the anniversary of our acceptance of Germany's challenge to fight for our right to live and be free, and for the sacred rights of freemen everywhere. The nation is awake. There is no need to call to it. We know what the war must cost, our utmost sacrifice, the lives of our fittest men, and, if need be, all that we possess.

The loan we are met to discuss is one of the least parts of what we are called upon to give and to do, though in itself imperative. The people of the whole country are alive to the necessity of it, and are ready to lend to the utmost, even where it involves a sharp skimping and daily sacrifice to lend out of meagre earnings. They will look with reprobation and contempt upon those who can and will not, upon those who demand a higher rate of interest, upon those who think of it as a mere commercial transaction. I have not come, therefore, to urge the loan. I have come only to give you, if I can, a more vivid conception of what it is for.

The reasons for this great war, the reason why it had to come, the need to fight it through, and the issues that hang upon its outcome, are more clearly disclosed now than ever before. It is easy to see just what this particular loan means, because the cause we are fighting for stands more sharply revealed than at any previous crisis of the momentous struggle. The man who knows least can now see plainly how the cause of justice stands, and what is the imperishable thing he is asked to invest in. Men in America may be more sure than they ever were before that the cause is their own, and that, if it should be lost, their own great nation's place and mission in the world would be lost with it.

I call you to witness, my fellow-countrymen, that at no stage of this terrible business have I judged the purposes of Germany intemperately. I should be ashamed in the presence of affairs so grave, so fraught with the destinies of mankind throughout all the world, to speak with truculence, to use the weak language of hatred or vindictive purpose. We must judge as we would be judged. I have sought to learn the objects Germany has in this war from the mouths of her own spokesmen, and to deal as frankly with them as I wished them to deal with me. I have laid bare our own ideals, our own purposes, without reserve or doubtful phrase, and have asked them to say as plainly what it is that they seek.

We have ourselves proposed no injustice, no aggression. We are ready, whenever the final reckoning is made, to be just to the German people, deal fairly with the German power, as with all others. There can be no difference between peoples in the final judgment, if it is indeed to be a righteous judgment. To propose anything but justice, even-handed and dispassionate justice, to Germany at any time, whatever the outcome of the war, would be to renounce and dishonor our own cause, for we ask nothing that we are not willing to accord.

It has been with this thought that I have sought to learn from those who spoke for Germany whether it was justice or dominion and the execution of their own will upon the other nations of the world that the German leaders were seeking. They have answered-answered in unmistakable terms. They have avowed that it was not justice, but dominion and the unhindered execution of their own will. The avowal has not come from Germany's statesmen. It has come from her military leaders, who are her real rulers. Her statesmen have said that they wished peace, and were ready to discuss its terms whenever their opponents were willing to sit down at the conference table with them. Her present Chancellor has said-in indefinite and uncertain terms, indeed, and in phrases that often seem to deny their own meaning, but with as much plainness as he thought prudent-that he believed that peace should be based upon the principles which we had declared would be our own in the final settlement.

At Brest-Litovsk her civilian delegates spoke in similar terms; professed their desire to conclude a fair peace and accord to the peoples with whose fortunes they were dealing the right to choose their own allegiances. But action accompanied and followed the profession. Their military masters, the men who act for Germany and exhibit her purpose in execution, proclaimed a very different conclusion. We can not mistake what they have done-in Russia, in Finland, in the Ukraine, in Rumania. The real test of their justice and fair play has come. From this we may judge the rest.

They are enjoying in Russia a cheap triumph in which no brave or gallant nation can long take pride. A great people, helpless by their own act, lies for the time at their mercy. Their fair professions are forgotten. They nowhere set up justice, but everywhere impose their power and exploit everything for their own use and aggrandizement, and the peoples of conquered provinces are invited to be free under their dominion!

Are we not justified in believing that they would do the same things at their western front if they were not there face to face with armies whom even their countless divisions cannot overcome? If, when they have felt their check to be final, they should propose favorable and equitable terms with regard to Belgium and France and Italy, could they blame us if we concluded that they did so only to assure themselves of a free hand in Russia and the East?

Their purpose is, undoubtedly, to make all the Slavic peoples, all the free and ambitious nations of the Baltic Peninsula, all the lands that Turkey has dominated and misruled, subject to their will and ambition, and build upon that dominion an empire of force upon which they fancy that they can then erect an empire of gain and commercial supremacy-an empire as hostile to the Americas as to the Europe which it will overawe-an empire which will ultimately master Persia, India, and the peoples of the Far East.

In such a program our ideals, the ideals of justice and humanity and liberty, the principle of the free self-determination of nations, upon which all the modern world insists, can play no part. They are rejected for the ideals of power, for the principle that the strong must rule the weak, that trade must follow the flag, whether those to whom it is taken welcome it or not, that the peoples of the world are to be made subject to the patronage and overlordship of those who have the power to enforce it.

That program once carried out, America and all who care or dare to stand with her must arm and prepare themselves to contest the mastery of the world —a mastery in which the rights of common men, the rights of women and of all who are weak, must for the time being be trodden underfoot and disregarded and the old, age-long struggle for freedom and right begin again at its beginning. Everything that America has lived for and loved and grown great to vindicate and bring to a glorious realization will have fallen in utter ruin and the gates of mercy once more pitilessly shut upon mankind!

The thing is preposterous and impossible; and yet is not that what the whole course and action of the German armies has meant wherever they have moved? I do not wish, even in this moment of utter disillusionment, to judge harshly or unrighteously. I judge only what the German arms have accomplished with unpitying thoroughness throughout every fair region they have touched.

What, then are we to do? For myself, I am ready, ready still, ready even now, to discuss a fair and just and honest peace at any time that it is sincerely purposed —a peace in which the strong and the weak shall fare alike. But the answer, when I proposed such a peace, came from the German commanders in Russia and I cannot mistake the meaning of the answer.

I accept the challenge. I know that you accept it. All the world shall know that you accept it. It shall appear in the utter sacrifice and self-forgetfulness with which we shall give all that we love and all that we have to redeem the world and make it fit for free men like ourselves to live in. This now is the meaning of all that we do. Let everything that we say, my fellow-countrymen, everything that we henceforth plan and accomplish, ring true to this response till the majesty and might of our concerted power shall fill the thought and utterly defeat the force of those who flout and misprize what we honor and hold dear.

Germany has once more said that force, and force alone, shall decide whether justice and peace shall reign in the affairs of men, whether right as America conceives it or dominion as she conceives it shall determine the destinies of mankind. There is, therefore, but one response possible from us: Force, force to the utmost, force without stint or limit, the righteous and triumphant force which shall make right the law of the world and cast every selfish dominion down in the dust.

Presidential Decisions

The State of War: The President's Proclamation of April 6, 1917.

Whereas the Congress of the United States in the exercise of the constitutional authority vested in them have resolved, by joint resolution of the Senate and House of Representatives bearing date this day "That the state of war between the United States and the Imperial German Government which has been thrust upon the United States is hereby formally declared";

Whereas it is provided by Section 4067 of the Revised Statutes, as follows:

> Whenever there is declared a war between the United States and any foreign nation or government, or any invasion or predatory incursion is perpetrated, attempted, or threatened against the territory of the United States, by any foreign nation or government, and the President makes public proclamation of the event, all natives, citizens, denizens, or subjects of a hostile nation or government, being males of the age of fourteen years and upwards, who shall be within the United States, and not actually naturalized, shall be liable to be apprehended, restrained, secured, and removed as alien enemies. The President is authorized, in any such event, by his proclamation thereof, or other public act, to direct the conduct to be observed, on the part of the United States, toward the aliens who become so liable; the manner and degree of the restraint to which they shall be subject, and in what cases, and upon what security their residence shall be permitted, and to provide for the removal of those who, not being permitted to reside within the United States, refuse or neglect to depart therefrom; and to establish any such regulations which are found necessary in the premises and for the public safety;

Whereas, by Sections 4068, 4069, and 4070 of the Revised Statutes, further provision is made relative to alien enemies;

Now, therefore, I, Woodrow Wilson, President of the United States of America, do hereby proclaim to all whom it may concern that a state of war exists between the United States and the Imperial German Government; and I do specially direct all officers, civil or military, of the United States that they exercise vigilance and zeal in the discharge of the duties incident to such a state of war; and I do, moreover, earnestly appeal to all American citizens that they, in loyal devotion to their country, dedicated from its foundation to the principles of liberty and justice, uphold the laws of the land, and give undivided and willing support to those measures which may be adopted by the constitutional authorities in prosecuting the war to a successful issue and in obtaining a secure and just peace;

And, acting under and by virtue of the authority vested in me by the Constitution of the United States and the said sections of the Revised Statutes, I do hereby further proclaim and direct that the conduct to be observed on the part of the United States toward all natives, citizens, denizens, or subjects of Germany, being males of the age of fourteen years and upwards, who shall be within the United States and not actually naturalized, who for the purpose of this proclamation and under such sections of the Revised Statutes are termed alien enemies, shall be as follows:

All alien enemies are enjoined to preserve the peace towards the United States and to refrain from crime against the public safety, and from violating the laws of the United States and of the States and Territories thereof, and to refrain from actual hostility or giving information, aid or comfort to the enemies of the United States, and to comply strictly with the regulations which are hereby or which may be from time to time promulgated by the President; and so long as they shall conduct themselves in accordance with law, they shall be undisturbed in the peaceful pursuit of their lives and occupations and be accorded the consideration due to all peaceful and law-abiding persons, except so far as restrictions may be necessary for their own protection and for the safety of the United States; and towards such alien enemies as conduct themselves in accordance with law, all citizens of the United States are enjoined to preserve the peace and to treat them with all such friendliness as may be compatible with loyalty and allegiance to the United States.

And all alien enemies who fail to conduct themselves as so enjoined, in addition to all other penalties prescribed by law, shall be liable to restraint, or to give security, or to remove and depart from the United States in the manner prescribed by Sections 4069 and 4070 of the Revised Statutes, and as prescribed in the regulations duly promulgated by the President;

And pursuant to the authority vested in me, I hereby declare and establish the following regulations, which I find necessary in the premises and for the public safety:

First. An alien enemy shall not have in his possession, at any time or place, any fire-arm, weapon or implement of war, or component part thereof, ammunition, maxim or other silencer, bomb or explosive or material used in the manufacture of explosives;

Second. An alien enemy shall not have in his possession at any time or place, or use or operate any aircraft or wireless apparatus, or any form of signalling device, or any form of cipher code, or any paper, document or book written or printed in cipher or in which there may be invisible writing;

Third. All property found in the possession of an alien enemy in violation of the foregoing regulations shall be subject to seizure by the United States;

Fourth. An alien enemy shall not approach or be found within one-half of a mile of any Federal or State fort, camp, arsenal, aircraft station, Government or naval vessel, navy yard, factory, or workshop for the manufacture of munitions of war or of any products for the use of the army or navy;

Fifth. An alien enemy shall not write, print, or publish any attack or threats against the Government or Congress of the United States, or either branch thereof, or against the measures or policy of the United States, or against the person or property of any person in the military, naval or civil service of the United States, or of the States or Territories, or of the District of Columbia, or of the municipal governments therein;

Sixth. An alien enemy shall not commit or abet any hostile acts against the United States, or give information, aid, or comfort to its enemies;

Seventh. An alien enemy shall not reside in or continue to reside in, to remain in, or enter any locality which the President may from time to time designate by Executive Order as a prohibited area in which residence by an alien enemy shall be found by him to constitute a danger to the public peace and safety of the United States, except by permit from the President and except under such limitations or restrictions as the President may prescribe;

Eighth. An alien enemy whom the President shall have reasonable cause to believe to be aiding or about to aid the enemy, or to be at large to the danger of the public peace or safety of the United States, or to have violated or to be about to violate any of these regulations, shall remove to any location designated by the President by Executive Order, and shall not remove therefrom without a permit, or shall depart from the United States if so required by the President;

Ninth. No alien enemy shall depart from the United States until he shall have received such permit as the President shall prescribe, or except under order of a court, judge, or justice, under Sections 4069 and 4070 of the Revised Statutes;

Tenth. No alien enemy shall land in or enter the United States, except under such restrictions and at such places as the President may prescribe;

Eleventh. If necessary to prevent violation of the regulations, all alien enemies will be obliged to register;

Twelfth. An alien enemy whom there may be reasonable cause to believe to be aiding or about to aid the enemy, or who may be at large to the danger of the public peace or safety, or who violates or attempts to violate, or of whom there is reasonable ground to believe that he is about to violate, any regulation duly promulgated by the President, or any criminal law of the United States, or of the States or Territories thereof, will be subject to summary arrest by the United States Marshal, or his deputy, or such other officer as the President shall designate, and to confinement in such penitentiary, prison, jail, military camp, or other place of detention as may be directed by the President.

This proclamation and the regulations herein contained shall extend and apply to all land and water, continental or insular, in any way within the jurisdiction of the United States.

Formal U.S. Declaration of War with Germany, 6 April 1917

Joint Resolution Declaring that a state of war exists between the Imperial German Government and the Government and the people of the United States and making provision to prosecute the same.

Whereas the Imperial German Government has committed repeated acts of war against the Government and the people of the United States of America; Therefore be it Resolved by the Senate and the House of Representatives of the United States of America in Congress Assembled, that the state of war between the United States and the Imperial German Government which has thus been thrust upon the United States is hereby formally declared; and that the President be, and he is hereby, authorized and directed to employ the entire naval and military forces of the United States and the resources of the Government to carry on war against the Imperial German Government; and to bring the conflict to a successful termination all of the resources of the country are hereby pledged by the Congress of the United States.

CHAMP CLARK
Speaker of the House of Representatives
THOS. R. MARSHALL
Vice President of the United States and President of the Senate
Approved, April 6, 1917
WOODROW WILSON

Footnotes

1. The Tariff Bill was signed Oct. 3, 1913; the Currency Bill, Dec. 23, 1913.

2. It had been the practice of our Presidents to send their Messages to Congress and not to read them in person.

3. The speech was made from a rostrum in the National Cemetery, on the battlefield.

4. General Victoriano Huerta had, on Feb. 18, deposed President Madero, and had been, on the 20th, elected President by the Mexican Congress. Three days later Madero was assassinated while in the custody of the new government. An army calling themselves Constitutionalists under General Villa, defeated the Mexican Federal forces in May. On August 20, Huerta declined the proposal of the United States government that he should cease to be a candidate for the Presidency.

5. In the *Areopagitica*: "I cannot praise a fugitive and cloistered virtue, unexercised and unbreathed, that never sallies out and sees her adversary, but slinks out of the race, where that immortal garland is to be run for, not without dust and heat."

6. Sir George Williams, 1821-1905, an English philanthropist, founder of the Young Men's Christian Association.

7. This was at Princeton, in 1902 and 1903.

Made in the USA
Monee, IL
22 April 2021

66505415R00134